ENOUGH SAID

ENOUGH SAID

BERNARD LEVIN

Jonathan Cape
London

Published by Jonathan Cape 1998

2 4 6 8 10 9 7 5 3 1

Copyright © Bernard Levin 1998

First published in Great Britain in 1998 by
Jonathan Cape
Random House, 20 Vauxhall Bridge Road,
London SW1V 2SA

Random House Australia (Pty) Limited
20 Alfred Street, Milsons Point, Sydney,
New South Wales 2061, Australia

Random House New Zealand Limited
18 Poland Road, Glenfield,
Auckland 10, New Zealand

Random House South Africa (Pty) Limited
Endulini, 5A Jubilee Road, Parktown 2193, South Africa

Random House UK Limited Reg. No. 954009

A CIP catalogue record for this book
is available from the British Library

ISBN 0-224-05169-5

Typeset by Palimpsest Book Production Limited
Polmont, Stirlingshire
Printed and bound in Great Britain by
Mackays of Chatham PLC, Chatham, Kent

For Lis – much
laughter, and more love

Acknowledgements

Yet again, my indispensable helper and friend, Catherine Tye, has thrown herself into the grind of checking and rechecking a new book. Oula Jones of the Society of Indexers has once more rubbed her hands with glee (I hope), as another of my books came her way.

Mike Shaw, my literary agent, kept everything on an even keel, and Tom Maschler, Dan Franklin and Charlotte Mendelson of Jonathan Cape gave sturdy help.

As for Elisabeth Anderson, a glance at the dedication speaks all.

Contents

Introduction: Bernard Levin

T HE FIRST BOOK I wrote – and it was an appallingly long
one, indeed it ran to some four hundred and thirty pages
– was about Britain and the Sixties. The Sixties – of course
– were held to be the dreadful poison that was ruining the
country for ever, with the most terrible bit being *That Was
The Week That Was*. People, by no means only hysterical
clergymen and Members of Parliament, actually said that the
country was changing for the worse, and that the disaster was
held to stem from *That Was*.

Today, many books have the most extraordinary titles,
but, seeking a title for my book, I thought "Britain and the
Sixties" was really snappy. I was on the verge of giving my
precious book that title, but my publisher thought it would
not be sufficiently snappy, so we looked about for a more
snappy one.

Then the real trouble started. Dozens of suggestions were
put up and tried, and all of them found wanting; more and
more claimed that the perfect title had been found, and even
more insisted that *that* one was the worst of the lot. Someone
suggested *The Pendulum Years*, we liked it, and all around
shook hands. There was not much time for getting the title
on the book, but in the end everything went smoothly.

Er, for a time. *Was* that the perfect title, or even half
perfect? More argument, and more. A cry was heard: there
was now no time to change titles, and *The Pendulum Years* it
was, and still is. But I remember vividly one who was against
our title, and she burst into tears.

But that was only the beginning; can you imagine the rest

of it? No, you cannot. There is nothing extraordinary about a writer writing. Take me and my words; they are all to be found in any ordinary dictionary, and I don't think that there are any dirty words to be found – I have never thought that foul words were smart or amusing. Nor do I sprinkle words or phrases in other languages to show off.

Yet when I draw back the curtain, and switch on the lights, I know that any ordinary human being will be shuddering; I say shuddering, but that is a very mild word for what is coming.

But now, gritting my teeth, I must tell you what you will not believe, or, if you do believe it, reel at the true horror and its widening. All the words I have written for *The Times*, most in the form of columns, have come from the same fingertips – mine. And how many words have I written and published? Why, *seventeen million.*

Now I must make clear that I have never worked in any other kind of trade. I know I was scribbling when I was 14, though I don't recall any claim to being a writer at that time. I think my mother suggested I should work in a bank, though if I had done so, there would have been a total collapse of the bank, not because I had been filching the money, but because of my total incompetence in the field of arithmetic. (That incompetence has remained with me for all of my life.)

What then? My father (who didn't stay long) suggested I should be a carpenter, but only a few days before, when my mother was out, I had sawn through all the legs of all the chairs, and no leg was the same length. Not a carpenter, then.

When University loomed, I put away such merry wickedness. I quickly discovered that, whatever I would be, I could not be a businessman. Nor could I draw or paint. Or sing. Or teach. Or dig. Or drive. Or cook. Or plant. Or be a conjurer. Or anything else, obviously ruling out robbery. I tried some bit parts when the University players came round, but I quickly discovered that I was not to be an actor either. I had made good friends, many of whom gave me good advice, but still I sought a trade, a profession, a craft, even a vocation if anybody would take me. (Nobody would.) Then, at University, when it was my turn to give a paper to the class, and the Professor had heard me read it aloud (that was the practice, and I suppose it still is), he, the Professor, said – and I can remember that Professor and his name, and his very words – not because his name was Smellie, but because I can still hear his voice, which had a little jerk between words, saying, "Levin, what you want to do is write". And I did. And I do. And will, as long as I can see the keyboard, though there are alarming voices saying that the keyboard is going to be scrapped and some dreadful new machine put in its place.

But I am wandering, and the echo returns: "Levin, what you want to do is write". Should I have done what he said? Could I have done something else? Or, more to the point, should I have written *and done something else as well*? Perhaps I could have done so, and perhaps my one profession has destroyed me. I know that many people envy me my success; should I shout at those who would follow me, and cry from the rooftops, "Go back, go back – run, run, run for your life"? Well, we do not need such lurid answers, but I do seriously urge anyone starting on a life of writing in newspapers and such to have another arrow in his or her bow.

But for me it didn't come out that way. Perhaps I was lucky enough to get started almost immediately. So I can only press the button, and indeed only one button. I must say that I have greatly prospered in my work; on that side, I make no moans. Come; how many men would change their jobs for mine? One in 10? One in 50? Surely one in a thousand, I should think.

Now nine of my collections of columns have been published, and the ninth (and last) is in your hands. Yet again there was a struggle to find a title for the book, but, as you see, the struggle is over. I do not remember who thought out this idea – the idea, that is, that there should be given to me a fixed chunk of *The Times*'s centre-fold, and that that chunk should always be exactly fifteen hundred words in length. I have toiled my inky way through nine anthologies, and if I should be so foolish as to list all the columns, there would be a pile of paper many yards high. There was a stab of pain in that question why, why, why did I become a writer, when there were hundreds of other professions? Why? Because I had not a scrap of any other talent. In this book you will find a moan or two which wishes that I had never picked up a pen. But I shrug, and smile, and here is the book.

But now the clouds gather. Apart from those who live in igloos and poke their noses out only once a year, we all know that for a good many years now the world as we have known it has been changing, and changing fast, and changing for the worse.

Ah, yes, that is what everyone says, so what's new? Something – I can call it terrible – and it has many branches. Let me start – at random – with a branch that at one time would not only get the police running, but would also shake the land from end to end. Come; when did you see a headline saying, "16-year-old girl drinks 60 pints of beer a week"? And you can only answer, never. (You see, the law says that children may drink in a pub or other such place if they are over 16 years of age.) No, don't shrug, and particularly don't wince, because beneath the headline, these words follow: "The case – described as 'horrendous' by youth workers – highlights the growing risk to Britain's teenagers from drink, now regarded by experts as a greater danger than drugs." So drugs are a danger, are they? Tut, tut. You will be worrying about violence next, ha, ha. Well, er, yes.

Another headline? Oh, we can rustle up hundreds. Take this one: "The gang boss aged 12 gets five years". You didn't know that children of that age could be locked up? Where have you been? Don't worry, I'll tell you where you have been: you have been living in the last 10 years or so. But back to the 12-year-old professional criminal – his name is Donovan Tull. "A court heard how the streetwise thug had terrorised the community where he lived." I'll say he terrorised the community. Enough? Good heavens, we've only just started. Because Donovan had a mate – name of Denzil Simms. And between Donovan and Denzil (high-class names, eh?) there was a mighty spree. Hark:

> Detectives believe that in six months he and his 14-year-old cousin carried out more than 200 thefts and robberies in South London. On one occasion they were arrested for a street robbery, taken to court and bailed into the care of social workers. Minutes later, they left the social worker standing on the pavement and robbed a lone woman a few streets away. In a matter of months Tull graduated from muggings and street thefts to robbing taxi drivers and then bookmakers, leaping the counter to snatch cash from the till and then running off. Hardly a day would go by without his committing a crime. Police said Tull would often not bother to disguise himself, believing he was virtually untouchable from going to jail. In one day, he robbed two bookmakers in succession in broad daylight, without trying once to hide his face. Neighbours on the Tanswell estate told how Tull would steal from flats and shops, threatening anybody who tried to stand in the gang's way. The landing outside his fourth floor flat was strewn with stolen handbags and other items, and turned into a shop for receivers. Tull and his gang became very well known among the South London bookmakers; they steam in, vault the counter, and take what they can from the till in seconds. There's hardly time to blink.

Now do not make the terrible mistake of thinking that the Tulls and Simmses are a pair of monsters who had their time and disappeared, leaving the respectable people to mop their brows and go about their business. The Tulls and Simmses have indeed gone about their business, happily for the rest of us in prison, where there is a straw's possibility that they might reform themselves. This business is not a one-off: it is

a hundred-off, a thousand-off, a countless-off. Our world is
changing for the terrible, and will not change back.

Still, we can borrow a few more headlines, with not a Tull
or a Simms, but something even worse. *Worse?* Try this:

> Violent teacher struck again on first day in class.
> A teacher with a history of violence against pupils
> found work at a comprehensive school and assaulted
> three children on his first day. Hartley (his name)
> admitted grabbing a 12-year-old boy's hair, hitting
> him twice around the head and dragging him across
> the floor by his tie. He then chased two 13-year-olds,
> bruising one of them on the arm and pushing the other
> against a wall.

Mad? No, surely not. Drugged? Not in this case. A quarrel
in the matrimonial home? Nothing like it. It is the time,
and nothing else. Once upon a time, no pupil would strike
a teacher; now we have a teacher who violently strikes his
pupils. We do get around, don't we?

Shakespeare knew, of course:

> Let fame, that all hunt after in their lives,
> Live register'd upon our brazen tombs,
> And then grace us in the disgrace of death;
> When, spite of cormorant devouring Time,
> The endeavour of this present breath may buy
> The honour which shall bate his scythe's keen edge,
> And make us heirs of all eternity.

But we do not need Shakespeare, or indeed any poet, to
tell us that the world is not what it was. Take one, ghastly,
statistic – the number of people killed by wholly random
and meaningless killers. Again and again, we see the same
dreadful answer to the same unanswerable question. Not a
week passes but that someone has been killed by kicking
or stamping as the killers enjoy their meaningless violence,
their total meaninglessness. For, make no mistake, hardly
one of those corpses died through their own fault, but from

someone else's lust for violence, and the latest horror is to stamp someone to death on the pavement.

Meanwhile, the Prince of Wales has been banging his head on a different wall; he said – quite rightly – that "Many people look in dismay at what has been happening to our language in the very place where it has evolved. They wonder what it is about our country and society that our language has become so impoverished, so sloppy and limited, that we have arrived at such a dismal wasteland of banality, cliché and casual obscenity." The Prince is right, of course, but he is far behind the times. When our farmers have to sit up nightly in patrols to stop the stealing of cattle and other livestock, the language has to take a back seat. And what about fraud in the Civil Service? *Fraud in the Civil Service?* Is it possible? Alas, yes, as the figures show: "Civil Service fraud has risen by more than thirty per cent in one month".

There is plenty more. Oh, plenty. Take this headline: "Girl of nine raped by five of her classmates." And try, "Five boys held after rape of 10-year-old". More, more! You want more? Oh, you shall have more. Try this, "A lollipop lady at the school said: 'It has gone downhill. The kids run riot in the streets. They are out of control and their language is filthy. The teachers don't seem able to control them'". Er, no . . .

That's nothing. Nothing. "A man obsessed by the break-up of his marriage murdered four of his young nieces and nephews by setting fire to their home . . . He was angry with Mrs Good for allowing his estranged wife to stay there . . . As most of the Good family slept, he emptied a can of petrol inside the hallway of the house in Sullivan Road . . . and set it alight."

And what about, "Two youths stole a family's pony before lashing it to a railway line with its head on the track and setting its mane on fire . . . Five-year-old Bobby . . . cried so loudly in pain that the passers-by ran to his aid as the youths fled . . . Bobby was saved when two boys heard him screaming and whinnying . . . The vet . . . had never known anything so completely evil . . ."

And that is only in this country. Look around the world, and shudder.

No one can count the thousands – the very many thousands – slaughtered in Algeria and now beginning to join the slaughter elsewhere. For many months, the mad Algerian Militants have been coming down upon a peaceful and decent world, a world which is now torn to pieces at a stroke. For the Militants have taken to slitting the throats of peaceful and decent people, and when I say throats, I mean hundreds. (Many go further and cut off the heads.)

And Zaire? "Thousands left to die as Zaire airlift begins." That's nothing – try "Massacre of Hutus". Meanwhile, "Big business scrambles for share of mineral wealth", and the share that they scramble for is that of Zaire, of course.

What has happened to the world that a nine-year-old girl can be raped, in England, in the open, and laughed at by her friends and fellow-pupils when the rape is over? What has happened in Britain when a man standing at a bus stop, waiting for his bus, saying nothing and doing nothing, is knocked to the ground by three hooligans and stamped to death, for fun?

I do not know. Don't tell me that there have always been brutal and criminal people, and there always will be, because it would not be true. Criminals and savages have always existed, true, but now the nature and depth signal something very different.

By now, my readers may be thinking that I have no thoughts other than the most hideous and sickening. It looks like that, but I assure you that I can speak and write about happiness, beauty, laughter and other wonders of the world (though not all the wonders). Indeed, I think I can blow away all the grimness of the world. Bragging again, my readers will say; but I ask you to stop and think. What is the only thing that sweeps away pain, wipes out anger, shrugs off poverty, smiles at ridicule, mops up tears and leaves one feeling entirely contented? Why, music, of course.

I truly believe that Shakespeare expressed more than mere words when he said:

> The man that hath no music in himself,
> Nor is not mov'd with concord of sweet sounds,
> Is fit for treasons, stratagems, and spoils;
> The motions of his spirit are dull as night,
> And his affections dark as Erebus:
> Let no such man be trusted.

Shakespeare was speaking with his tongue in his cheek, I am sure, but he was not speaking with his tongue in his cheek when he said – and they were some of his very greatest words

> How sweet the moonlight sleeps upon this bank!
> Here will we sit, and let the sounds of music
> Creep in our ears; soft stillness and the night
> Become the touches of sweet harmony.
> Sit, Jessica: look, how the floor of heaven
> Is thick inlaid with patines of bright gold:
> There's not the smallest orb which thou behold'st
> But in his motion like an angel sings
> Still quiring to the young-eyed cherubins;
> Such harmony is in immortal souls;
> But, whilst this muddy vesture of decay
> Doth grossly close it in, we cannot hear it.

One of my dearest friends "hath no music in himself" (he will recognise himself at once, when I say that he is exactly 10 years older than me). He is no gloomy figure – indeed, almost anything will make him laugh, but I shake my head in wonder when he tells me that the only music he will listen to is Gilbert and Sullivan, which he sings in an appalling – nay, hideous – warble. (I have written elsewhere about the possibility of my never finding music, and whenever I think about it, I shudder.)

So we soothe the savage breast with music, do we? But behind the curtain the stewpot still bubbles. I tried to give you brightness, my readers, in that mess of foul stew, but I fear that I have failed. I was not just giving you a catalogue of crimes and other wickednesses, I was driving into my readers' heads, and into my own, that terrible thought that the growing pile of awfulness might never be shovelled away.

Have you seen – it has been shown many times on television – a gigantic pile of used motor-car tyres – hundreds and thousands of them? Indeed it is a strange sight, this Everest of tyres. Yes, but there is another side of this great mountain: nobody has found a way of disposing of these now useless objects; to burn them would choke the country, there can be no pit big enough to hold them, and – worse than all – the mountain is growing as more and more cars are sent for scrap, and there are at least four tyres for every car.

So I retreat, cowardly, to my music. There will be sneers and cries of "running away". I have an answer; I have spent at least a third of my adult life looking at dreadfulness and fighting – not, I admit, with fists and clubs, but with words – words which I have tried to use to stem the tide of evil. Have I had any success? Yes, a good measure of little bits and pieces – who will demand of me more?

Some years ago, I was walking down Regent Street, and as I passed the doors of Dickens and Jones, I saw two young lads – I guess they were about 13 or 14 – and each of them was stuffing a large and presumably valuable scarf beneath his jacket, obviously stolen.

Did I cry, "Stop thief", or run after the boys and try to catch them? I am sorry to say that I did not. I am not sorry for Dickens and Jones, who would not be ruined by the loss of two scarves, but I am sorry for the young thieves. I should have run after them, because if that was the start of a life of crime, they may continue to live in crime for ever. I hope not. And to blot out the pain (dammit, it was my pain, and not that of the young thieves), I turned to music, which when used properly is the greatest solace in all the world.

That evening, I tried to soothe my disturbed feelings with music. But what music? It could not be Beethoven; I would have been crushed beneath those mighty wonders. Well, then, Mozart. Mozart has the great, the very great and magical touch of being able to do anything that is wanted, but that evening I wanted something rock-solid in its profundity. Wagner – ugh – in spite of my great and deep passion for Wagner, his music that night would have made me throw myself out of the window. Even Schubert would not quite do, and Haydn, I feel, lovely as he is, can be too soothing.

Yes, that evening it had to be Bach. I know every bar of every chosen piece, and each one is more wonderful than the last: *Sheep May Safely Graze*, a handful of *Brandenburgs*, the *Mass in B Minor*, the *St Matthew Passion*, and finish with the *Goldberg Variations*. Many will disagree with that choice, but if a man may not sit by his own fireside and listen to Bach, the world has turned upside down. And so, slowly, those thieving boys faded from my memory, and Bach took the stage. And, as he did so, I looked out of the window – it was a cloudless night – and I looked into the immensity of the numbers of the stars, and as I stood there, I felt a drop of moisture trickling down my cheek. And there were more such tricklings before I went to bed that night.

News from the zoos

I FIRST ENCOUNTERED MR John Aspinall some years ago when he was running a gambling house – a very smart and elegant gambling house abutting on Berkeley Square – where the champagne flowed like Niagara. I have a faint memory that he was always getting entangled with the then laws of gambling, and always coming out successful. From time to time I dropped in and lost a few bawbees; I was never a serious gambler, thank heaven, but the ambience was so pleasant and absurd – it amounted, of course, to foolish people truly believing they could win millions – that I could while away an hour or two sketching out in my mind the novel about gambling that I would one day write. Aspinall made a fortune from his gamblers, but to give him his due, he was a very successful businessman even without them.

I don't know how much attention Aspinall now gives to the cries of *faites vos jeux*, but few, in the old days, would have guessed what he would turn to. For Aspinall, with or without the whirr of the roulette-wheel, has long ago turned to the growls and roars of great animals; his transmogrification was manifestly no joke, nor was it something to take up on Friday and drop, all passion spent, on Sunday. He established Howletts Zoo in 1958, and since then, almost half a lifetime, he has taken the role of zoo-keeper, and taken it so passionately that it is no metaphor but the literal truth that he has come to love animals more than human beings. (He said some time ago that half of his best friends were wild animals.)

Now Aspinall, in his other life, is not a lunatic. A man who sets up zoos and includes the most fierce and dangerous animals in the world is not playing Pooh-sticks. All care had to be taken, and of course it was. But Aspinall has his theories about the rearing and keeping of animals, especially the great cats, and Aspinall's theories are in the limelight today, not least because a year ago one of the keepers at Howletts Zoo was mauled to death by a tiger. A tragedy indeed; but when I say that this is the third such death caused by the great tigers, it is surely time to examine not the tigers but Aspinall's theory.

Aspinall's theory says that wild animals should keep their wildness (he has recently started to send orphan gorillas back to the jungle), and to make sure that they do he "fed them only every four or five days to mirror their wild state". Now I am entirely ignorant in the behaviour of wild animals, or indeed caterpillars, but even I can understand that if you take a jungle tiger weighing five hundred pounds, and feed it only every four or five days, the tiger is likely to eat anything in sight which it believes edible, including mice, stray dogs, visitors, the railings and, *in extremis*, Mr Aspinall.

Mr Aspinall is great on bonding, that is "people should bond with the animals soon after birth, developing a relationship of trust and affection". (In case some of you have got the wrong end of the stick, I should make clear that it is the animals that should be doing the bonding soon after *their* birth.) But there is no suggestion that Mr Aspinall is ordering his staff to go into the tigers' compound; on the contrary, the keepers are plainly the most fervid tiger companions, and the head keeper, after saying that there is "an inherent risk in handling a tiger" (well, yes), says that it is "a desirability that they remain wild and keep the instinct and ability to kill".

Apart from me, whom or what are they thinking of, when they say that the tigers should keep the ability to kill? If you say that without killing power the great beasts would pine and become milksops, you must answer this question: why did you bring these noble but savage animals halfway round the world in the first place for people to gawk at?

Mr Aspinall and his colleagues argue powerfully against the more usual means of taming a tiger, such as electric prods and meat given or withheld. Even I shudder at that, and so should anyone who has any feeling. But that only multiplies my questions. Recently, there has been a swell against zoos, any kind of zoos; perhaps it is time to abolish the whole business. But assuredly, if we did, we would have lost something precious. It is not only that children go wide-eyed when such amazing creatures as the rhinoceros, the alligator, the kangaroo and indeed the parrot come into view; it is we, the grown-ups, who are reminded of the almost incredible variety of living things in our multitudinous world.

Yes, but Aspinall does go rather far. To bond with a tiger on short commons must be a wonderful experience – if, that is, the tiger doesn't get you first. In Howletts Zoo, three men have died at the claws of a tiger; they were seasoned experts and Aspinall had taken every precaution (including of course going into the tiger's lair himself), but there is an obvious hole in the certainty. Aspinall, his team, you, me, the man who caught the tiger in the first place, any passer-by – anyone can see the great mistake: nobody, *nobody* can see into the mind of a tiger.

> Tyger! Tyger! burning bright
> In the forests of the night,
> What immortal hand or eye
> Could frame they fearful symmetry?

> And what shoulder, and what art,
> Could twist the sinews of thy heart?
> And when thy heart began to beat,
> What dread hand? and what dread feet?

If you won't take it from Blake, then take it from Professor Paul Bateson of Cambridge University's zoology department, who says rather sensibly that ". . . a tiger could behave like an overgrown kitten one minute and a highly motivated hunter the next, and it is sentimental and naïve to think that closer relationships between keepers and big cats would always be friendly".

But whether the tiger is friendly or hostile, Aspinall gives more to the enemy every time he opens his mouth, *viz.*, "Captive animals should be treated as honoured guests." And he makes it even worse still, by saying, yes, the honoured guests are dangerous, ". . . but it is also dangerous to cross the road".

When shall we – that is, the British people – see animals straight? Do you remember the gigantic uproar, a year or two ago, when a very splendid cow (I think it was a cow) which had won prizes for its size and magnificence was going to be slaughtered? No matter that a hundred cows are slaughtered every week or so without anyone screaming the place down or even noticing, the nation rose as one, demanding the head of any farmer who would touch a hair of the by-now sanctified beast. Did those who demanded blunderbusses, debates in Parliament, boycotts, masked avengers – did they pause to think how much veal they had consumed in the previous few months? Nay, a much more terrible thought comes unbidden: were there some among the save-the-cow contingent who didn't know where their milk comes from?

Well, Aspinall knows where his tigers come from, and it is quite clear that every one of Aspinall's colleagues is willing to put his head into the tiger's mouth. Moreover, this particular argument would be trivial were it not for the danger. For the battle is between Aspinall and all his colleagues on the one hand, and the law on the other (there must be a funny side if the Health and Safety at Work Act has got into the business). The argument goes on while the tigers prowl about their demesnes, but the law says that the keepers may not go into those demesnes *with the beasts*.

Don't bother to whistle; these amazing people (Aspinall the most amazing) are going to sit down and weep if they are not allowed to go into a tiger's den with the tigers. This is not just bravura; it is their profound but wrong belief that tigers and human beings truly can cohabit. Yet I have to say that there is some mighty evidence on Aspinall's side.

The wolf also shall dwell with the lamb, and the leopard shall lie down with the kid; and the calf and the young lion and the fatling together; and a little child shall lead them. And the cow and the bear shall feed; their young ones shall lie down together: and the lion shall eat straw like the ox. They shall not hurt nor destroy in all my holy mountain; for the earth shall be full of the knowledge of the Lord as the waters cover the sea.

The Times, 24 November 1995

Banks? Try cliffs

A S MY REGULAR readers will know, I have a very considerable number of King Charles's Heads. (I use that familiar trope, but to my shame I have just realised that I don't know exactly what it means. I would not be surprised to find that a great number of my readers do not understand it either. And when it comes to the phrase's provenance, it seems that hardly anyone gets the right answer first go. So I looked it all up in Brewer and discovered that it means an obsession, something the afflicted cannot stop doing, and it comes from Mr Dick, in *David Copperfield*.)

But now to our muttons (and where did *that* phrase come from?) – for I am coming back to the wonders and lunacies and excuses and squirmings and incompetences and genteel robberies and mistakes and mistakes and mistakes and mistakes and many more mistakes on the part of – yes (but who else could it be), the bankers and the financiers, from the humblest high street bank that has just got two decimal points adrift and insists that it was the customer's fault, to the greatest international muck-up whether honest or dishonest, if indeed there is any difference. (*I* don't think there is any.)

Let us begin with a *bonne-bouche* before we tuck in. (The cream was supplied by our dear sister the *Sun*.) A boy of 15 thought it might be fun to pull the tail of a bank, with no criminal purpose. A high-street bank was selected – it was Lloyds in this case, but of course it could have been any of them and almost certainly will be sooner or later. Our young hero, wearing jeans and a jersey indicating that he follows Aston Villa, walked into the bank with nothing but a home-made ID card and announced that his grandmother had just died and left him six hundred thousand pounds, and he would like to open an account. Whereupon and instantly, without checking of any kind, the bank stuffed seventy-five pounds into his jersey; and when the boy said that he was going to get two cars immediately, one a Ferrari, the manager rang round insurance brokers for quotes. Nor was that all; he said that the first instalment of the bequest was just coming along, and it would be £43,000.

The boy, whose hand I should feel honoured to shake, said: "I did not know exactly what I was going to say – it all just came off the top of my head and I made it up as I went along. I only went in to see if I could open an account but as I got deeper and deeper into the story it took on a life of its own."

Mark my words: that boy will go far. But whether Lloyds Bank will go anywhere at all is another matter.

Now for something serious. Mr John Schultz is a restaurateur; his place is near Wisbech. For six years he had been – come, we are plain people, so let us use plain language – diddled by the Midland, over a loan and a current account. The Midland denied it, so Mr Schultz engaged an independent financial examiner, a Mr Radin, to look at the books. He discovered that indeed Mr Schultz had been paying too much, by a hefty £5,800. The Midland paid out, and I should think so.

But then Mr Schultz discovered that his partners – in the family – had been short-changed by the Midland to the tune of another £13,000. The Midland coughed up again – though with less than it should have been. And then came the very thing which make the banks hated. *Hated*, I said, not found bothersome or time-wasting or expensive, but hated. Hear Mr Schultz:

I could never get a straight answer out of the bank. Many of my letters went unanswered and I didn't get anywhere. It put me under enormous pressure and stress, and threatened the viability of my business. I felt like I was banging my head against a brick wall.

And Mr Schultz topped the story by saying that he had had to deal with ten – *ten* – different bank managers as the Midland switched his account. Now hear Mr Radin, Mr Schultz's hero:

> For six months after I started investigating, the bank insisted that nothing was wrong, and made excuse after excuse. I discovered that every aspect of the Oldee Mill's business loan that could go wrong had gone wrong. We found interest charges were too high, bank charges inflated and transaction charges incorrect. Nobody would grasp the nettle and deal with the problem.

And do you know what the Midland said at the end – that is, when it was all over after *six years* of incompetence and more from them? They said: "We are a service-oriented organisation and determined to get things absolutely right. We treat complaints very seriously." (If they treat complaints very seriously like that, how do you think they treat them when they are doubled up with laughter?)

That's Lloyds and Midland; now for NatWest. Come to Wallingford – a very nice place in Oxfordshire. Here, as usual, the problem is bank charges; the customers say they are exorbitant, and the banks say when businesses go bust it is the recession's fault, not the banks'. An action group was formed, and an expert, Dick Sargent, whose company is Audit, was summoned; his job is precisely to see whether the recession or the banks are pushing Wallingforders into bankruptcy. He looked, and claims that the bank had overcharged every one of the businesses in the action group. NatWest denies that. Well, they would, wouldn't they? And Audit carefully said that ". . . although banks have occasionally undercharged, the difference between what should have been charged and what was actually charged almost always favours the bank".

Almost always favours the bank. Say it again. Again. Once more. Because Mr and Mrs Crudgington would like you to do so. Or at least I think they would.

The Crudgingtons were not the only ones in the area to feel the pinch, and of course the argument – banks or recession? – goes on. But the Crudgingtons have rather more to argue about. Mrs Crudgington had begun to worry about excessive charges in 1991, but was told that they were correct. The Crudgingtons discovered, however, that what they had been told was – to put it bluntly – a pack of lies. And it took *13 months* for NatWest to pay back £11,155 in interest, £443 in charges and £4,447 in auditing and legal fees. And again we hear the same stinking story, this time from Mrs Crudgington, who says – as thousands and thousands and thousands say – "What angers me is the evasiveness and the delay in the bank admitting it was at fault". And I doubt very much that the Crudgingtons – Mr Crudgington is bankrupt now – finds very funny the NatWest television advertisement in which a bank manager is seen sailing a boat in stormy seas, just to visit a small businessman.

A good many years ago, there was a move to nationalise the banks; it must have been under the Labour Government, or at least the argument must have started in the Labour Party. It was no wild, crazy idea, and was argued seriously. The banks smiled at first, but when it was seen to be a viable notion, the Tories began to worry. The idea of nationalisation faded, and the Tories settled down happily. As I recall – it *was* a long time ago – there was, as a sop, some kind of overseeing of the banks, but that died out too. Now, all we have are the ombudsmen; good as they are, for one rapped knuckle a hundred corner-boys get away with it.

Perhaps we should look at that idea of putting the banks into some kind of quarantine; at the very least, there should be some real force – from outside – that would make a real bruise on the banks' hides. For do not believe that these shocking instances are just a sprinkling: they are a steady downpour.

And there is the worst to come. We are now regularly told that more and more bank staff are becoming redundant; the human being versus the machine. Perhaps that was inevitable, and we cannot all become Luddites. But it means – oh, how it means – that for every unanswered letter, for every mistake, for every lost document that the human being brought down, there will be fifty when the machines are doing the work.

Ah, well. We can fall back on *Schadenfreude*. Nomura Securities, Japan's largest firm of stockbrokers, has been fined £641,000 for violations of American securities laws. And – we can still laugh, thank heaven – Nomura says that the violation was a technical matter.

Stop Press. A startling headline reads: "Barclays Bank pays police in dud £50 notes." Better not linger, you might discover what the headline is about.

The Times, 8 March 1996

No! No! Sing!

IT WAS ONLY a few weeks ago that I wrote, yet again, about the Holocaust. On that occasion I was discussing, first, the mad or evil (or mad *and* evil) men who deny that the Holocaust ever happened, and next, the much more evil men – yes, there are some – who wallow in the Holocaust, loving and revering Hitler. Hark to the American Gary Lauck, perhaps the most Nazified figure in this entire midden (he is so steeped in Nazism that he has grown a moustache exactly like Hitler's, and although he is entirely American, he deliberately speaks with a German accent): "In my opinion the Jews were treated too humanely. We must never make this mistake again."

So what is there more to say, after that? Two things: the first thing was encapsulated by a Holocaust survivor, who said, "I believe no culprit should be allowed to climb into his grave without being unmasked". And the second thing? The second thing is what I propose to write about today.

I have been rebuked for my belief that the few old men who murdered Jews and somehow found asylum in Britain should be left in peace, though their victims could find no peace except in the grave. (One of the accused could be seen on television a few days ago; very old and no doubt ready to deny everything.)

When *will* that tap stop dripping? The answer is a grim one: it will stop dripping when, and only when, every person who has drunk from it or washed in it is dead. Again and again, some elderly man or woman is found to be a survivor of the Holocaust, and it is sometimes a very delicate matter to discover on which side that person lived. But now we have another problem. We have, still living among us, one of those elderly figures – she is just 80 – who cannot be simply categorised as another old and doddery figure, of no importance except to her own family. For this person, you see, is famous. Very famous. Very famous indeed.

True, she is famous only in the musical world, but in that world she still shines above us like the stars, for a star she was throughout her wonderful career. That career was based in Britain – indeed, she lived in Hampstead – when, of course, she was not flitting about the world doing her work. In 1979, when her British husband died, having worked tirelessly for her fame, she retired to Switzerland. She is not a recluse by any means; in 1992 she was decorated by the Queen as a Dame of the British Empire. And now, someone has written and published a book about her and her career.

Tush: there must be a dozen books about her and her career; I have one on my own shelves, and I would feel odd if I hadn't. For you see, the famous person we are discussing is Elisabeth Schwarzkopf, one of the most wonderful opera singers the world has ever heard.

I started with the words "For you see", but you cannot possibly see until I have explained. I said that someone had written a book about Elisabeth Schwarzkopf, and such books are standard in the operatic world; but even the most self-satisfied luvvie (and the luvvies in the world of the opera are self-satisfied indeed) would shudder on seeing such a book as the one that has just been published, written by Alan Jefferson (who he?) and published by Victor Gollancz. (Gollancz himself died many years ago and his business was long ago swallowed up by Cassell, but the publishing world has a generous and charming practice which leaves intact the imprint of a long-dead publisher.)

Now the book says, in the most vigorous terms, that although Elisabeth Schwarzkopf was indeed a most wonderful singer, she was also a deep-dyed Nazi throughout her entire time in Hitler's Germany and quite possibly after. (There is another wry aspect to this story: Gollancz himself would have been horrified twice over to learn that Madame Schwarzkopf was being attacked, once because of her miraculous singing, and second and more important because Gollancz spent thousands of hours on reconciliation between Germany and Britain – indeed, the world.)

And here we are again. But we are no longer talking about the doddery figure with one foot in the grave; we are talking about a musician of genius and her past. And her past, for many people, is more interesting than her genius, *particularly for those whose relatives died in the gas-chambers*. Before you shout me down, kindly listen to this:

> I obediently declare herewith: none of my parents or grandparents has ever belonged at any time to the Jewish religion, nor have I ever been married to anybody of non-Aryan descent . . . I vow to be true and obedient to the Führer of the German Reich and people, Adolf Hitler, and to fulfil my duty conscientiously and unselfishly.

That, as you may have guessed, was the form of induction into the Nazi Party. And that was Elisabeth Schwarzkopf signing on as a fully fledged member, number 7,548,960. *Now* you can shout. Particularly because there is proof that, after the war, when the Nazis were being sorted out from the innocents, she claimed that she had never been a member of the Nazi Party, and repeated that lie several times until finally she gave in and told the truth.

Now then; singing beautifully and being a Nazi is not necessarily the same thing, nor the opposite of it. If you made a list of artists – in music, in the theatre, in painting and sculpting, in writing itself – and then counted up the whole number of German artists who carried on their trade after being fully inducted into the Nazi Party, how many would the list contain? And then, after the war, count the number of such figures. Three-and-half, would you say? Where is the ruler that always rules straight?

Elisabeth Schwarzkopf signed up as a Nazi, true to her leader, Adolf Hitler. And what did that mean? That she would, every Saturday, murder a specified number of Jews? Reader, would *you* like to live between the devil and the deep blue sea? Her signing on as a Nazi meant nothing other than "I want to go on singing". Who shall be so pure and white to say no to Adolf Hitler, when saying no is likely to mean losing a job, and indeed a life. Yes, there were heroes, who died for being heroes: come, Mr Jefferson, with hand on heart, would you swear that if you had a choice between signing on as a Nazi and being hung from a fine wire you would not choose the signature?

The trouble with this terrible problem is that Elisabeth Schwarzkopf learnt to sing, and to sing so beautifully that her singing was heard all over the world. If she had only learnt double-entry book-keeping, not only would she have had no reason to tell lies about her past, but she would have been much less likely to be obliged to sign up as a Nazi against her will.

How many human relics of the war and the Holocaust are there left? How many prominent persons in the arts and sciences who lived through hell and saw the rainbow in the end? These are no less or more cherishable human beings, for all their prominence. Fear of a dreadful death, in those days, hung over the great and the low together.

Who was Elisabeth Schwarzkopf to change the world? In a sense, and a rather powerful sense, she *did* change the world, at least in one tiny corner. In my own youth I heard her sing again and again, and the sounds that came from her were not the thud of the jackboot, I can tell you. Come: she signed up on a wicked piece of paper; did that make her wicked? Did she ever push a Jew off the pavement? Did she demand space in the Nazi newspapers to denounce Jews? How often did she go about with members of the Gestapo telling where Jews were hidden?

Take it from me, you pillow-heroes, when *your* time comes, most of you will suffer just as much trembling of the hands as any ordinary coward like me. Who will demand that Elisabeth Schwarzkopf must be braver than anyone else?

Not me. She was weak, perhaps, and – more to the point – she wanted cheers. What artist of the stage doesn't? (I don't think even Haitink would reject them.) But above all, in this story, there hangs one more aspect, and it is this. We cannot measure, let alone understand, what a life in the Third Reich meant. When you and I can understand it, then, but only then, may we rebuke Elisabeth Schwarzkopf. I think the rebuke will be some time coming.

The Times, 12 January 1996

Choose your partners

H OW LONG AGO it was, how long! How long ago it was
that apartheid ruled in South Africa and black men and
women were thought of as creatures hardly different from
animals! How long ago it was when white men as well as
black could be, and were, thrown into jail on the slightest
pretext and kept there for years! How long it was, how long,
the time that Nelson Mandela spent in prison for disagreeing
with the dreadful rulers of South Africa! (To be exact, it was
26 years.) How long ago it was that Alan Paton wrote *Cry the
Beloved Country*, and because by then his name was so widely
known around the world, the rulers of his beloved country
did not dare to imprison him or have him silenced!

Yes, it was a long time ago, and Nelson Mandela has since
shaken hands with the wicked and absolved them. And so, at
last, we can shut that door for ever, can we not?

No, for some of the graves in that story are still crying out
for justice, and as the earth heaves, they say that their voices
will never fade until that which was wrong is put right.

Now for the story.

It starts with John Lloyd, and I should first warn you
that Mr Lloyd is putting his own case and is not exactly
rushing to give the other side, where he might find an
argument or two. Yet this is a truly tragic story and it has
many facets.

Mr Lloyd, when he lived in South Africa, hated apartheid,
as any decent person would, and he conspired with others to
do as much damage to the hated State as they could. To this
end they blew up electricity pylons, radio masts, and suchlike,

but, he says, did not seek to kill or injure any person, however
steeped in apartheid evil.

One of the leaders at the head of the organisation Mr Lloyd
had joined – they called themselves the African Resistance
Movement – was Hugh Lewin, and although he and his band
did not expect to topple apartheid, they were sufficiently
successful to make the forces of government think them a
serious danger. So far, so good. But then came the news
that Lewin and others had been caught. One of these was
John Lloyd himself, and he was in turn imprisoned and
interrogated.

Then came the bomb – the bomb that brought down
not a pylon, but a human being: Ethel Rhys was killed
by a bomb deliberately left on a bench in a Johannesburg
railway station by one John Harris. (There is a tiny clue to
the feelings of John Lloyd. He has written about the bomb
and its aftermath, but it seems that the pain, understandably,
precludes him writing anything about the dead woman and
even her surviving granddaughter.)

Now the pace quickens. John Harris was caught (and
subsequently hanged). Lloyd had said that he would not
testify against his mates – Hugh Lewin and the rest – though
he did. But he did something else, and that something is
what the brand-mark on his soul denotes. He sang like any
canary thus:

> I agreed to give evidence against Harris because he had
> so violated our code. I can't know whether I would have
> made a different decision had I been at liberty, or if I had
> shared a cell with colleagues.

Do you shudder, reader? I did, when I first read Lloyd's
apologia; that phrase "he had so violated our code" (that
is, that they would not harm other people). Was he playing
God? Or was he the arbiter in a truly difficult position? It is
difficult to say, but those who still hate him would, I suppose,
call him a stool-pigeon.

Whatever went through Lloyd's mind as he turned state's

evidence against his comrades, it must have been a dreadful blow – not only, of course, to Harris, but to all his former comrades. And having done his work – it is time for another shudder – Lloyd was given immunity from prosecution and moved to London. (Well, if he had still been in South Africa when any of the men he fingered finished their terms and got out, Lloyd might have lost a lot of teeth at the very least.)

Let the dead bury the dead. But the dead will not stay dead. This story is only half way through, and more pain, much more, will be felt.

Because, you see, the figures in the story didn't vanish when they left the stage; Hugh Lewin went to prison for seven years because Lloyd betrayed him. He also betrayed Baruch Hirson, who was in the same boat, and who went to prison for *nine* years. Dreadful; it is very easy to point a finger, but we must remember the conditions in which the fingers were pointed. Young men, facing years of prison, will look at horror, and turn away.

Lewin, understandably, would spit in Lloyd's face if they met, and that is not just a figure of speech; Lewin says that Lloyd is "a Judas Iscariot who should have the decency to piss off out of politics".

And Baruch Hirson says of Lloyd that "The fact of the matter is that such a man is not fit to hold public office, particularly since he made no effort to apologise to any of us or to John Harris's widow. Such a man is not fit to hold public office."

And Harris's widow herself says: "What he has done is not honourable. Worse than that, it is ignoble. He should stand down."

And Glynis Burleigh, whose grandmother was killed by the Harris bomb, and has had to have 40 skin grafts from the effects of it, says: "Unlike him, I could not run away to England and begin a new life." Refusing to forget Mr Lloyd's history, she said: "He cannot whitewash the past and pretend it did not happen. He is not a fit candidate."

But what is all this about politics, public office, candidates and standing down? It stems from the extraordinary fact that John Lloyd, with a past like his, is trying to become an MP – a Labour MP, for Exeter.

Take him back all those years; assuredly he cannot have forgotten them. Here is a young man who thought, not ignobly, that to set bombs among machinery would be to bring a moment or two nearer the purging of South Africa's apartheid evil. But then, after a time, the world shifts for him; he who was betrayed, betrays in turn; who would not betray under torture? But what his erstwhile comrades will never forgive was that John Lloyd gave evidence in court against his comrades, who went to prison and stayed there for years. Later on, Lloyd sought to be an MP, and he is now close to becoming one, on the Labour side. (If you open the window, you can hear Tony Blair groaning.)

Over the years, we have had all kinds of people in our Parliament, Commons and Lords; some have been very odd, and some of them have been very bad indeed. Some have lived a very pure life, while others haven't. Even in my lifetime, I have seen more than one MP thrown out for behaviour that even the House of Commons could not stomach. (The members of the House of Lords, being peculiar *ab initio*, don't count in this examination.) But I do really, I do really think that somewhere in this complicated world a line must be drawn. And I do really think – I do, I do, I do – that the line in question must be drawn on the unsunny side of Mr Lloyd becoming an MP.

Interviewed when he was seeking the Exeter candidacy, he spoke of being arrested for his political views, and said: "I was arrested and detained without trial for about 120 days. I didn't think I was a revolutionary and I didn't think I could keep quiet after that, so I decided to leave."

A reasonable reply, though he might have added a word or two about the planting of bombs, let alone the betrayal of John Harris.

I conclude with two versions of Lloyd: the first is his.

I was approached by a very hostile woman . . . who asked me to sign an affidavit saying my evidence against John Harris was untrue. I first of all agreed, and then I thought it through. Such a withdrawal would have been of no weight . . .

And the second version is from Jill Chisholm (a journalist, friend to another accused):

With Harris on death row . . . [I] . . . came to London to plead with Lloyd to retract his evidence . . . He was not prepared to change his evidence or make any statement or any clemency bid at all. My impression was that he was concerned about how people would view him if he retracted his evidence.

Choose your partners. But don't choose Lloyd for our Parliament.

P.S. He did not become an M.P.

The Times, 19 January 1996

Keeping it in the family

WICKEDNESS, THY NAME is legion. In Britain, every day, nay every hour, a crime is being committed. Every hour, do I say? Every minute, surely, and I would not argue if someone said it must be every second.

Yes, but "a crime" can be something from a savage murder to someone picking up a few coins dropped from a short-sighted lady's reticule and not giving them up. We must define our terms. Violence, surely, must be high on the ladder, and I *think* that we must differentiate between violence in the home and elsewhere. Then there is the confidence trickster: he too can be a mild nuisance or a real swine. (Are there still hayseeds in New York who are tricked into thinking they have bought Brooklyn Bridge? I bet there are.)

No doubt there have been many men and women who have stolen from their relatives. Indeed, huge sums have been wheedled out of their loved ones, and it seems that the larger the sum, the deeper people go into the mire. As for the City folk and the countless millions that go to and fro, dropping a few million into the wrong pockets, they should get their full and a bit over, but usually don't.

But there is something especially horrible when the thieves are deeply loved in the family *and* are the ones who are robbing those who love them. And worse yet when the family that is being robbed is not at all rich, but lives most modestly, and has to.

And that is the kind of criminal I am to discuss today.

First, for what actually happened. There is a woman, her

name Diane McManus, who wanted money. (Oh, money, money, money, when will human beings stop wanting that terrible and poisonous stuff? Never.) She wanted money, not for giving the children of the orphanage a treat, not for giving thick new blankets to the poor men who sleep in doorways, not for the rebuilding of a dozen leaky churches, but for buying herself a brand new sports car, costing £12,000. And for a new garage and new kitchen costing £40,000. And for things she cannot remember, costing £60,000.

Now then, let us say that she wanted money, as most of us do. She was not poor, but she wanted real riches. So she went to her father and stepmother and told them that she was dying of cancer, a singularly powerful lever. The older couple sold their holiday bungalow to get funds for the dying Diane, but that was not enough. So the parents gave her their savings. Cancer, you know, is a dreadful malady, and it can take a great deal of money to sustain the sufferer. Our Diane needed more money, much more. Her father raised more money – these doctors do not come cheap, but for a beloved daughter, no sum is too great. More money, more money. (There was one point – it was touch and go for a few hours - one when an actual doctor was getting close to examining the supposed sufferer; she told the family that that doctor had been killed in a car crash.) Then her father, practically ruined, yes, but my beloved daughter must have the most gentle rites – more money – thought that he would go to the Medical Negligence Board, for Diane had said that on one occasion there had been negligence. Diane said that they would get compensation automatically from the board, so he would not need to go to it, but he wanted to go, and told his daughter he was going, whereupon the whole edifice of lies and thieving collapsed into the sand – for of course if her father had gone to the board he would have discovered that there was no negligence, no cancer, no dying and no more lies. So Diane broke down and said: "There's no compensation, Dad. I've conned you. I've ruined your life." And indeed she had.

★   ★   ★

And then the headlines began: "'Dying' woman conned her parents out of £100,000", "Cancer lies cheat a trusting father" and so on.

It is no use saying that the parents were dreadfully naïve. Have *you* ever been told that a deeply beloved member of your family is very slowly dying, and if you had, would you, do you think, announce that there must be an examination in case the sufferer is conning money out of the family? Anyway, however childish the wronged father was, it is not he and the rest of the family who need close examination. (The details of the examination will not take place for some time, because Diane has been put behind bars for three years, but there is plenty to go on.)

For a start, there is the extraordinary matter of Diane's dreadful swindle. It is one very close to the clerk who steals the money, convinced that he will get it all back and more as the wheel begins to spin. But there is one enormous difference; in this case there is no wheel. Diane knew, and must have known, that none of all the money she was stealing would ever be brought back. I find it difficult to believe that she, knowing how it would and must end, nevertheless did it.

Take her words when the bomb had gone off: "There's no compensation, Dad. I've conned you. I've ruined your life." It sounds like a rather hurried elocution lesson from a somewhat downmarket teacher. Put it parallel to the remarks of the ruined parent: "When she was recovering at home we would visit, and she would be lying on the sofa covered with a blanket and really looking ill. I know I have been conned, but when you see your own daughter in that state and she says she's got cancer it doesn't enter your head that it's all a lie."

I don't think that the focus was the £12,000 car; experts tell me that a £12,000 car is only a medium-money one. Perhaps there was no exact moment, and night after night she tossed and turned, and came back just as tormented in the morning. You see what I am getting at. The woman had never cheated or stolen; so the question is "At what point did she go over the falls?" And, of course, why?

To start with, she knew that her thieving was from her family. Does that make her crime better or worse? It can be either; within the family circle the horror is doubled because the thief knows that there was no great fortune to rob, but within the family circle there are – must be – at least the dregs of love that would still tug at the heart.

So what about the stranger? The blow is surely worse; out of the clouds comes nothing that can mean anything, until the ripples of horror; yes, there is horror in robbery even if there is nothing physically alarming. But none of these explanations makes any sense. The girl (well, she was 26) was an ordinary girl who wanted to have lots of money, and took it; it is just possible that she was so far in the heavens that she thought she would not be prosecuted. Perhaps that is why she robbed the family rather than a stranger who would bring the police.

When she was in the dock, her lawyer must have had the very devil of a job to find anything that he could say on her side, but he did come up with an interesting idea. He said that Diane "was motivated by jealousy, revenge, emotional insecurity and a desire for attention". There was nothing to back this up, but it is quite possible that it is true, or partly true. After all, Stavely near Chesterfield could hardly have been a great centre of work and play and politics, music and theatre, beauty and writing. But where would the money come from? Alas, we know, and so does Diane, and so do the warders.

But turn the page. Diane's parents are ruined. When Diane went into the dock, it was to admit that she had squandered £100,455, two-thirds of her parents' lifesavings, and that not a penny of it will ever be seen again. And the other third? It had vanished entirely – not even the thief could say where it had gone.

A thief by any name is still a thief. But if you can read the story of Diane and her parents without feeling a chill run down your back, you must have a nonpareil spine. "There's no compensation, Dad. I've conned you. I've ruined your life." And she had. And she will never fully understand what she did in doing that.

To hate a child of one's own loins must be a terrible thing. But to ruin a father and mother for life is also terrible. God forbid that any of us might have to spin such a coin.

The Times, 25 October 1996

Only man is vile

C OME, LET US put all care aside for a change and think only about merriment, wassail, laughter and the pleasant side of the weather. And we shall start with a most striking headline: "Cars overturned as mob attacks National Gallery". Bravo! How wonderful it is to be living in a country so thirsty for art that it can never be slaked, and – as the headline tells – Trafalgar Square has been full of people fighting, literally fighting, to get a mere glimpse of the Degas and the Stubbs at the National Gallery.

No, alas, readers, I am cheating; I dare say you realised that. But if you didn't, try this:

> England football fans went on the rampage after the national football team's Wembley defeat last night, throwing missiles at police and bystanders, looting shops, and burning cars . . . crowd-control barriers were overturned and a hot-dog stand smashed by thugs eager to take on the police in a pitched battle . . . shortly after midnight the mob surged to the north of Trafalgar Square, standing on the steps of the National Gallery, throwing missiles through its windows . . .

We might as well toss in a few headlines, for instance: "Russian student stabbed five times in the neck and chest after his attackers heard his accent . . . Dozens of cars set on fire . . . Groups of yobs intent on confrontation . . . Riot stirred up by four gangs" – and of course – it is absolutely *de rigueur* in these merriments – "MPs say tabloids are to blame for football violence".

And that is only football. There are lots more from other sources.

Take the 74-year-old Betty Ellis, who was in Dachau concentration camp and lived to tell the tale. But Nazi *gauleiters* are nothing to the children of Birmingham today. A 10-year-old knocked on her door, asking if he could get his football back from her garden, and when she let him in, he and another boy allegedly knocked her to the ground, broke a couple of her ribs, and ran off with her purse. To which she said: "You just don't expect children to do that sort of thing." Oh, Madam, you had better start expecting *right now*.

By now the theme of my column must be coming clear. But I must say that I am not just piling up a heap of dreadfulnesses (though I could pile up an Everest of them in half an hour); my purpose is to make clear the differences of our horrors and the horrors of other countries. I begin with Sri Lanka.

> What though the spicy breezes
> Blow soft o'er Ceylon's isle;
> Though every prospect pleases,
> And only man is vile?

"And only man is vile". You're telling me, Bishop, especially when I see a headline reading "Troops kill 200 rebels in Sri Lankan assault". The Tamil Tigers want a separate state; the leaders of Sri Lanka do not want to give them one. Silly? "Sunday's fighting . . . has claimed 300 lives." How silly can you get?

And Peru's long struggle against the Shining Path guerrilla group has taken a turn for the worse: "with a deadly series of bombings and attacks . . . more than 35,000 people . . . since 1980 . . . government has detained more than 500,000 suspects . . ."

And then again there is Seoul, South Korea, where "prosecutors demanded, on Monday, that a former President, Chun Doo Hwan, be executed, and that his successor, Roh

Tae Woo, be imprisoned for life for presiding over some of
the bloodiest days of South Korea's authoritarian past . . .
Both men are also accused of using bribes to amass hundreds
of millions of dollars in secret political slush funds."

And what about that startling headline "Algeria buries murdered bishop"? If the murder of bishops is to become a
frequent occurrence, things have come to a pretty pass, but
the truth is that the murder of bishops is indeed going to
grow; you only need the mad Islamic fundamentalists, who
have killed and will continue to kill.

And what of the power struggle in Indonesia? Suharto was
and is nothing but the head of a murderous regime of thugs,
who like having their opponents killed if they can get away
with it, which they can. And I remember vividly the apologies
for the regime by Patrick Nicholls, MP, who was very cross
with me because I wrote 1,500 words on the genocidal regime
that slaughtered countless innocents in East Timor (experts
say probably about 200,000). I wonder if Mr Nicholls, MP,
is having second thoughts now about what happened: if so,
I shall be the first to congratulate him.

And why – Mr Nicholls, MP, may say – is this story being
brought up again now? It is because the oppressed people
of East Timor, and indeed the Indonesian opposition, have
once again found a hero (actually a heroine) to plead their
case before the bar of decency, truth, honour and democracy
– four things that Suharto knows not of.

The heroine is Megawati Sukarnoputri, and we might start
with the obvious. The obvious is that Suharto and members
of his family and friends have accumulated vast wealth;
the corruption is so gross that the middle classes, who are
well-off by Indonesian standards, flock to Mrs Megawati.
But beyond those who can (again by Indonesian standards)
get by, there are by World Bank definitions *30 million living
in absolute poverty*. You ask: "How can that be tolerated?"
You are naïve; by proportion, Indonesia has one of the
largest armies in the world, and the irony is that only the

army could – and one day may – throw out Suharto and his thieves.

Indonesia? It is a long way away. In our country, one in 10 – more likely one in 50 – could point to Indonesia on a globe.

Then we learn that there is more and more violent crime in the nascent South Africa, where we thought, because black had turned to white and vice versa, all would be well for ever.

In this tiny collection that I have put before you today, there are no fewer than seven warring tribes, some of them internecine, others awaiting a chance to strike; many don't know or care what they are going to fight and kill – great heaven, I swear that there is not a Tamil Tiger in the universe who truly understands why he is killing or being killed.

Now let us go back, for a moment, to Mrs Betty Ellis. Take the words that she said as soon as she was capable of speech after being assaulted: "You just don't expect children to do that sort of thing." I made a harmless joke, but burnt into my mind and soul in that moment was something very much greater than any joke.

Look through that catalogue of horrors, of countries where no man or woman is truly safe. Look thoroughly, because I have the list at my hand: Sri Lanka and the Tamil Tigers; Peru and the Shining Path; South Korea; Algeria; Indonesia; South Africa. And I have not mentioned Burundi or Grozny.

We pick up *The Times* at breakfast, and all too frequently we find in it a murder or a brutal robbery. But just as we shake our heads in sadness and horror, we stop, or we should. Because we have realised that in our country such crimes are the rarity, and in every one of that catalogue of countries it is the norm, and for mass murder of children we have to go to Dunblane and a raving lunatic. (But I must not cheat; springing from Belgium, a new horror has grown, and we learn that the number of paedophiles grows apace in our country.)

Perfection is not to be found this side of heaven. But

a reasonable measure of ordinariness, calm, decency and laughter, we can expect. So how do we secure it? After all, the peaceful places of the world come down to a sprinkling of Western Europe, Australia and New Zealand, my beloved India (hanging on by its teeth), Canada (but alas not the United States), bits and pieces from this or that continent. In how few countries – how few? – can people be sure that when they lie down to sleep they will also wake.

We all think grimly: "Suppose I had been born somewhere else – somewhere terrible?" After all, we are only a tiny bundle among the huge numbers. And indeed I might have missed being born in Britain; both my grandparents and my father were born in Russia, and they might have stayed there, to be murdered by Stalin or Hitler.

Go down the lines again – the lines of Sri Lanka, the Tamil Tigers, Peru's Shining Path, Seoul, Algeria, Indonesia, South Africa. And pause for a few moments in silence. And if tonight you wake screaming, thank your forebears that it was only a dream.

The Times, 13 September 1996

The unhappy spy

WE ARE BIDDEN not to speak ill of the dead. Today, I break that rule. The world of espionage has faded; some now argue that it was a waste of time on all sides. There has been something of a flood of memoirs, not very interesting and not very true. But once upon a time men and women died in the secret service of their countries, just as though they had died on the front line and reckoned not the price.

But there were others, of a very different kidney; the traitors. These men and women were on the enemy's side; they worshipped Stalin, and wanted the whole world to worship him too, and those who would not worship were to die.

Many did die, and badly. But John Cairncross died in bed. For John Cairncross was the Fifth Man.

Oh, how many decades have passed since those names – Philby, Blunt, Burgess and Maclean – were on the front pages of every newspaper? How many generations have been and gone since the four plus one finished their treason? How many jokes have been made about them, how many arguments have been left unsettled at chucking-out time, how many books on the subject have been written?

And how many honourable British men and women, working for their country and their country's good, died because of *their* activities?

John Cairncross came back to Britain to die; well, better perhaps to die than to tell terrible lies as he did in his heyday. It is said that he finished the book he was writing – the book about his treachery, and which was supposed to finance his last years. (He was a British citizen, so he could not have been made to go away and stay away.)

You will, as you read this, find that you are hearing a tone more savage than is my wont. If you have begun to think that I am being beastly to an old, frail, dead man, reflect upon what he did, and consider how many innocent men and women died for their country because John Cairncross was a traitor to his. And I warn you that nothing of what he wrote can be believed without independent corroboration.

Let us go back to those days. Philby was the spymaster-general who had penetrated the heart of British security; after a time he became suspect and was about to be arrested, when he fled to the Soviet Union, where he lived until he died. He lived well, very well, because not only had he brought with him an immense quantity of vital matter, every scrap of which would harm Britain and her allies, but he also had a touch of genius, which led him to a very high position in the Soviet Union in its counter-espionage department; that, also, meant that he could live high on the hog, as the Soviet leaders did. Burgess and Maclean had an appalling shock; they brought little of use to the Kremlin, and when that little was expended they sank into the poverty, dirt and wretchedness in which the Soviet citizens lived.

Then there was Sir Anthony Blunt, who cared for nothing but art and a ripe bumboy, and who had been an early believer in the wonders of the Soviet Union. When he was discovered as a Soviet arm, MI5 struck a deal, in which Blunt was to be "covered", and would in return identify everyone he knew about. (The deal went on for a long time, but in the end he had nothing more to give, and his cover was opened; belatedly, all his honours were taken from him.)

And then it was the turn of John Cairncross. But that turn had to wait many years, until Cairncross's Soviet controller, all passion spent, revealed that, yes, Cairncross was the Fifth Man.

I go back to my warning that nothing Cairncross said could be believed on his own word. He did, after all, have decades to brush up his story. He claimed that not only was he not a part of the Cambridge spy-ring, but that he did not even know Philby, Burgess, Maclean and Blunt, until they met in the war.

That matters little, and the British secret service was anyway a crumbling edifice; that was why Cairncross was not immediately spotted as a traitor, even when correspondence between him and Burgess was found *after* Burgess and Maclean had fled to the Soviet Union. (According to Fiona Barton, who had apparently spoken at length with Cairncross, he was not arrested but told to leave the country and not return, and for all we know he might have usefully fingered many more of his kind as he went.)

Then, after almost half a century of exile, he returned, thinking – rightly – that an old, frail, ill traitor would not be arrested and prosecuted. Mind you, his garment was soiled not only by his treason but by ordinary crime; he was imprisoned for a year in Italy for smuggling contraband currencies. Anyway, death ended it all.

There is now no use in trying to sort out which of the traitors did which crimes. All the five are dead, and if Cairncross had lived he would have lied as much as he needed to. But what we know for certain is that Cairncross betrayed his country and people and went on betraying his country and people. Whether it was he who led the Soviet spymasters to many brave British agents, whose fate was terrible, or whether he acted in a different play, we shall perhaps never know; the dead cannot speak. Philby certainly had had more killed than any other agent – surely there must by now be a student writing a thesis on Kim Philby and his satraps. Why, if Cairncross had lived, he might have said that Soviet agents and British ones do the same job and run the same risks, so what's the difference? (Oh, how I groan and writhe when I read again that shameful paragraph of my greatest hero E.M. Forster in which he said that terrible and monumentally foolish thing: "I hate the idea of causes, and if I had to choose between betraying my country and betraying my friend, I hope I should have the guts to betray my country.")

But at one point Cairncross not only argued that a British agent was equal to an enemy one; he argued that the enemy was much better than the Brit. He could not get out of those pincers, because what else was he doing in his years of treason other than silently crying hurrah for the Soviet Union and down with his own country?

Those words of Harington can stand another outing, I think:

> Treason doth never prosper, what's the reason?
> For if it prosper, none dare call it treason.

Did the Burgesses and Macleans and Blunts and Cairncrosses – yes, even the hard-headed Philbys – believe that they would wake to a world presided over by Stalin? And did they not tuck away the thought that they would be tremendous figures in that world? For among the lies Cairncross told is the one that he wasn't betraying Britain, he was only helping the sore-beset Soviet Union.

One mystery remains for me. I have never fully resolved it. How long did it take for the traitors to realise what they had done and how wrong they were in doing it? In a sphere a million miles from Cairncross and his like I put up *The God that Failed* – some half a dozen or more chapters, organised by Arthur Koestler and Richard Crossman, each of these having once fallen into the siren call of the Soviet Union. All of them got out, well in time, and there was nothing underhand to be ashamed of. And remember Anthony Hartley's apophthegm: "If anyone, after the seizure of Czechoslovakia, still clings to Stalin, that person has failed as a human being." Indeed, I myself was a tiny Stalinist from the ages of 12 to 18. But I, too, got out well in time.

But others didn't. Why? The easiest answer for someone who did not get out is that having wasted most of his or her life it had become impossible to admit it. Yes, but there are those who cannot *see* that they are wasting their lives. When the British Communist Party dissolved itself for good, having at last realised that their own god had failed, I got bundles of papers each claiming that while the old Communist Party had dissolved itself, *we* have kept the faith. I nearly passed out when I realised that each of those bundles contained a separate neo-Communist Party. (I don't think any one of them had more than six followers.)

In all his roster of *mea culpas*, John Cairncross never once actually denounced what he did and lived by, all those evil years ago. Is it possible that, deep down, he died still believing what he believed to begin with?

The Times, 13 November 1995

Beggars can *be choosers*

OUR DEAR SISTER the *Sun* has got tidings for us all, and very gloomy tidings they are. The *Sun* has made a random survey of 1,000 people, asking their opinions, and more to the point their experiences, of crime. On the whole, they are against it; indeed, if the attitudes of *Sun* readers were put into force, there would be hard labour in prisons, a justice system less concerned with the rights of the accused, a smaller divide between rich and poor people, a stronger government (ha ha), vigilante-style citizens' watch schemes, and hanging. *Lots* of hanging.

Moreover, 91 per cent (actually, a *staggering* 91 per cent) blame the rise in crime on the breakdown of family and community values; 80 per cent think that violence and crime on television contribute to the rocketing figures, and a staggering 97 per cent (there's a lot of staggering in this business, particularly when you add on all the rocketing that goes on as well) blame the increased use of drugs and alcohol (there goes my last bottle of *Gruaud-Larose* 1970).

Silly old *Sun*, eh? But at some point you have to stop giggling and face a different kind of figures. These are to be found neither in the *Sun*'s survey, nor in your uncle Fred's opinion (hang the lot), but in the dispassionate figures which are to be found in Her Majesty's Stationery Office. There, they do not comment on the figures, but only put them before us, to make of them what we will. And the most recent ones tell us that in the last year there have been 311,400 muggings, which include murders (numbers not specified), and sex offences, which include 5,100 rapes.

And – I nearly forgot – that number is 11 per cent higher than last year. Now giggle at the *Sun*.

I recently wrote about my astonishment at finding beggars everywhere today, and my astonishment has grown even greater; poverty, we know, can be found practically anywhere, but when I compare the poverty of my childhood to the poverty of today, not only do I feel that I should climb up a lamp-post to tell them that – compared with pre-war and long after – they are living in the most extravagant luxury, but that I should climb down the lamp-post to hobble home shaking my head at the most remarkable thing about this business: it is that contemporary beggars have no shame. Now *that* was different in my day.

But that brings me to something which might only be a straw in the wind, but which I fear may become a world in a hurricane. For this story has already started.

The central figure does not mind having his name and indeed picture blazoned upon the pages of a newspaper, although when I say that he does not mind, it is not to be thought that he wants to glory in the limelight. Such fripperies mean nothing to him; name, figure, actions – he cares for nothing and for nobody. He is 22 years old and at the moment he is in prison, but when he comes out, he may very quickly go in again, and go in and out until he dies, and if so he will die young and very badly.

Meanwhile, he boasts that he makes £125 a day at begging; it may well be true. Indeed it probably is, because throughout this story he has lived by drugs, lies and thieving. But there are two other figures in this story; they, too, have also been in the same limelight, but they wish – oh, how they wish! – that they had never found themselves in this tragedy. But alas, when the story opened, they were already bound inextricably to take their part in this terrible play: for you see, the one is the prodigal son, and the two are his parents. And the parents, at the end of their tether and a long way further, say that their son, the child of their loins, has brought them "nothing but hell and heartbreak".

How did he get that way? Assuredly, not from his parents. He said that his parents refused to speak to him; it was plainly a lie, and what a lie, for his parents come very close to sainthood in their refusal to cut him out of their minds and hearts for ever. His mother says: "I have never stopped loving him. He is welcome back tomorrow – and what really hurts is he knows that." His father says: "I took him [in prison] tobacco, sweets, socks and deodorant. I would wash my hands of him but I can't."

But I ask again, how did he get that way? The obvious and presumably correct answer is that he took to drugs. Yes, drugs destroy their victims, but no one forced him to take to drugs; *that* is the mystery. People of my generation avoided the temptation altogether, not least because that temptation did not exist. When I was a student, the most terrible thing we could swallow was a second pint of beer; as for cannabis, we literally did not know what the word meant, let alone set eyes on it. But suppose the plague had descended much earlier, and I had been tempted to try a little here and a little there – what then? I don't know, that's what. I tell people that the reason I have never touched drugs is because I have Wagner, which is a much more powerful essence, and there is something in it, but not much. What I want to know is: where were the channels that opened the sluices to hell? And why did no one slam the sluices shut? The drug "barons" are the only people I can think of whom I would like to see hanged, yet the question remains, for no one actually pushed drugs down any young throat.

Besides, I am writing about one particular fool, who doesn't think he is foolish, and many would agree that he isn't, if they, too, could get £125 a day for sitting about and asking the passers-by for money.

For sitting about and asking the passers-by: I come back to the incredible sight (well, it was incredible when I was a poor boy) of people, mostly young, *begging* for alms. No doubt many of these are truly without means, but no doubt

– starting with our prodigal son – more are begging because begging is easier and more lucrative than seeking work, and very much better than finding it.

There is a scene in *Umberto D* (if I have got the right film – I see, on the average, two films in three years), in which the poor but utterly respectable old man has no money at all, and realises that he has to beg. He stands at the edge of the pavement and puts out his hand, palm up, as he hears a passer-by who he hopes will put a few coins into his hand. But just as the footsteps are coming close, he is swamped with the shame of having to beg, and he turns his hand palm down, as though he were just seeing whether the rain had stopped. The old man had felt the burning fire of shame, and he calls up every scrap of his respectability, but now it is clear that a generation has grown up which not only goes a-begging, but feels no shame in doing so.

Hear again the parents of the prodigal son: "We are decent working-class people, so imagine how we feel at seeing our son reduced to this at 22. We genuinely did everything we could. Our son repaid us with a life of crime, drugs and now doing what he does best – getting other people's money." It is very unlikely that the son has closely studied the scriptures; if he had, he might have come across St Luke, and read, "I cannot dig, to beg I am ashamed". Unfortunately, he came across the mammon of unrighteousness first, and decided that that was much more his style.

Will the clock be put back? *Can* it be put back? Who is there to put it back? It is clear that the "decent working-class people" who sired the prodigal son in this story cannot do it. Neither can a string of imprisonments, and shame seems to have vanished for ever. True, in the *Sun*'s survey (with which I started) 91 per cent held that the reason for crime was the breakdown of family and community values, but few if any of that 91 per cent have gone to the length of discovering how to remake the family and community values.

Meanwhile, the prodigal son has been offered a job by his elder brother. Shall the family "Bring hither the fatted calf, and kill it"? For the only alternative is that sooner or later "He would fain have filled his belly with the husks that the swine did eat". Which will he choose?

The Times, 28 July 1995

Out of fashion

DE MINIMIS NON CURAT LEX, Oh, yes? I have always rightly treated that claim with the greatest of suspicion, and again and again I have found that so far from it being even slightly *minimis*, it is all too obviously piled high with every kind of *curat*, to say nothing of shovelfuls of *lexes*. But this one beats the lot.

It begins "Liza Bruce, the top fashion designer . . .", and instantly I am lost in a forest of creatures which prowl and prowl and eat people like me unbuttered. For I have never heard of Liza Bruce; much less do I know that she is the top fashion designer. Yes, yes, I have been remiss, culpably remiss, but there it is: as far as Liza Bruce goes, she might be the girl who invented the *de minimis* bit.

But now I am about to know a great deal about the subject, and possibly more than I wish, because

> Liza Bruce, the top fashion designer, is to take High Court action this week against Marks & Spencer, claiming that Britain's biggest high-street retailer has copied her swimwear design.

Cor! Nay, cor blimey! But it gets better, much better.

> She has instructed Mark Stephens, senior partner at the law firm Stephens Innocent, to serve a writ this week. A separate action for criminal proceedings against individual Marks & Sparks directors is also being considered.

> Ms Bruce, dubbed the "queen of cling" (though not by me) in the fashion world, is recognised as one of the world's leading

designers for swimwear (though not by me). Her outfits sell in top stores such as Harrods and Harvey Nichols for more than £100 (though not to me). But she claims that Marks & Spencer – dear old Marks and Sparks, no less – has "ripped off" her unique swimsuit style and is selling the goods at a fraction of the price.

Not so, says Sir Richard Greenbury, chairman of M&S, who will contest any legal action. He says it is a "spurious claim", and after "an internal investigation (but not by me) decided there was no substance to the allegation".

Meanwhile – oh, yes, you know what is coming, you frightful cynics – Ms Bruce's lawyer, Mark Stephens, has opined (though not to me) that the claim for damages "is expected to be between £300,000 and £500,000 but could be substantially higher". Aw, come on Mark, lad, don't be a skinflint; go right up to the million, or a couple of millions more, just for fun. After all, you're already saying that a criminal action is "a serious possibility", and if it is pursued, those found guilty of copyright theft can be fined, or in extreme cases, imprisoned. Shucks. Only fined? Only imprisoned? Hang them, lad, hang them! (You know, it's a funny thing; we all talk about it, but has anyone ever actually boiled a lawyer's head for a turnip? Isn't it time that someone did so?)

Now you wouldn't guess, from my august position and lofty mien, that I come of a line of poor Jewish tailors. Indeed, it was I who finally broke the chain, and I sometimes wonder whether I would have been happier if I had left it alone. (At least I can tell you something you can't do and I can: I can sit on the floor, cross-legged, without discomfort.) I tell you this, not for my biographers, but to establish my credentials in the world of *schmutte*. My first thought when I met this preposterous nonsense in the form of Marks & Spencer *v* Liza Bruce was to hark back to my grandfather's iron (we didn't have electricity so the iron was heated by gas-flame) and to the magic moment when he spat on the iron to make sure that it was neither too hot or too cold.

*   *   *

At this point I must make a diversion. I knew nothing of
Liza Bruce and her problems (or her enemy's problems) until
I read the story in the *Sunday Times*, and a pretty giggle it
gave me when I did. But for a considerable time I could not
think of lawyers or the price of clothes or the astounding
and terrible news that Diana Ross (who she?) might not
have her new swimsuit in time. (In time for what? Search
me.) But all this was ignored, as I say, because when the
Sunday Times published the story, it simultaneously put, and
in colour, pictures of two models, of course wearing the two
disputed swimsuits, and the two models in question were so
stupendously beautiful that the very pictures of them nearly
stopped my heart for good. Reader: it is all very well to
discuss the rights and wrongs (if any) of Marks & Spencer
v Liza Bruce, but when such beauty floats before my eyes,
I don't care if *no one shoots the lawyer*, and I cannot say more
than that.

Meanwhile, I come back to the nonsense in hand, still
adamant that I will not take sides. My rule, as my regular
readers know, is either to go in boots and all, or to sit on
a bough making noises uncannily like a real cuckoo; in this
case I shall be a bystander to the end. But that does not mean
I cannot comment on the passing show, provided I display
no bias. And I have to say that the first rule in these matters
has been broken, on Ms Bruce's side. For the first rule in
these matters (well, in practically all matters) is "Don't overdo
it", and she did. Take this, for instance, a passage from Ms
Bruce's lament, that goes like this: "It was a callous misuse
of all that my label stands for. I trade on my name, and the
creativity and exclusivity which goes with it. My losses will
be inestimable."

Now, now duckie; your losses will *not* be inestimable; they
will be estimable, a very different thing. If you want to go to
law – oh, don't go to law, don't go to law, *don't go to law* –
do anything at all rather than go to law, if necessary shooting
your own lawyer to prevent it. But if you must, do not give

the impression that life holds nothing more for you after the tragedy of the swimsuits. I repeat, I take no sides in any of this, but if – *if* – I were to give you advice, it might take the shape of stopping for a moment to tell yourself that a consignment of swimsuits that have been turned into a tug-o'-war will neither destroy your entire livelihood nor make you a laughing-stock.

Here, I must pause to make sure that I have been even-handed, for I promised not to take sides, and I must put something in the other scale. Shall I proclaim, then, that I use the sausages Marks & Spencer sell for hitting burglars over the head and for little else? Or that I think that their bread is the most dull imaginable? Or that whether the disputed swimsuits were good, bad or indifferent, Marks & Spencer could well afford to make swimsuits that would hurt nobody's feelings, let alone pocket?

Perhaps the heat got to everybody in this ridiculous story. What else could bring sensible people into such an argie-bargie that when they wake up, they will wake up blushing? Well, it filled a space in the papers, and the two beauties were sights for sore eyes. But it did something else.

Now as I write, I do not know whether legal procedings are in train; the fierce words, the howls of "We wuz robbed", the cries of anger and even tears, suggest that if it all goes on like this we shall be on the edge of bloodshed very soon. The clue word is "obstinacy", and it ought to be painted on every wall in the land. We have succumbed to it, hundreds of times, and felt ashamed that we did succumb; but we have soon succumbed to it again, even when we have just heard the very echoes of our previous folly.

Do you really think that all of this shouting and weeping and hating – particularly the hating – could not have been settled over a cup of tea, a glass of decent wine, or the blood of a lawyer? Perhaps, over the centuries, mankind could dispense with heels; they would get smaller and smaller (rather like the appendix), until the human heel disappeared entirely, whereupon we could all rejoice because there would be none anywhere, and no one could *dig in his heels*.

Meanwhile, I remember that a frightful row is going on; on one side of the row is a swimsuit, and on the other side there is – well, well – a swimsuit. Please, antagonists, go to bed and get a good night's sleep. When you wake, you may find that the problem has been solved. Or better, that it was a dream.

The Times, 21 July 1995

The sins of the father

T HE OTHER DAY, one of my kind readers wrote to me and asked me "to write something funny and cheer us all up". Murmuring under my breath that in these days there is precious little to be funny about, I complied, and the reader who had begged for amusement wrote an even more kindly note to thank me. Little did he know – little did *I* know – that hovering above both of us was a story so awful, so full of pain, so terrible not only for the man in the centre of it but for all mankind, that my first reaction was that I would never laugh again.

You think I am exaggerating; I wish I were. Read on.

Does the name Adolf Eichmann mean anything to you? No? Then you are a lot younger than I am. That doesn't matter, but if I may say so you are inexcusably ignorant. For Eichmann was a part – a very substantial part – of the Holocaust, and if you don't know what the Holocaust was, you should go back to school. (If, indeed, the broadminded teachers of today have the space and time to include it in their curriculum, and don't prefer lessons in how to spot and rebuke those who fail the tests for political correctness.)

Adolf Eichmann organised, supervised and carried out the extermination of roughly three-quarters of the Jews of Hungary. This, incidentally, was no mean feat, because Budapest was something like 180 miles from the gas-chambers, and he had to convey his doomed charges there. Well, no one has ever said that Eichmann was not efficient.

When the war ended, Eichmann would certainly have been executed had he not fled, under an assumed name, to

The sins of the father

South America and lived there with his family. (One day, I hope someone will explain to me why South America was – and still is – so eager to give shelter to some of the greatest criminals in the world's history.) But in 1960, Israeli commandos kidnapped Eichmann and brought him back to Israel, where he was put on trial, convicted and hanged. (He was cremated, and his ashes were sprinkled in the sea; not even a flake of ash could be allowed to stain the soil of Israel.)

So what is this all about, if it is not a history lesson? It's like this; there is no rule or bar that can prevent mass murderers begetting children, and Adolf Eichmann sired four. And Ricardo Eichmann, the mass murderer's son – an infant, you must remember, when his father was hanged in Israel – has now decided to speak out and announce that he, the gentle, ordinary professor of Middle Eastern archaeology with the German-sounding name, is the son of Adolf Eichmann, the mass murderer.

What is the correct approach for a man who is about to announce that his now deceased father had murdered approximately three hundred thousand men, women and children? I don't know; do you? More to the point, does he? Well, he has had time to think about it; he is 40 years old, and it would be foolish of us to start dissecting the mind of a man who has been dissecting his soul for almost his entire life.

But surely, never have the familiar words been spoken so painfully: "The fathers have eaten sour grapes, and the children's teeth are set on edge." Again, we must not try to tell Mr Eichmann what he has known and brooded over through all these years, but it is impossible for us to shrug and go away without asking ourselves the obvious question, which we would have to ask if we had found ourselves in Mr Eichmann's position: "My blood is his blood – what does that mean for me?"

Pause, reader; I am not playing conundrums. Over there, a harmless-looking professor (and he *is* harmless) is trying to cleanse his blood. He knows, or if he doesn't know, his colleague the professor of haematology will soon tell him, that there is no point trying. Your blood, examined most rigorously, will be the same as mine. Quite: but try telling him that, in the silence of the night and with his memories.

Oh, memory, memory, that murderer of sleep! "Methought I heard a voice cry, 'Sleep no more! Macbeth does murder sleep', the innocent sleep . . ." And indeed the innocents slept no more, because Professor Eichmann's father decreed that they should die. And die they did.

This, as it happens, is by no means a unique situation; there were hundreds, indeed thousands, of mini-Eichmanns, who drove the sheep to their last pasture, and many of those murderers must have had children. Moreover, a few years ago, in Israel, there was a colloquy for the children of the killers. Professor Eichmann seems to be a well-balanced man, but you can't tell me that he never wakes in the night, shuddering, or indeed screaming – perhaps screaming so loudly that his own two children, aged eight and six, are awakened and have to be hushed to sleep again.

Exercise your imagination; there are grotesque blunders to steer past: "And what did your father do, Ricardo?" The answer can hardly be "He murdered Jews", but neither can it be "Oh, he bought and sold rare postage-stamps".

For that matter, I have been told that there are several Hitlers in the German telephone book, through no fault of their own (the Führer left no issue), and for that matter the name of Hess can be found 19 times in our own (plus one Eichmann).

What's in a name? It all depends. Professor Eichmann did not change his name, though when his father fled from Europe it was under a pseudonym. But I am wandering; what I am talking about is not names but wickedness – a wickedness that the world had never before seen, and Professor Eichmann, for being born and for nothing else, has got mixed up in it.

What about the extra gene and such fashionable nonsense? Please, executioner, it wasn't my fault, I was born that way.

Ah, now we are getting to the heart of the story. Professor Eichmann is an ordinary, decent, honourable man, but he got that way by being an ordinary, decent, honourable man, *and because he wanted to be those things*. His father was an evil, murderous, dreadful creature *because he wanted to do other things*. Both got what they wanted; one to be an academic, the other to be a mass murderer. The fact that one is living an ordinary life and the other was hanged does not change the picture.

We make our own lives, and if we find that at the end we have wasted them, there is nothing to be done except shrug.

> And that inverted Bowl we call the Sky,
> Whereunder crawling coop't we live and die,
> Lift not thy hands to *It* for help – for It
> Rolls impotently on as Thou or I.

There is, however, another question with no answer. Could Eichmann the murderer or Eichmann the professor have changed course? If I argue that both of them made themselves, surely they could have changed tack. I was recently watching a television programme about the Nuremberg trials; the commentator was clearly an expert, and when he got to Goering he made a powerful argument, saying that, in effect, the monster could literally not understand the idea of right and wrong. Yet at least one of the indicted at the Nuremberg trials *did* truly realise his own evil. Perhaps some can and some can't.

But one avenue is closed. I do not believe that you or I could fathom the mind of Adolf Eichmann. I doubt if anyone really could, including himself. There are, true, levels of evil – for instance today, and in Britain, not a day goes by but an elderly, frail lady is assaulted, sometimes so hideously that her relations are unable to recognise her. That indeed, is evil, but I still see a gap between that and the millions boiled down for soap.

So we come back to the mystery of the two Eichmanns,

father and son. All the studies of Eichmann the murderer conclude by saying that he was a nonentity, a reed in the wind, a man who did nothing other than truly obey orders. It seems that he did not even relish the job of killing Jews, as many did. He was told to kill Jews, and Jews he killed. I believe that if half-way through the Holocaust he had been told to stop killing Jews and to start killing left-handers or redheads instead, he would not even have wondered at the change, but would have carried on until he was told to kill people shorter than five foot three.

We leave Eichmann the son to his strange life; we leave Eichmann the murderer to *his* much stranger life. There is no answer that makes sense. Perhaps a prayer might do.

The Times, 14 July 1995

Swept under the carpet

CHEER BOYS, CHEER, your mother's sold the mangle, dee, da, dee, da dee dee dee dee; there can hardly be another song dedicated to a mangle, but it is unlikely that the well-known song would warm the hearts of the people I am going to talk about. Indeed, when they hear the very word "mangle" they wince; but their wincing is nothing to what they feel when they hear the apparently harmless words "vacuum cleaner".

But I am going too fast; be patient a little while, and you will be rewarded with the story, the glorious story, the wonderful, splendid, rousing, immortal, hilarious, magnificent, tremendous, rollicking, story – yes, I tell you, that the very same story has come back into the news, and with a very considerable *whump!*

For those who have not followed one of the greatest cock-ups of the 20th century, I must introduce Messrs Hoover, but for a few minutes before I explain how Hoover and the great disaster got together I must set the scene properly.

First, we know that many brandnames have become *words* with use, and indeed have entered the loftiest dictionaries; the maker of many a product – say, an electric bread-slicer – can frequently be found proudly saying that *his* bread-slicer is the Rolls-Royce of the breed, and I don't think that the people who actually do make Rolls-Royces are displeased.

If they are, they must be daft to reject such free promotion, when many a Saatchi would sell half a dozen of his brothers to get the billboards for nothing. Mind you, there are such people; the (rather American) word "realtor" bristles when it is not written as "Realtor", and – much dafter – the Weight Watchers scream the place down if they are called weight-watchers. (I know – let's all go round to where they live, shouting "Yah, boo, rats to you and your barmy upper-case" and then deliberately paint "realtor" and "weight-watchers" on the pavement outside their houses.)

But although I sing the mangle, the world has passed it by, and now we must bow to the Hoover. And the bow must be a profound one; I know of nothing that matches the extraordinary lead that Hoover won and kept over any of its rivals. I do not know, and cannot find out, whether there was a Mr Hoover with an innovative turn of mind, or whether the original inventor greatly admired the American president of the same name, or the two sounds "hoooo" and "verrrr" were so beautifully onomatopoeic that the maker fell in love with them, but Hoover it was, and Hoover it still is. So much so, that the very word was incorporated into the language: whatever brand of vacuum-cleaner the housewife had, it was spoken of as "the hoover". More, it became a verb, "to hoover". and the housewife would say – does still say – that she has been hoovering the carpet. What the rival firms did, and do, other than splutter, I don't know.

Ah, but "Pride goeth before destruction, and an haughty spirit before a fall". The Bible got it right, very right, very right indeed. And Shakespeare got it right too, with "If you have tears, prepare to shed them now". For some clever-dick in the Hoover company (I don't know whether he was shot, or disembowelled, or tied up in a sack and thrown into the sea – presumably the Black Sea – or hanged, or suffocated, or – well, anyway, he must have been made away with), came up with a wheeze in the shape of a come-on. (A come-on, in this context means getting something for nothing.)

Now whether the sales of Hoover had been a bit sluggish for some time, or some of Hoover's rivals were looking smug, or that special new device for the Hoover wasn't catching on, I don't know, but surely a really exciting come-on would turn the tide.

The only question was: what is the come-on to be? And then stepped forward the man who was in time to suffer a wide variety of discomforts, and he said: "I know – let's tell every customer that if he or she bought more than a £100-worth of goods from us, he or she would have a dream gift: no less than free air tickets for two, either for continental Europe or the United States." And so it was.

But then some mathematical genius worked out that £105 was very considerably less than the price of a flight to Europe or America; all the would-be free-flyer had to do was to cough up £105 and name the date. Cheers, folks.

Then, back home in Hooverville, the penny dropped – too late. A public and unambiguous promise had been given: a hundred pounds plus fourpence on the counter and Hoover is bound, foot and throat.

There followed the wailing and sprinkling of ashes on the head: to no avail. But also came something rather less amusing.

Hoover wriggled, and when I say wriggled, I mean what I say. From then till now, practically every day there has been a story in one or more newspapers in the shape of a Hoover-wriggler doing his morning wriggle. The disaster (for Hoover) took place three years ago, but Hoover has still not paid out, in flights, all the promises that Hoover made.

And now it seems possible that Hoover is going to do the Great Wriggle and get away scot-free.

How? Perpend. Hoover is a part of a larger business called Maytag; Hoover is one of its subsidiaries. But Maytag, in a cunning and – as far as I can see legal – twist, has sold Hoover to an Italian company. (A shifty little statement from Maytag says that the decision to sell Hoover was not related to the Hoover catastrophe. You can believe it if you want to – it's a free country, innit?)

But not only did Maytag sell Hoover, it sold it without requiring the purchaser to honour Maytag's liabilities and without paying its own losses (*viz.* the flights).

So shabbily did Hoover behave in the honouring of its

pledges, that some of those who were manifestly due to have flights (and hadn't got them) took legal action; some of those actions are still unfinished, but I don't know whether they cover all the losers, or only the specified ones.

This is a rather nasty business. Maytag/Hoover made a colossal mistake, and some 220,000 people took – quite legally – the advantage of it. Nor was it the kind of mistake that normally leaves a nasty odour; a huge promise was given, openly and truthfully, and the only nasty odour in this case is the way Hoover got out of its pledges. I can hear some people saying that the initial claim by the lucky ones was greedy. No; it was not. It was the come-on that was greedy; Hoover advertised widely and unambiguously, in effect saying: "Buy £105 of our goods and we shall give you a pair of flights, no holds barred." Then it came unstuck. The £105 promise was given and kept. The flights promise was given and not kept.

But there is yet another nasty bit to deal with. Hoover had the impudence to go to law, to have 127 cases struck out; the people in these cases were ones who had not had their promised flights, and Hoover was trying to stop them going to court for their promises.

The judge immediately quashed Hoover's scandalous claim, and *the very next day the great sell-off took place*. Such manoeuvres cannot, of course, be done on the spur of the moment; the scammers had obviously been working on the scam for some time, and the 127 cases formed the whistle that said "Go".

It is no use saying that we should boycott Hoover and its products. As I say, this business must have been gestating for a considerable time, and in that time the participants had worked out a scheme that was watertight; to give them their due, they made it not only watertight, but thickly covered in pitch.

I must make clear that although this business is and has been shifty and indeed grubby, it is not criminal. Not even the wriggling out of the promise of flights was contrary to the criminal law, though Hoover could be pursued in the civil courts, or rather would have been pursuable in the civil courts, if the villains had not scarpered in time – that is, sold Hoover and quit.

It started in laughter, but there were tears before bedtime. I could wag a finger, and say that people who want something for nothing are bound to be disappointed, but it wasn't quite like that, was it? But there is one small bit of the jigsaw that I still cannot fit in.

What did more than two hundred thousand people do with more than two hundred thousand unwanted Hoovers?

The Times, 7 July 1995

When obstinacy is idiocy

W E HAVE BEEN here before, and it will go hard but we shall be here many times again. That, you may think, must be boring, but it isn't; indeed, the longer it goes on, the more fascinating it becomes. I, for one, hearing of it this time, plumped up the cushions, and had a decanter handy, in rich expectation, nor was I disappointed. And now you want to know what I am talking about. You shall.

The very headline is ripe for agogness, for it reads, in its entirety, "Postman harboured 30-year grudge over fine". Roll that round your mouth, shake your head, sigh audibly, look at the nearest person and inevitably look away. For a human being has passed this way, and another will shortly do so, and so will many, many others, until the earth stops going round and goes back to its original cold, and serve it right.

Meanwhile: "Postman harboured 30-year grudge over fine".

Thirty years? *Thirty?* And what, you obviously want to know at once, was the terrible thing that caused the terrible grudge? You shall know when I get to the point, though I think that some of you, having seen the answer, will wish that you had not.

Thirty years is a long time, and counting in days it comes to some eleven thousand. Eleven thousand? Do it in hours, and it comes to more than a quarter of a million. And minutes? Call it 16 million, and don't bother with the seconds.

But you must bother now, because the human being takes over; the Reluctant Postman's heart beats at roughly the same rate as his opponent's, which is some 75 times a minute. Oh, dogged postman, how are you at arithmetic? For if you have even a smattering of that simple mystery, you will be able to say how many times your heart has beaten in those 30 awful years, and beats yet.

Very well. Thirty years ago, postman Martin Fitzgerald was reported by a policewoman for riding his bicycle after dusk without lights; the policewoman's name was Stella Kilvington. For the offence he was fined five shillings.

Five shillings.

Five shillings.

I see blank faces around me; all right. "Shillings" were coins, five of which in today's currency would be 25p. He had been fined 25p and for 30 years, *30 years*, he had nursed a hate of the officer who booked him, all the while insisting that he had not broken the law.

Time went by for you and me and the world, and indeed for Policewoman Kilvington, who retired from the force in 1966. But it did not go by for Martin Fitzgerald. For him, time had stopped 30 years ago, and still the thought of the five shillings burnt in his pocket and "Still it cried, 'Sleep no more!' to all the house: Glamis hath murdered sleep, and therefore Cawdor shall sleep no more, Macbeth shall sleep no more!"

The years passed; and still no recompense came for him; Policewoman (retd) Kilvington had long forgotten everything about the five-shilling fine, which only stoked the fires for Mr Fitzgerald, as he went deeper and deeper into oblivion, until he could bear oblivion no more. He would tear off the bandage and make his enemies see the bruises. He did, by sending offensive Christmas cards, until the law stepped in. And now if you have shivers, prepare to shiver them now, for law or no law, nothing could shake his immovable belief that he was right and everybody else was wrong. From beginning to end his flag flew, and from beginning to end, it said "I am right". Now just for a moment, let us try to put ourselves in Mr Fitzgerald's place. We deny the charge, we go red in the face, we splutter with anger when we go into the dock, knowing that we are innocent and that we did *not* ride a bicycle after dusk without lights. And then, when Pelion has been piled on Ossa, we are fined 25p. We go home raging at the injustice, we swear very shockingly, we say things about the magistrate that the magistrate's young children should in no circumstances hear, and for days, perhaps weeks, a month even, we growl at the wrongdoing, and then we get on with our lives – though occasionally, perhaps once a year something jogs our memory – and we mutter about "that bloody copper" and put our thumbs to our noses.

That is what *we* do; but it is not what Mr Fitzgerald does, and what I want to know is exactly where the chalk line runs; where we remain on one side and he the other.

Obstinacy: we are all obstinate about something, but we do not destroy our lives over it. Injustice: there is enough injustice to fill the world, our little drop would not be noticed. Envy: he has much, I have little, I burn with the way the world has been made, but I promise to work harder and get more. Dishonesty: he didn't get that huge house and Rolls-Royce honestly, and so what? Luck: Why don't I get it, when my neighbour does, because that's how the luck goes. Oh, yes, we have all crossed our arms and played Luther at Worms; here I stand. But we go indoors if it starts raining. A very dear friend of mine, many years ago, was embroiled in a matter in which he was being swindled by a crook. There was no doubt at all that the crook was swindling him, but my friend alarmed me by saying that if all failed he would kill the crook. I looked at my friend, and I suddenly realised that he meant it.

I spent the night talking him out of murder, and as a *bonne-bouche* persuaded him to give in to the swindler altogether.

There is a much grimmer story of those who will not give in: it is the terrible picture of Hitler, in the last hours, with a map in his hand that was disintegrating as he twisted it, demanding to know "When will Wenck and the Ninth Army join?" though he was in the bunker and there was no Wenck and no Ninth Army left.

There are, to be sure, examples of heroic obstinacies; who would not admire the Spartans at Thermopylae? And, a few steps down, we must, however grudgingly, admire that tiresome nuisance called Charles de Gaulle.

One of these days, I shall write a book called *How to give in gracefully*, but it will be a tremendous flop. (Tim, the beloved cat of my infancy, would royally wave away a mouse, but that was because it was beneath his dignity to kill it.)

But human beings – oh, human beings! Let us go back to the beginning with the postman and his grudge.

There is something that I did not tell you at first, and I shiver again when I tell you now. When Mr Fitzgerald was prosecuted he was 52 years old. That means that he was 22 when he had his brush with the law. At 22 did he really give up his future to spend his entire life pursuing five shillings, or did he just stoke the fire from time to time?

> Truly to speak, and with no addition,
> We go to gain a little patch of ground
> That hath in it no profit but the name,
> To pay five ducats, five, I would not farm it;
> Nor will it yield to Norway or the Pole
> A ranker rate, should it be sold in fee.

But it seems Mr Fitzgerald thought it worth most of his life to nurse his grudge where they "Have in these parts from morn til even fought, and sheath'd their swords for lack of argument".

Well, our hero did not lack argument; for him, there was one cause, one fight, one victory. I wonder whether he brandished his grudge among the villagers where he lived and worked, or hugged his burning outrage lest someone might come along and pour water on it? It cannot be that he found himself a failure when it all happened, because he was only 22, and it would be a very gloomy youngster of that age who was already despairing. But then, when evening came and he rode his bicycle without lights – or with lights for that matter – his world and life more or less ended.

What waste! What tenacity! What folly! Did he waver at moments – perhaps at anniversaries? Did he ever think that *he* might have made a mistake in the first place? We all make mistakes, so why not him?

Did he, does he, think that it was all worthwhile? Should we pity him? I do, surely, but for all I know he would spurn an outstretched hand. And – it is almost sacrilege to ask – has he given up his cause, or does he fight on still? But the waste! The waste!

The Times, 9 June 1995

The fence and the bench

WHO SAID "STOUT fences make good neighbours"? Whoever he was, he must have been barmy. Unless, of course, he meant that stout fences are useful for hitting the neighbours over the head with. But did you ever see, did you ever hear of, did you ever imagine, did you ever shake your head in wonder at, anything like the fracas between the Kingstons and the Wards?

Yes, frequently.

Because, you see, when neighbours fall out they do not do it by halves. And when the falling-out is in the depths of the country, it is 50 times worse than it would be if it were taking place in my own dear Wimpole Street. I am no master sleuth, but when I heard that something was taking place in "Wootton Road, a quiet residential area in Wootton village near Bedford" rather than "the Old Kent Road, from which you will be lucky if you get away with nothing but a couple of stab wounds", I hastened to the village shop to buy a deckchair wherein to make myself comfortable at the ringside. For I knew for certain that a ringside seat was going to be useful.

Let us look back for a moment, for surely the trouble didn't start the moment the Kingstons' removal-van arrived; there must have been a period when if a Ward had run out of milk and the village shop was shut, a Kingston would leap to the rescue, and when a Kingston's Sunday newspapers hadn't been delivered, a Ward would pass theirs on as soon as they had finished reading them. Or so I like to think, softie that I am. Anyway, if there *was* a calm before the storm, the hurricane that followed made clear that from now on smiles would not be exactly *de rigueur*.

I return to where I started. My investigations show that, in the country, 93.7 per cent of quarrels and indeed murders are brought about *by fences*. And it was indeed a fence that caused the very large hole in Mr Kingston's pocket. You see, Mr Ward had decided to change his fence. It had been a chain-link fence (whatever that may be), and Mr Ward decided to replace it with a wooden slatted one (whatever *that* may be). Then he went on holiday with his family.

Friends, if you live in the country do not change your fences; but if you must, do not go away on holiday. For when Mr Ward returned he found the new fence uprooted and flung in his front garden. And the rest you know. (Well, almost. It was part of Mr Ward's evidence when he was listing the things Mr Kingston had said; the list was long, dreadful and of course untrue, but it included the amazing claim that Mr Ward had attempted to procure a boy for sex "outside Wootton Post Office". I must say that even with someone like Mr Kingston at the helm, that surely goes too far.)

Again, I must stress the problems caused by living in the country, for the countryside is a very dangerous and unpleasant place. To start with, you can't get to sleep for the rustling of the leaves, nor wake up without the mooing of the cows (if it is cows that do the mooing – it might be the chickens for all I know), and the smells are fit to poison your entire family with one sniff. I really do think it is about time my prescription was carried out: *viz.* cover the entire countryside with an even layer of tarmac.

But – and now I am not joking – I believe that things like the Ward–Kingston battle do not take place in town. Oh, plenty of bad things do happen on the pavement, and the bad things are mostly the violent ones; the country loses points for its absurdity and meanness, but scores for its unviciousness, while the town loses points for the violence and gains for the vast variety of things to do. I do believe that the Ward–Kingston imbroglio and its outcome has at bottom the terrible truth that the country is *bored*. And how could it be otherwise?

Go back a moment to the things Mr Kingston said about Mr Ward. I reject (rightly, I am sure) the theory that Mr Kingston was truly mad. He wasn't, but what he *was* was absolutely uncontrollable in his raging vendetta against Mr Ward. But that is the beginning of the story, not the end. For we must ask ourselves what the terrible rage was made of, that he could live for three years without softening, and watch himself go down to financial ruin into the bargain at the end of it?

I won't run through the entire catalogue of vilification again; we have heard it a dozen times, and Mr Ward is entitled to his peace – after all, he had to carry the burden throughout the three years. But one item, easily missed in the overplus of awfulness, was the fact that Mr Kingston had twice been bound over by the magistrates to keep the peace. And how had he been breaking it? He had assaulted both Mr and Mrs Ward, *and he had threatened to dig up the remains of the Wards' son, who had been killed in a road accident.*

Yes, it does look like madness, but I insist again that it isn't. So what is it? Oh, reader, dear reader, it is that terrible Thing on which I have broken a thousand thousand lances, that Thing which I can fluently name in a hundred languages, that Thing which makes the angels weep, that Thing which has to be spoken with words that are all too well known, so frequently have they been used, and which still go like this: "I beseech you in the bowels of Christ, think it possible you may be mistaken."

I wonder – I am sure we all wonder – whether Mr Kingston now thinks it possible he may be mistaken. Of course, he has had a bloody nose; after all, the costs amount to something like £20,000, and he may lose his house. But that's obvious; what I want to know is: does he still hold to what he said when he started? We would say, of course not. Don't be so sure; if not he, the world is filled with such obstinacy; indeed,

I had a dear friend who died of it, though countless hands had been stretched out to save him.

There is an obvious clue. Mr Kingston could surely not have believed the appalling untrue things that he said about Mr Ward: presumably he just wanted to hurt Mr Ward and recked not the price of his wrecking. One day, perhaps, Mr Kingston will be taken aside by someone he trusts, and asked how he could behave like that. But I hope I will not be within earshot; the risk of finding that Mr Kingston had not wavered an inch would have me bursting into tears.

Ah, but tall oaks from little acorns grow. Note the name and profession: Mr Justice Michael Davies. It was he who presided over the Ward-Kingston case, and if somebody doesn't stop me, I think I am going to climb onto the nearest roof and sing the praises of this very justicer. Indeed, I think I have found the judge whom I have sought these many decades – and just as I was going to give up the search for ever he came galloping over the horizon on a horse so white that I had to don dark glasses.

The Ward-Kingston case was for libel, without a jury. (Me! Me applauding a libel case without a jury – *Me!*) But this judge was manifestly sensible, and my cheers could be heard on Aldebaran. Instead of the lunatic hundreds upon hundreds of thousands of pounds that juries have been giving to slimy crooks, Sir Michael gave Mr Ward £1,000 plus costs. Not because Mr Ward's case was thin – it was massive – but because he took into account that the posters were only put up locally, and because all the witnesses testified that they hadn't believed the allegations anyway.

But he went even further, this notable Solomon. When Mr Ward said that Mr Kingston had ruined the lives of the Wards, the judge very gently pointed out that he hadn't. And Solomon did even better. Hark unto this: "In settling on the award, the judge said he tried to place himself in the role of a jury which does not always award large damages in cases of libel."

Oh, for benches crammed with judges like this one! Come,

if he aspires to be Lord Chief Justice I would be perfectly happy to shoot the present incumbent. In any case, may he dispense wisdom and truth for many years to come. And may he be spared more such cases as that one.

The Times, 1 August 1995

Murder most foul

A GLOOMY SUBJECT today, I am sorry to say, with not even a giggle somewhere to lighten the burden. I chose my subject from a very deep well of evil, and before my readers say that they don't want any more such matters I do assure them that the evil is so remarkable that I sat up with a bang when I learnt of it. Truly, the story is not the story, but the amazement it gives off.

Try speaking this sentence aloud and don't peep at the answer: "He was my hero. He still is. He will remain one of the greatest men of our time." Well? Winston Churchill? De Gaulle? Harry Truman? Alexander Fleming? Einstein? Frank Lloyd Wright? Give up? The man who was a hero, who will remain one of the greatest men of our time, was Adolf Hitler. And the man who said Hitler was one of the greatest men of our time was François Genoud, a rich Swiss banker, who died a few weeks ago, at 81.

Now my readers are a motley crew, which is right and proper, but I presume that none of them admires the Nazis, let alone insists that Hitler will remain one of the greatest men of our time. Of course, there are loonies in every crack and cranny, including that man who pretends to believe that there was no Holocaust, but although I will offend some of my readers, I have to say that though François Genoud stank of evil from his childhood to his grave, it is hard not to admire a man who can continue to hold such beliefs throughout a long and passionate life.

Look at the catalogue. He bankrolled groups of Nazis and of fanatical Arabs; he got war criminals out of Europe; he held

Nazi money by stuffing it into Swiss banks; he gave money for the defence in the trials of Eichmann, Klaus Barbie and Carlos the Jackal; he had already, during the war, held the writings of Goebbels and Bormann in safety; he had earlier met the Grand Mufti (equivalent to the head Nazi), he ran what he called the global war against Zionism; he had Hitler's "Political Testament" translated into many languages, and he topped it all when he shook hands with Hitler.

Mad? You could call it mad, but it is not enough to say that he was steeped in Nazism, and it seems he was no ranter or screamer like his hero Hitler. I think that if you met him (Heaven forbid) you would at first think that you had met some kind of businessman ticking off in his head which of his subordinates should have a rise; there is no reason to believe that he ever struck anybody.

And yet, and yet . . . what makes a man like this into what he became? It seems that in the Genoud household, the infant Genoud would certainly not have got such ideas. His father was a respectable manufacturer of wallpaper, and it would be stretching things to believe that young Genoud was so delicate a figure, and that papa sold wallpaper so ugly, that our evil youngster was instantly turned into a lifelong Nazi. But all the signals seem to show that there was nothing crazy in Genoud. He met Hitler and shook hands, but surely that would mean something more substantial than a handshake? Of course he had been infected with the poison of anti-Semitism, but that doesn't answer the question; nothing does. It seems clear that Genoud would not kill anyone himself, but from his words I can only deduce that he liked the thought of murder.

"The thought of murder": roll those words round your tongue. Here is a man who does not shudder at such words, but feels a glow of pleasure. We, the sane majority, are brought up sharply when murder is discussed, and it is notable that when the word is used in jest ("I could have murdered him!") there is usually something in the air that immediately sours the jest.

We know and obviously understand that murder is the

greatest of all crimes; to take a sentient being and rob him or her of life is the wickedest thing any person can do. It is said that the abolition of capital punishment in countries such as ours is due to the danger of getting the wrong man, but I think that there is a stronger element: the deep horror of taking human life. (Before hanging was abolished in Britain, I can remember the tremendous stir; at the time of a hanging, hundreds clogged the pavements, banners demanded clemency, dreadful voyeurs had a good time.)

We talk of murder as though it is obvious and the punishment likewise ("an eye for an eye"), but murder is probably the most difficult crime to grapple with. Some kinds of murders, indeed, are hardly seen to be such. In India, for instance, the law demands that an offender knows the danger he might produce, which rules out a claim of recklessness or ignorance. In Japan, I gather, a murder within the family is thought of as the worst kind, and even today, in Italy, I believe mitigation rules and a passionate deathblow can be overlooked when honour is at the stake.

There can be little argument as to the horror that Shakespeare felt when murder was spoken of; he was not just shocked but longed to "Revenge his foul and most unnatural murder", and went on to describe "Murder most foul, as in the best it is, but this most foul, strange and unnatural". But darkest of all is the murder of Duncan by Macbeth:

> Methought I heard a voice cry "Sleep no more!
> Macbeth does murder sleep", the innocent sleep,
> Sleep that knits up the ravell'd sleave of care,
> The death of each day's life, sore labour's bath,
> Balm of hurt minds, great nature's second course,
> Chief nourisher in life's feast—

We are now in a world in which murder is almost trivial, so frequent has it become. But that frequency is not just a matter of numbers. Nor is it a matter only of brutality, though I think that meaningless savagery has risen very greatly. The truth is that murder is slowly merging into "ordinary" crime.

But murder is not an "ordinary" crime, and any country that begins to believe that it is, has begun sliding into the void.

Yes, yes, there are terrible wars going on, and when those terrible wars are over, other wars – just as terrible – will break out in turn. But I am not talking about countries in which murder is just as frequent as pickpocketing. I am not quite old enough to remember "Murder, Inc." – the clusters of American gangsters who killed for money. If you wanted a man killed, the price was fixed and the man was no more. There was a ladder; if you wanted a man maimed, a man robbed, a man threatened . . . there was a price at any level.

I am, however, just old enough to remember the break-up of "Murder Inc." – which had a group who turned informer, and "grassed" on the killers. It is said that nearly a hundred gangsters were put behind bars.

But now? I return to the difference – the difference between murder and all other crime. Some would say "What's the difference?"; some would admit there's a difference but say it doesn't matter. But it is a big difference, and it does matter. It matters, of course, because in every crime but one, the crime can be rectified.

But that is not the point. The point is that if we believe, or even begin to believe, that murder is only a different kind of crime from bank robbery, say, we shall turn the human creature into just another ordinary creature.

Let us come back to where we started. We saw a rich man – a cultured, knowledgable, intelligent man – whose only apparent wish was to admire and almost revere Adolf Hitler, and to follow him. He shelled out much of his money in keeping the flag of Hitler flying, and when Hitler shot himself in the bunker, Genoud, sad but not giving up, hauled out the precious documents – Goebbels's diaries. What a waste of a human being! If, indeed, he was one.

The Times, 9 August 1996

A different colour

I T IS WELL known that God does not make mistakes, and I accept that, but sometimes – and more frequently as time goes on – I begin to think that He is pulling the leg of the lot of us. Oh, we know the bit about the mystery and wonders to perform, but some of the things He has been doing recently suggest that we are being had. What, for instance, was He up to when He had the idea of colouring some of us white, and some black, and some yellow, and others a sort of reddish-brown, and indeed practically every shade of colour in the paintbox, whereupon He tossed us out higgledy-piggledy to get acquainted with each other.

Again, I do not wish to get into an argument with the Almighty, but if that isn't the biggest plonker in His universe I don't dare to think what the bigger ones look like.

These musings of mine have not been called up at random. The question above is being tested to its snapping-point in Australia, of all places, and the story was first found in the *Guardian*. Take a deep breath.

It happened in a Qantas aeroplane (yes, yes, I know there should be a 'u' after the Q, but that comes from being upside-down all the time), in which a white lady was sitting among three Aborigines, and let me tell you that Australian Aborigines hold the record for blackness. Now, the three black men were not in any way annoying or being unpleasant to the white woman; very much to the contrary, because these Aborigines were her friends and colleagues, and they were all flying on a joint mission.

But, alas, the stewardess did not know that.

So, coming down the aisle, and seeing a white woman among Aborigines, she said: "If you don't feel comfortable sitting there, we understand the situation and are happy to move you." The white lady indicated that she was perfectly happy, but later on, another stewardess, in the kindness of her white heart, told the lady that there was a window-seat available, which, in the circumstances, could mean only one thing – that the white lady would be unhappy among Aborigines. The lady once again indicated that she was not, repeat not, unhappy among Aborigines, and there the matter ended.

Or rather, began.

Because, of course, when the story broke (it is not clear who broke it), merry hell broke out. The cost of damage-limiting alone must have come close to bankrupting Qantas for ever (and remember British Airways holds a 25 per cent stake in Qantas), and letters of apology were flying so thickly that they blotted out the sun for days. Inevitably, some Aboriginal centres demanded a head or two, saying that "Qantas is constantly using images of Aboriginal children . . . to encourage people to fly in their aircraft to the outback, but they don't want their passengers to sit next to us".

Now share with me, please, an experience that I have had only a few minutes ago, as I was writing. In the previous paragraph, what I first wrote was not: "The cost of damage-limiting alone must have come close to bankrupting Qantas for ever (and remember British Airways holds a 25 per cent stake in Qantas), and letters of apology . . .", but it was: "The cost of damage-limiting alone must have cleaned out every chemist's smelling-salts shelf . . .".

I changed the wording because I felt that the introduction, *with its reference to smelling-salts* (by which, of course, I meant that some of the people involved in the *brouhaha* would be fainting from shock) would be picked up and read as though I was saying that Aborigines smell unpleasantly.

Before I continue, please fill in this quiz-paper: Is B. Levin (a) mad; or (b) racist; or (c) both; or (d) none of

these; I *think* the answer is (d), but I am not entirely
impartial.

When you have made your decision, I propose a harder
test. Go back some time: when the uproar among our
potential prime ministers was at its screaming height, I
thought that some laughter would be useful, so I imagined
– in all good fun – Portillo praying that Heseltine would "be
discovered in bed with 14 fat ladies and a dog". ("Ha, ha",
or, possibly, "That Levin fellow goes too far".) But although
those were the words you read in the paper ". . . discovered
in bed with 14 fat ladies . . .", they were not the first words I
wrote in that sentence: the first version read ". . . discovered
in bed with 14 black ladies . . ."

A new quiz-paper, but asking the same questions, *viz.*, Is
B. Levin *now* (a) mad; or (b) racist; or (c) both; or (d) none of
these. Again, I choose (d), but again I have to rule myself out
while the Sanhedrin is in session. But what I want to know
is: who are the members of the Sanhedrin?

First, obviously, the law. I do not think that I am giving
away the secrets of News International when I say that this
column was examined by a lawyer, and that anything by me,
or indeed by anybody else, is inspected by a lawyer if there
is even the slightest suggestion that trouble might follow its
publication. (We have even turned it into a verb, and as the
evening draws on we can hear cries of: "Has it been legalled
yet?") I scrupulously obey the law, and always shall; but I
am not going to admit even the tiniest crack in the fabric
through which anyone – lawyer or layman – might widen
the law without full and proper right. When I first wrote ". . .
black ladies . . .", I could certainly have been in bad taste,
but I do not know whether I would have been breaking the
law. And I rather think that a lot of other people, including
lawyers, don't know either, not because the lawyers are not
good enough, but because the law is not good enough.

Am I, or am I not, breaking the law when I say quite
innocently ". . . and 14 black ladies . . ."? If I am told yes,
I shall demand to see the statute, and when I have seen it and

understood it, and agreed that it is in force, I shall never use those words again (I must add here that I have no intention of ever again using those words in any context, not even if all the lawyers in the land and millions outside it fall on their knees and beg me to say them). I shall always bow to the law, but only the law, the whole law, and nothing but the law.

Of course, those stewardesses – obviously a pair of innocents – should not have been so appallingly clumsy; if they had stopped to think what they were doing they would have blushed and changed the subject. But were they breaking the Australian or any other law? (I ask, can you be breaking a law five miles up which can be put in force only on the ground? If so, I am going to spend a lot of time in aircraft murdering my enemies.)

Clearly, the three Aborigines did not take umbrage; good for them. I trust that a few sensible words to the stewardesses would suffice. So everybody is happy? Ah, not quite.

Suppose a traveller finds him/herself to be the only white person in that section, all the others being Aborigines? And suppose the white gets up, carefully and without speaking, and crosses the aisle into a group of white travellers? The only conclusion that the Aborigines can come to is the obvious one; that their colour – and only their colour – gives offence.

Let me go back to the beginning, when I was complaining that the Almighty was winking; a dangerous belief. But wasn't He? The terrible question, embedded in the argument over colour, must be terribly asked. It is: "All the beautiful words, and all the money, and all the arguments, and all the laws, and all the fights, and all the despair, and all the suppressed hate, and all the unsuppressed hate – have we not, when we tot up the score in the field of differences of colour, discovered that they have made things not better, but worse?"

I don't know. I don't think anyone knows, though thousands upon thousands claim, very noisily, that they do know. But if the Almighty *is* pulling our legs, He can – and perhaps should – stop all the laughter. If we all got together and painted ourselves in one equal shade, we would have nothing to worry about – at least not in the trivial matter of the colour of human skin. Well, what's wrong with that? Nothing? Then let's get down to it right away. Oh, of course, when we agree on the colour.

The Times, 30 September 1995

Waiter, the soup's too hot

I RATHER THINK that it is I who should be called to settle the row now going on about restaurant charges, though none of the restaurateurs has as yet even asked my opinion. More fools they.

To begin with, the fracas is not just about hiked prices – those have been going on for many years, and the customers likewise have been complaining since – well, since ". . . the woman saw that the tree was good for food, and that it was pleasant to the eyes, and a tree to be desired to make one wise, she took of the fruit thereof and did eat, and gave also unto her husband with her; and he did eat . . ." (Mind you, there is another bit about being cursed above all cattle, and above every beast of the field, which suggests that Adam and Eve were vegetarians. I should sincerely hope not.)

But before I get into the fray, I must offer my credentials. To start with, I will have you know that I am a Chevalier de la Confrerie des Tastes-Fromages de France, and I have a scroll, together with a beautiful green sash and a medallion to hang on it. More to the point, eating good food and drinking good wine (in particular with good company) has been my hobby throughout my life.

And why not? There are people who collect rare stamps and glow with pleasure when they find a beautifully kept Penny Black; nobody says the collector is a fool. There are other people – many – who stand on the touchline of a soccer or rugby game in cold and rain to cheer their idols; why not, if it pleases them? There are those who can pore over a chessboard for hours – and without actually playing, but just following a printed game played years ago.

I love good food and enjoy it, just as those who enjoy their own hobbies do.

Yet, there is one difference; a strange difference, which I have written about before. The worst that can be said of the stamp-collector is that he is wasting his time in trivialities; the worst said of the Cantona-follower is that he gets too angry; the worst of chess is that the spectators get bored.

But the man who makes food his hobby will be laughed at, sneered at and even shouted at. I will take good odds that there will be several letters in my postbag when this column is published, letters which denounce me as a voluptuary; my only consolation is that half of them can't spell voluptuary and the other half don't know what it means.

No, dammit; that is *not* my only consolation. I have many consolations, among which will be found my pleasure in good food.

But now to the subject I was supposed to be discussing: the Earl of Bradford's assault, not on restaurant prices, but on restaurant money tricks. The Earl has put forward a measure, called the Restaurant (Service and Cover Charges) Bill, the purpose of which is to bring Britain into line with the rest of Western Europe in the matter of paying for meals. Let me make all clear.

If you have a restaurant meal in France, you will be given one bill at the end of it. The bill will include all service and other charges, and no one is expected to give more nor do they. The same is true for Belgium, Germany, Holland and indeed all the Western European nations.

Except Britain.

Except Britain.

In Britain, your bill can include – openly and without blushes from the *patron* – separate cover charges, separate vegetables (this is not a joke), separate coffee, even separate *petit-fours* (this is also not a joke). And there is no rule covering all these things in all restaurants; two restaurants side by side in the same street can be charging in vastly different ways.

The Earl of Bradford – three cheers for him; no, six – has now taken up the cudgels, and if he wants a cudgel with nails sticking out, I'm his man.

Naturally, most of the most expensive restaurants are screaming the place down; just look at a few here. But before you do, take the measure not just of the prices but, much more significantly, of the way the restaurants wriggle out of their claims to be modest when the bill comes.

For instance, at Kensington Place (which has the remarkable honour of being the noisiest restaurant in London), "the service charge is left to the discretion of the customer . . . although parties of nine or more are told there is a fixed charge of 12½ per cent". Then comes the *coup de grâce*: ". . . if for any reason a party questions this, we would shrug and refund it," says Tim Brice, the manager. ". . . Happily, so far, no one has complained."

Happily, so far, no one has complained.

Oh, yes? Just picture the scene; here is a diner, just finishing his meal. There has been no complaint about the food and wine and service. But the diner doesn't want to pay for the service, and he refuses to tip. A certain *froideur* would ensue, would it not?

Or take the same road to the Pont de la Tour, which is owned by the Terence Conran Group (as is everything except Mount Everest, and there is a bid out for that now) – and which demands 12½ per cent irrespective of the number of the party. "Should a customer question the charge," says its man, "I would ask if anything was wrong, but he or she would not be forced to pay the tip."

Just one more: James Ward of Orso, near Covent Garden, says: "Tipping is discretionary, while there is a fixed service charge of 12½ per cent on parties of 10 or more, but there would be no question of enforcing the charge if the customer did not want to pay."

The only words fitting this catalogue are "Come off it".

Legally, of course, the service charges (which, in a very great number of restaurants, including some well-known ones, are dreadful or invisible), need not be paid, and that is the screen behind which so many restaurateurs hide. But, dear reader and eater, have you ever seen, in a respectable restaurant, a customer raising his voice not to blast the food, with which he is wholly content, but to argue about the tipping? No, dear reader and eater, you haven't. Nor have I. Nor has anybody else. Nor does the picture need a very large major-domo to browbeat the customer who refuses a tip, in whatever guise.

Let me turn the story just a little. One day, in New York, I was dining alone, but when I had finished my meal (a very good one, as I recall), I saw a friend on the other side of the restaurant, who beckoned me over. He motioned me to sit down, and he was very angry at something connected with the tip. I calmed him down, and another friend joined us. In helping my first friend to stop seething, the third voice said words that I have never forgotten, though this all happened a good many decades ago. He said: "You never tip an equal."

I have used those words in countless forms and places, and with countless effects. For they are packed with meaning, are they not? I look up from my desk at *The Times* and I see a colleague, a colleague who has recently given me a bit of help. I have thanked him, but in doing so, I would never have thought of giving him money, nor would he have thought to take it. *You never tip an equal.*

When you think of it, do you not feel that the entire business of tipping is not only distasteful, but shocking and almost evil? During my first visit to New Zealand (and I hope it was the first of many), one of the most striking items that I took into my mind and heart was the fact that there was in New Zealand no tipping. It wasn't a rule, much less a law; but the weight off my shoulders when I learned that wonderful truth will never fade from my memory.

Come, Lord Bradford and your colleagues; there will be

Members of the House of Commons, and also some in the Lords, who would like to scupper your splendid Bill; I regret to say that (some? many? all?) of those who fight it are in one way or another tied up with the catering and restaurant world.

The last stand of the "Keep tipping alive" team will be a false and indeed almost criminal claim: that tipping has to go on because, in many places, the tippees cannot live decently without tips. It answers itself: try using decent wages for those who have none. Meanwhile, let us remember those potent words: You never tip an equal.

P.S. He lost.

The Times, 17 February 1996

Taleban meets Caliban

S TOP PRESS. THIRTY-FOUR killed in Algeria ambush by Muslim fundamentalists, in Algerian town of Laghouat. Passengers of a bus were told to get out for identity checks, and one by one their throats were cut. (This news was relayed to the world a fortnight ago in a one-column *Times* story well down the page.)

No doubt my readers are horrified by this story, but I have to say that it is by no means remarkable, for the story has been replicated in Algeria approximately 30,000 times over not many years. The other side of this terrible argument is by no means unwilling to shoot first and toss a hand grenade after; many an Algerian soldier has shot a fundamentalist without asking him first if he would like a cup of tea.

And if my readers are bemused by this tale of murder most foul, and wonder why and how it comes to pass, I can tell you. The beautiful and holy Muslim religion is not a charnel house, though the fanatical wing of it is making it into one. Remember, those who cut the throats are not Christians or followers of other religions, they are brother Muslims, presumably doing it so that the fundamentalist Muslims will eventually take over the entire Muslim world, and there will be only fundamentalists.

Anyone with eyes and understanding must have seen over the years, and not very many years, that the Muslim religion is becoming much more prominent in Britain. That prominence gives shame to the other religions in Britain. For instance, the Christians are getting fewer, or if not fewer, not going deep into their souls; we Jews are getting less and less interested in our beautiful religion; the minor religions show no sign of growing.

But the Muslims take their wonderful religion seriously, and that is one reason that they multiply. And, incidentally, how many people who dip into the Christian Bible or the Jewish Talmud ignore the Koran?

But there is another side to the religion of Muhammad. Indeed, there are many sides, but they all seem to come together, and they all seem to say that there should be but one religion, and that one the Muslim.

The fighting in Afghanistan has been long and bloody, nor is it settled now. The Afghan capital is still besieged, but for the moment Taleban – the name of the new rulers – reigns. And the first thing that they did when they had conquered was to hang the former president, Najibullah, and leave him and others hanging for a few days. It seems that whatever is the nature of the new rulers, it does not encompass any kind of religion other than the Muslim one. And moreover, the nature of the new Muslim rulers is the kind that does slit throats.

Moreover, it took not days but mere hours to make clear that anyone who lives under the fanatic wing of Muhammad is to live under a reign of terror, though Muhammad surely did not want that. But the fanatic wing of the Muslim religion had conquered, and was now in the hands of that religion. And the words of the trumpet that sounded were: "We will punish all those who do not follow Islamic teachings, whether educated or uneducated."

Eyewitnesses in the capital say they saw armed Taleban fighters thrashing two women with aerials ripped from a car; the women were apparently guilty of not wearing strict Islamic dress. Women who fail to wrap themselves in these robes are horribly beaten. (You can see, on any pavement in London, women shrouded entirely in black cloth except for a quarter-inch slit for their eyes. But in their case it is not enforced by secular law.) In Kabul, on the other hand, a married couple, riding together on their own bicycle, were beaten because they were riding too close. Men who do not have beards are told that they must grow one or be beaten perhaps to death. A butcher had two of his fingers cut off for selling meat at the wrong price.

Television sets must be destroyed, as must videotaping and cassettes. Games like soccer are forbidden. Pet birds are illegal, and because they may not be fed they must die. Playing chess or card games is forbidden. Praying at home is banned; it must be done only in the mosques. Girls may not leave their homes, nor may they talk to men other than relations. Nor may they go to school or learn. Women with serious injuries can be dragged back to their homes. Music is banned (any kind of music). A couple having an affair are stoned to death. Anyone found drinking liquor will be stoned to death.

In hospitals the patients are dying, because many of the doctors are women, and thus may not work. Take this: "A short distance away a woman doctor was pleading with the mullahs, saying she had to work because she had three patients to operate on. Her plea was in vain; they sent her home." (Presumably, the patients died.)

Black-turbaned Taleban fighters move through the streets five times a day, beating men into the mosques for prayers and ordering shops to close. Women may not enter mosques. Indeed, if they are even seen out, or wear modern clothing they are whipped. A thief, if caught, has his hand cut off.

The number of women who were working before Taleban arrived was roughly 250,000; none of these is now allowed to work. And tens of thousands of people are daily fleeing from Taleban troops, some because of the hideous life that now lays before them, others because study and work and climbing the ladder and even laughter would disappear.

There is hunger in the orphanage, and not a single toy; the place is filthy. One woman does what she can, all the time in fear of being beaten if Taleban members see her. (At this point it is surely proper to hail Christopher Thomas, our man in Kabul, who brings all this awful news to *Times* readers.)

We should have known, though who could have even

guessed? Did you or I give more than a glance at the murder case in Leeds, in which "a Moslem killed his sister-in-law – he drove his car three times over her – after she had walked out of her arranged marriage, saying that she had brought shame on the family". (He was jailed for life, but for all I know he might even now be pleased with himself.)

There is a great deal more to say about this almost incredible story, and I shall certainly say it. But I want to go back to where we started – that is, the way in which the Islamic peoples take their religion.

I mentioned earlier the 30,000 deaths in Algeria which were solely concerned, on both sides, with Islam. On one side is a country struggling to keep its head (Algeria was moving towards real democracy when she had to break off because of the fight against the fanatics). And on the other side is a country in which the number of innocent people murdered per week is counted, and the higher the number, the greater is the delight of those who are doing the counting, because Islam, it seems, wants it this way.

It is difficult to believe that the mad savages in Taleban are of the same belief, but it is true. I look at the Koran very infrequently, but even from my glances at it I instantly find myself in a world as beautiful as it is wonderful. The language in the Christian Bible is so wonderful because of the translations, and the Hebrew ones are similar because they are so profound. But the Koran is a poem in itself, and it is impossible to understand why some Muslims want to exterminate not only non-Muslims, but countless men and women who do follow the teaching of Muhammad.

Can anyone make sense of the horrors of Taleban? Why are there no wedding-parties? Why may people not listen to music? Why may we not play chess? Why must I grow a beard? Why should children not be taught? Why must people be stoned to death if they drink a glass of wine?

I don't know. But what I *do* know is that the Muslim breath of life is a wonderful one, but the ravings of Taleban are poisoning one of the greatest teachings, in the shape of the Koran and all it tells us.

There are, of course, hundreds of things it tells us, but assuredly it does not tell us to go to Algeria, to get out of our bus on the pretence that we have to have identity checks, and, one by one, have our throats cut. Truly, Taleban has come to Caliban.

The Times, 18 October 1996

Don't hit back

L ET ME INTRODUCE Mr Andrew Malone, a reporter on the *Sunday Times*. Mr Malone was just outside King's Cross Station, waiting for a friend. While waiting, he was eating a cheeseburger. A man came up to him and said: "Give me your burger." Mr Malone refused, which was his first mistake.

He saw the man go over to another man and talk to him. Mr Malone looked in the direction of the pair, which was his second mistake. Mr Malone's third mistake was not to go immediately to the taxi rank, get into a cab and go away, waiting friend or no waiting friend.

Then the burger-lover and his companion – but if Mr Malone is yet capable of speaking for himself, let him do so. This is what he said:

I was knocked to the ground. The two men started kicking me on my head, my hands, my body. I saw a woman's face looking at me in horror; pinstriped legs scurried past. I managed to clamber to my feet and stumble down the concourse, but my assailants caught me again. The smaller man started first. I pushed him off and was getting to my feet when the tall man kicked the side of my head, knocking me down. I tried to get away, running across the traffic to an island in the middle of the road. But they caught up again. I was kicked back on the pavement and the taller of the pair jumped on my leg. I was unaware he had snapped the bone – all I could focus on was the skinhead on top of me shouting:

"Cut his f—ing throat." The taller man stood over me;
I couldn't see a knife but I feared the worst. In panic I
found myself on my feet again, shouting at them: "What
are you doing? What's this about?" My voice sounded
disembodied, but the words registered with the taller
man. He dragged his friend off and the pair disappeared.
Still nobody came to my aid.

Now, a test for my readers. What was the worst of Mr
Malone's ordeal? That the villains continued to run after
him even when he was running away from them? Wrong.
That he was under genuine threat of having his throat cut?
Wrong. That he heard the disembodied sound of his own
voice? Wrong. That neither of the men had asked for
money or Mr Malone's wallet? Wrong. That he had lost
his cheese-burger after all? Wrong.

Alas, you all know the answer already. The six words: "Still
nobody came to my aid".

Sooner or later – probably sooner – those words will fade
from human memory, and scholars of what is left of the
English language (mainly grunts) will scratch their heads and
try to make some sense of them. And why? Because it is
already too dangerous to go to the help of someone who
is being attacked, *even a woman*.

I italicised those three words, to register my horror at the
very idea of a woman being attacked, and from my use of the
word horror in this context you should be able to work out
what my age is. For there is a divide – a huge gulf – between
those who take for granted that wherever they go they are
in peril, and those who, once upon a time, did not need to
hurry past a rough-looking figure, because a rough-looking
figure need not also be a bad one.

Very well. But I do not think that I am living in the past
when I see a headline reading "Obituary column burglars
preyed on the bereaved".

For the story tells of thieves, two of them, whose practice it
was to scour the national newspapers daily, though they were

interested only in the obituary columns. Why only those? You may feel sick at the answer, but here it is.

They noted the deaths, got the dates and times of funerals, hung about when the mourners were going into the church, and then sped to the empty houses, broke in and stole whatever of value they could find. No fewer than 14 homes had been thus ransacked; one of the men was sentenced to 10 years, and the other to seven.

I am not so silly as to think that there were no thieves and other crooks when I was a youth. But I truly do believe that when I was a youth, that horrible mourning theft did not, and could not, take place.

And if you think that that is a one-off crime, and nothing else so macabre could happen today, try this headline, "GP accused of cashing dead men's pensions."

You will be, I think, all the more nauseated, when you read the full story. For the doctor – some healer! – got the sum of £150,000 by collecting the pension books of his patients when they died. He signed the death certificates, and then continued to cash their social security benefits. (He went to prison for three years.) And again, I say that of course crooks abounded when I was a child, but I do not believe that that happened or could have happened.

And what about the crooked policeman? Ah, you say, those bent coppers are always on the lookout for someone to stitch up, and lots of them are not above breaking into the warehouses they were supposed to be guarding – what about them, eh?

And again, I say that there are and were indeed crooked policemen, but I do not believe that half a century or so ago a policeman, however crooked, would have done what today's headline announces: "PC jailed for theft from pensioners".

For the bent copper in this case was called to investigate the disappearance of £6, and, having done his investigation properly, he stole the entire sum – £440 – that the octogenarians had. And yet again I say that that would not have happened 50 years ago.

So we return to Andrew Malone and his broken leg. He tells us that a woman going past Mr Malone, who was by then being kicked and punched on the ground, looked at him in horror, but she did nothing – not even seek a policeman. He tells us, also, that "pinstriped legs scurried past", but the said legs did not pause in their scurrying. But he says: "The attack had lasted barely a minute, an outburst of savagery such . . ." – but now, reader, try to finish Mr Malone's sentence ". . . outburst of savagery such . . ." Go on, try, all you have to do is finish Mr Malone's sentence, and you do the crossword quickly enough, don't you?

Very well, you give up. What Mr Malone said was: "The attack had lasted barely a minute, an outburst of savagery such *as happens across Britain every day.*"

Mr Malone, I take it, has good evidence for that quite remarkable statement, and presumably he is not just drawing on his bruises and his broken leg. But if it is correct, and what happened to Mr Malone happens every day, it is time, I think, to change our attitudes rather quickly and rather firmly.

When did beggars first appear in substantial numbers in Oxford Street and in the equivalent of that thoroughfare in other cities and towns? It cannot be more than two or three years, and I think that the beggars followed hard upon the sleeping-rough.

It is too late now to separate the real beggars from the fraudulent ones, and for that matter it is too late to separate the real sleeping-roughs from the frighteners. For if, as Mr Malone tells us, brutal violence is the norm today, the whole edifice of begging, sleeping-rough, drugs and rampant theft is destroying the age-old compassion of the Samaritan.

The Times, 30 December 1995

The Bard in every home

Among my vast number of oddlinesses, some of which have had bystanders seriously worrying, I include the practice of tearing paper. I am not quite so barmy as to sit about doing nothing but tear pieces of paper for hours on end, but when I am, say, clearing out a cupboard, and finding in it a bundle of papers which have no more use, I do get a mild pleasure from tearing the papers before I put them in sacks for the rubbish-men. This almost invariably means that very large numbers of papers more or less vital to my life have been accidentally scooped up with the useless ones, so that I spend the next month trying to remember what the precious papers, now lost for ever, were about. (Perhaps the worrying *should* go as far as men in white coats.)

But from time to time, I accidentally fish out a piece of paper, which for the life of me I cannot place. One of these has just popped out, and I am intrigued to know how it got there, because it has plainly been mouldering in a cupboard for two or three years. Clearly, it is from *The Times*, but it has no byline and is headed just "By a staff reporter". (If the writer of the article is still on the staff and sees this, would he or she please let me know, so at last I can give some credit where it is due. *No one spoke.*)

But this little bit of sleuthing means, for me at least, a wonderful vista of glory, and I am not exaggerating when I say that. For the heading of the article is "Teach the Bard to five-year-olds", and the entire article is a beautiful plea to get the immortal lines of Shakespeare into heads so young that when they grow up they find Shakespeare in them for life. And to find that you have Shakespeare in you is second only to finding Heaven.

And I should know. For at my public school, one of the minor punishments for minor transgressions was to be given by the prefect or teacher a poem or a part of a poem and commit it to memory within a specified time; at the specified time, the transgressor had to repeat the poem, now booklessly, and woe betide he who had not got the lines into his head in time. (You know about my magic carpet, the discovery that I had a memory so perfect that I could recite two thousand lines of Shakespeare, or anything else for that matter, without any books. Alas, poor Yorick, the magic carpet burst into flames three or four years ago, and now I have to look up everything and anything I want to know.)

But let me alone, and let us contemplate what that eager chunk of newspaper could come to: "Teach the Bard to five-year-olds". First, let us tackle head-on the claim that if you stuff Shakespeare down a child's throat he will hate Shakespeare rather than love him when he grows up. The child who wants to run out and play rather than read Shakespeare is a real figure, but the same child, 20 years on, will bless the parent who demanded an evening a week of the boring Shakespeare.

In the Royal Society for the Encouragement of Arts, Manufactures and Commerce (and what a magnificent name!) Shakespeare must, of course, have a high place. And the RSA gives him one: "His output was prodigious, and his plays contain the whole range of human emotions, relationships, and situations. The themes are universal, encompassing every aspect of human endeavour. His language, rich in its imagery and dramatic power, moves fluently from heroic verse and lyricism to the broad humour of the street. His plays are read and performed in many languages and have been turned into ballets, operas, music scores, films and cartoons. Moreover, the acting of Shakespearean pieces by pupils is a means of exploring text and is a valid teaching approach. Seeing professional actors perform Shakespeare could also inspire curiosity and further study."

And that is how I came first to Shakespeare on the page, and from there on, Shakespeare on the stage.

Many years ago – oh, all right: 49 years if you must – there was a music-hall less then 100 yards from my home. I had been reading Shakespeare voraciously for some years, but I had not seen any of it on a stage, though that was not strange, because I had never then seen *any* play. But Donald Wolfit (yes, yes, you haven't the faintest notion of who Wolfit was) brought his ragtag and bobtail company to the Camden High Street music-hall.

I was, of course, dumbstruck. True, I was about 14 or 15 and as I say had been reading Shakespeare for a considerable time. Nevertheless, the transition from the page to the human being is something I have never forgotten, and never will. In one of my own books – *Enthusiasms* – there is a substantial chapter entirely about Shakespeare, and as I have said, there was not a day when at least half a dozen pages weren't turned.

One of the most stirring moments of my life took place in the United States, in Washington DC, where a very grand party was being given in the Folger Library – that mighty collection of everything in the world about Shakespeare. I had been asked to organise something for the evening, and I brought over two of Britain's finest players. I wrote a massive Shakespearean trumpet, made up of some of the hundreds of phrases that we use casually which originally came from Shakespeare. Maggie Smith and Alec McCowen spoke the lines wonderfully, but my finest hour was the utter silence as the two players rolled the words into the air and I realised that practically no one in that great hall had before known that so many hundreds of phrases were from Shakespeare.

But come, turn the pages, and with no more ultimate purpose let me recall just a few words of the millions he wrote.

How all occasions do inform against me,
And spur my dull revenge!

'Tis one thing to be tempted, Escalus,
Another thing to fall.

There is a world elsewhere.

    Perdition catch my soul
But I do love thee! and when I love thee not,
Chaos is come again.

If every ducat in six thousand ducats
Were in six parts and every part a ducat,
I would not draw them: I would have my bond.

Good shepherd, tell this youth what 'tis to love.

I dare do all that may become a man;
Who dares do more is none.

'Tis the time's plague, when madmen lead the blind.

The last of all the Romans, fare thee well.

I should like to know how many homes have a copy of
Shakespeare. I wish every home had at least one. I seem to
have nine, not including the original seven-volume None-
such and the later four-volume edition, and I even have the
Bowdler, which I find delightful when I get to the words he
had to expunge, such as "What bastard doth not?", but even
"his mother's milk". Bowdler must have had a fit when he
came to

She lov'd not the savour of tar nor of pitch
Yet a tailor might scratch her where'er she did
itch.

I also have a concordance, but alas, I now have to use a
magnifying-glass.

    Once upon a time, it is said, there was a Bible in every
home. I shudder to think what the numbers must be now.

And if the Bible has vanished, Shakespeare is going also. Ah, but that tiny newspaper cutting, years old, shows that Shakespeare can be digested by five-year-olds, which means that the Bard still lives, and still teaches.

But don't just tell me: tell Shakespeare. When the plebs crowded the arenas for another new work of Shakespeare, few there were who could read or write. That didn't stop them, nor did the rain. How can we bring back that feeling, that longing, that belief that every day has some Shakespeare in it? There can be only one answer: start with the children.

I was lucky; I met Shakespeare early. But now children do not need to be lucky, for that mysterious but wonderful piece of paper has demonstrated that even to the youngest, Shakespeare can be not only not boring at all, but a glory and shining path for ever.

The Times, 27 December 1996

Fools and their money

W HAT IS IT that draws me – and obviously draws thousands more – to back-to-back horror stories concerning money? We who are drawn know that there are two kinds in these stories: the plainly crooked ones whose feet can be heard tripping down the stairs to get away, and the equally plainly greedy ones who have lost their money (sometimes to the plainly crooked) because they were greedy.

Very well, you say, there are crooks and there are softies, and both of these types are so old that they go back to Adam and Eve, *viz.* "The serpent beguiled me, and I did eat". More plainly, I ask what is my favourite question in these matters: why do sane, decent people, again and again, persuade themselves that 10 plus 10 make 50?

We don't have to go back to the great BCCI scam to find that there is a sucker under every tree. But the Titan Business Club, to give it its full name, did actually do that very thing. In this case,

> as many as 12,000 investors paid between £2,500 and £3,000 each to join the Titan Business Club ... The new recruits were expected to recoup their money by persuading four or five other people to join up at ... meetings held around the country.

And as the story began to rise in the courts, it was Robert Miller of *The Times* who perhaps did most to alert the world to what was going on at Titan.

But listen to this: "Patrick Minford, one of Britain's most respected economists and a member of the inner circle of six 'wise men' who advise Kenneth Clarke, the Chancellor, was retained as a special adviser to the American version of Titan." Well, well; it seems that "one of Britain's most respected economists and a member of the inner circle of six 'wise men' who advise Kenneth Clarke, the Chancellor", may not be quite up to seeing that two and two make four, not three and a half.

But let us now leave that "most respected" booby, and turn to those who were convinced that money would rain from the clouds if there are enough people to believe it. *And every now and again there are enough people to believe it.* For the Titan Business Club is only one of thousands – literally thousands – which try the old trick, again and again, and with a wink and a nod catch their mouse. The hair of my hero, Tony Hetherington (of the *Mail on Sunday*), has gone grey repeating the rubric: every – *every* – chain letter, whether it is the child's one, saying that it mustn't be broken or pussy will run away – to, well – look at Titan ... But pussy's bewilderment does not take huge sums of money; yet the money the Titan swallowed was real money.

Come, I have money in my bank at roughly $5\frac{1}{2}$ per cent, and the sum grows modestly. I am content with that tree and what grows on it, Now then: how does it come about that reasonably intelligent people somehow begin to believe that their $5\frac{1}{2}$ per cent can burgeon overnight to 10 or 15 per cent or even more? But that is what they came to believe, and £17 million of their money has gone missing. And to rub in the salt, the experts tell us that the money was not stolen but "lost". But I do not intend to go through the details of where the money went and why and how. What, for me, is fascinating in this story is what the people thought and said when they saw their money disappearing down a deep dark hole. We all like money and what it can bring us, which is roughly what the people who swarmed around the fatal BCCI believed. But where was the broken bridge, and why did the suckers not notice that the bridge was broken? To this day, there are people who are still saying that they have been swindled by BCCI. But these people have forgotten how the catastrophe began. I for instance did not put my money – not a penny of it – in BCCI, though then BCCI shone like the evening star, and looked marvellous.

But why and how did it look marvellous? For, after all, there is only one way to measure marvellousness when we are talking about money. We talk about the golden gleam, and what the recipient will do with the new-made money, but that is all talk. And – believe it or not – the people who put their money into BCCI did so because the rates of return were enormously higher than anything they had previously met.

But now look at this, from *The Times* – only a few words: "Thousands of angry investors who joined Titan . . . may form a protest group to recoup losses now believed to top £17 million, after the scheme was closed down in the High Court yesterday."

Oh, yes, they may form any number of groups, and dance round the maypole for hours and hours, but the £17 million will never come again. And my modest millions are safely stowed in a bank, but not – oh, not – in the Bank of Greed and Morplease.

Greed? Well, of course there is a substantial element in it, but I do not believe that it is only greed which is behind these crashes. The element I study looks the same as folly, but is not quite the same. It is something – only something – like the wheel in the gambling saloon, where people mutter: "One more throw and I can get my money back twice over."

Ho! says the wiseboy, *I* would never be seen gambling; that's for fools – and he immediately puts £17 million into a business that even I, pitifully ignorant man when money is to the fore, can tell that the sound we hear consists of money vanishing, never to be seen again. And

don't think that the Titan business is the only absurdity
where money is concerned. Just now a page from the
Financial Times fluttered onto my desk. I glanced at it,
and then looked more closely. And then I was transfixed,
for the paper was headed "International corruption: a survey of business perceptions". I trembled with joy for such
a list – there are 54 entries, each a single country, and
I opened one of my best bottles. Dammit, if I was to
have an evening of pure joy, I wouldn't let anything mar
it.

The list gave ratings out of 10: if any one country had been
perfect, it would have scored 10 exactly; the worst of all was
0.69. Ready, steady, go.

Gentlemen, place your bets. Which country of the 54 came
closest to perfection as the cleanest?

No dear, we all wish it were Britain, but it isn't, though
it gets pretty high marks. Come, try your hand.

Yes, New Zealand, which scored 9.43 out of 10.

Now look at the end of the column to find the most
corrupt country in the world. It is, not surprisingly, Nigeria,
with 0.69 out of 10. But I find the second most crooked
astonishing: it is Pakistan, with exactly 1 out of 10. Now
Pakistan, everyone knows, is a savage and brutal place,
particularly with its brutal religion, but to find that it is
fifty-third out of 54 in the corruption league is alarming.

After New Zealand, as exemplars of probity, we find Denmark, Sweden (boring, it is said), Finland (I once went galloping over the frozen ice pulled by a pair of thundering horses),
Canada, Norway and Singapore (but Singapore bullies and
twists its way to success), Switzerland, The Netherlands,
Australia, Ireland (hmmm), and us. We beat Germany, Israel,
the United States, Austria, Japan, Hong Kong and the French
(who are six places below us).

And so the corruption and fraud goes on, among the
scamsters, but also in governments and everything they touch.
Be warned:

Corruption in trade and government procurement around the world has worsened, with companies offering illicit payments winning 80 per cent of their bids ... business newspapers and magazines almost read like police blotters ... state-owned industry officials demanding bribes, corporations making payments to politicians for contracts, costs of projects being inflated to cover kickbacks ...

Mutatis mutandis this must all be true throughout the world, including Britain. The Titan Business Club came from the United States, but when it reached our shores there were few to cry "No", and thousands to cry "Yes". And of those thousands who cried "Yes" and lost all their money, there are dozens who are even now looking for the same brand of mousetrap. And that will be the story to the end of time.

The Times, 23 August 1996

But put the books back

W HAT IS IT that makes people (I say people, though I cannot recall a female case) want to steal books, and only books? There is almost certainly a Latin word that means "theft of manuscripts", and at first we are tempted to admire the miscreant; ah, we say, this is a man who could not afford to buy books, but loved them so – or even needed them to write an imperishable masterpiece – that the crime is excused. But although knives and forks, to say nothing of credit cards, are stolen aplenty, nobody discusses the matter as though some strange magic is afoot. It is books, and only books, that stir the pot so strangely.

What about the people who do the book-stealing? I have often read about them and their peculiar malady. Only a year or two ago there was a man whose house was so full of stolen books that he was in danger of death from them – not, as you might think, because the heaps would collapse upon him and crush him, but because he could not move about in his home even to use a saucepan or open the refrigerator (which, anyway, was full of books). Aha, we say, this man wants to gobble up all the knowledge in the world, and has just started on his amazing voyage. But the most strange and touching part of his story is that the books were not stolen to get money by selling them – it transpired that they were not stolen even to be read; the thief (thief is almost too strong a word) had not opened even one of them.

Do not jump immediately to the conclusion that the man was mad. I have never stolen a book, but I cannot pick up any new book without sniffing it and stroking it, irrespective of its content; hardly as crazy as the house-full man, but distinctly odd. Anthony Powell called one of his novels *Books Do Furnish A Room*: a wicked jab at those who hardly ever open one.

But books, alas, are stolen for a variety of reasons; one of these reasons, however, is a very sad one. There are people who steal books *for money*. And as I write those words, I feel a shudder, and I think you do too. No names please, but an Oxford don, not long ago, stole virtually a library of rare books. The books were far from the wicked don's own world, for he lectured on Baroque music, but stole from the mathematics shelves. And the mathematics in question was no mere child's 10-times-table, but *Principia Mathematica* itself, Newton's theories of motion and gravitation. (And did he see the apple fall? I hope so, just as I hope that Archimedes cried out *Eureka!* and Galileo after all muttered *Eppur si muove*.)

Did he think, that Oxford book-robber, that he would never be found out, or did he sweat nightly from the thought that there might be a tap on his shoulder? Some would say he was crazy, considering that what he had stolen was precious and well-known, and moreover that the biggest prize was one of the rarest and best-known books in history and that he was offering it around the town, claiming that it had belonged to his grandfather. Surely, some dark angel was keeping him afloat?

Not a bit of it. The erring don had made a considerable pile long before his collar was fingered; he had bagged 78 books or manuscripts, every one of them a jewel. (Nobody seems to know whether any of the treasures was damaged. If so, a double curse upon him.) The 78 treasures were by no means the only booty; in the end, he admitted charges of theft and deception, and – in the time-worn words – asked for 113 similar offences to be considered. They were duly considered, and he went to prison for two years.

But not before – and I think it will curdle your blood – he gave as a reason for the thieving *to pay off his mortgage*.

The story doesn't quite stop here. The Newton book had been sold to a London dealer, who sold it to a New York dealer, and it was finally traced to an American collector. No doubt he was sad to see his new prize go back to where it came from, but all's well that ends well, though actually not all *was* well, for a dozen or so of the treasures have never been found.

But those tales are mere children's toys compared with what Joseph Bellwood managed. His speciality was cutting out the plates from precious volumes, and if there were prizes for the cutting out of plates from precious volumes, there would be no challenger, because all the challengers would have gone home hours ago.

Bellwood stole 1,149 plates. What they are worth is still being argued over, but estimates vary from £16,000 to £37,000. When he was on bail he was ordered not to go into any library (what? even my beloved London Library?) – a very sensible order. He gave many confusing statements, culminating with these remarkable words, given by his counsel: ". . . he does not wish to see a library again after the problems he has experienced". That, you might think, is no ordinary robber; he has none of the obvious thief, and is worlds away from the man who stole the precious Newton. Have we here, I ask, some parallel to the man who filled his entire house with books and almost suffocated?

Again, I draw your attention to the oddness of book-thieves; I bet you anything that Bellwood's haul did not include men's wallets or ladies' handbags. I will go further: I would not be surprised if Bellwood, asked whether he stole jade necklaces, shuddered at the thought, and grew angry at the accusation. He went to prison for four years.

I started this exploration by asking what makes people steal books, when they do not, and would not, steal anything else. But the oddness of books goes further. Perhaps you have never heard the name of Leo Ormston, much less know what he does for a living. Well, he does it in Newcastle upon Tyne, Northumberland, Gateshead and Sunderland – something of

a broad remit. He goes *incognito*, disguised in shabby clothes
and shoes. Disguised? In shabby clothes? Why? Because he has
been beaten up, he has had rubbish thrown down at him from
a high block of flats, and even been threatened by someone
wielding a machete. So *what* does he do for a living? Is he an
undercover policeman? A cat burglar? A beggar? No, he is a
gamekeeper, not a poacher. What he does for a living is to
go round and get back the overdue library books of the area.
Now will you believe that books are different from anything
else at all?

But do you see the thread that runs through all these conduits?
People steal books to plug the holes in their mortgages. People
steal books when they do not wish "to see a library again after
the problems they have experienced". People steal books and
fill their houses with thousands of them, never opening even
one. More sonorously, Milton said "As good almost kill a man
as kill a book: who kills a man kills a reasonable creature, God's
image; but he destroys a good book, kills reason itself, kills the
image of God, as it were in the eye". Milton, it is true, did not
stop to think about *bad* books; some say that the bad book will
kill itself, or at least the good book must prevail.

It is astonishing to me that there are cultures which have
no written form of communication; if I am not mistaken,
the Native Americans (oh, no, no we must not say "Red
Indian" these days, we must say American Indian, a flabby
version of what was once bright and bold and real) are one
example, and another is or was the people whom Peter
Shaffer made uncannily real in his play *The Royal Hunt of
the Sun*.

It is truly awesome to think that the public library has
existed some three thousand years. Were there people who
took the scrolls home and didn't bring them back? I fear
that when all the public libraries are on computer, something will go terribly wrong. I am sure the Dewey system
will be sniffed into oblivion. But does anyone now know
what Andrew Carnegie has to do with public libraries?

Ah, well, Anthony Powell was right, and for some 1,500 words I have been agreeing with him; yes, books *do* furnish a room.

The Times, 21 June 1996

Sing it!

OH DEAR, OH dear, and again oh dear, and yet once more oh dear; in short, oh dear. But why this catalogue of moanings? Ask Professor (of course he would be a professor – they always are) Brian Newbould, who is Professor of Music at the University of Hull. And why, you ask, should a harmless and useful Professor of Music be hauled up before the Levin Assizes, where he is to be reprimanded for nothing less than the heinous crime of *lèse majesté*? But when I tell you what *majesté* has been offended (ah, but he never took offence, so gentle and loving he was), many of you will say that for our professor hanging would be too good.

No, no; put away your ropes. Professor Newbould has only done what dozens and dozens before him have tried to do. He has taken in vain the name of Franz Schubert, by wasting his time (the professor's, not Schubert's) trying to fit endings to the pieces which Schubert never finished. And the prof, as if asking for the thunder, has begun his absurd endeavour with the *Quartettsatz*, and he thinks he "has written his interpretation of how the second, *andante*, movement would have concluded".

Now, now, if the good professor would go away and rub his head with beetroot-juice, we would need nothing more, unless, perhaps, he is serious in his belief that he can finish what Schubert – *Schubert!* – didn't.

Once upon a time, I heard the *Octet* out of doors, in Austria, and on an exceptionally balmy evening. There was a gossamer breeze so gentle that it hardly rustled the musicians' pages, and as the light faded, the very birds fell silent and clambered onto the branches of the trees to hear the sounds made by an immortal bird. Immortal? Yes indeed, but he had to hurry, for he lived only 31 years: he walked in the funeral procession of Beethoven, whom he worshipped, and the next year he was himself dead. Let professors alone; they die like the rest of us, and we rarely hear of an immortal one.

But I think I know something that was close to an immortal friendship. And not just a friendship, but a friendship that brought into the world two of the world's musical master-pieces, masterpieces that stand only a single rung lower than the very greatest of all.

The friendship was at first a working friendship – indeed at first it was almost not any kind of friendship, but a chilly arms-length recognition – and much time, patience and forgiveness had to be expended before two men who had been made for one another by heaven finally realised that heaven had been waiting. The two men were Giuseppe Verdi and Arrigo Boito.

For those of my readers who do not know who Boito was (I take it that no one reading this doesn't know who Verdi was), allow me to take a moment for enlightenment. Boito was foremost a writer of libretti, but he was also a composer; his opera *Mefistofele*, however, is the only work of his that has lived. (It is revived from time to time, and is well worth a hearing.)

But Boito was the man who gave up 20 years of his life to serve his hero, Verdi; he was librettist, archivist, support, librarian, copiest, corrector, shield (from sightseers, autograph-hunters and such), refuser of invitations, and loving friend. And at last, the correspondence between the two men has been translated, so those like me who cannot read Italian can joy in the joy the two men had. (First, though, I must commend the superb translation by William Weaver; no one could guess, with this one, that it had come from another tongue.)

I said that the two men had joy in the work, and joy it must have been; hard work, but joy. There was no deference

to Verdi, though Boito throughout addresses Verdi as Dear
Maestro, and signs off as A. Boito, and the composer almost
invariably writes Dear Boito and signs off G. Verdi.

We must remember that although a great deal of work
went into revising and polishing the enormous number of
operas Verdi wrote before Boito arrived, this symbiotic pair
wrote from top to bottom only two works: *Otello* and *Falstaff*.
(I have to confess that I am something of a Verdi heretic;
I enjoy him – who doesn't? – but I hold that only those
two operas are truly works of genius, so I now find myself
somewhat vindicated.)

But of the 300 letters that passed between the two men,
the very first one shows how deeply entwined Boito already
was: he had finished the libretto of *Otello* and sent it to the
composer with these words:

> Illustrious Maestro, In sending you the certificate of
> ownership of the libretto of *Otello*, I would like to tell
> you once again that my pen will be entirely at your
> disposal for any revisions that may seem necessary in
> the above-mentioned operatic text. Happy and proud
> at having been able, in this instance, to associate my
> name with your glory, I declare myself
> Your most devoted
> Arrigo Boito.

There is, of course, a considerable proportion of technical
matter in the correspondence, though so clear and interesting
is it that there is no temptation to skip. And if there were
such a temptation it would be instantly overcome by the first
words of letter 33:

> Dear Maestro, You must not believe I have forgotten
> the Moor of Venice. I have thought about him, but
> until now I have not had the necessary tranquillity to
> work at my desk.

But only two letters later, Boito is saying this:

> The siege of foreigners has not yet ended. The poor

wretches who live in Milan are subjected, during these days of expositions and congresses, to the torture of formalities and social ceremony, the most stupid and cruel torture conceivable. For more than three weeks I have been a martyr of this inhuman business: my day is destroyed and evening arrives without my having written even half a page.

Boito's silent vow to serve his great master was sustained to the end, but there was a price to pay. Boito's *Mefistofele* had been a disaster at its première, though it swiftly made its way into what would today be called the charts, and he was naturally delighted when the first thumbs down were turned into cheers. But it encouraged him to go on with his next and only other work: *Nerone* ("Nero"). From the outside, and now that all the participants are long dead, we can think it both touching and hilarious, but for Boito it was none of those. The letters are spattered throughout with references to the shadow of *Nerone*, which Boito was never to see on a stage; but that was the least of it: again and again, we find Boito saying that he is now getting down to *Nerone*; again and again, we find Verdi encouraging him to get on with *Nerone*; again and again we find Boito changing this or that in *Nerone*, again and again we find a quiet sigh from Verdi. But the last twist of the knife was yet to come: Boito died, and six years later, Toscanini conducted the first – and, alas, the last – performance of *Nerone*.

Still, we must remember that Boito was not only a friend to Verdi, much less a servant; when the two of them are going over a knotty problem, Boito again and again offers an answer, and Verdi is happy to take his suggestion.

And consider this. Verdi was a stickler for exactitude, and he could be very testy; we find in the letters a good deal of growling (much of which was soothed into benignity by Boito). But though Verdi often did *not* take Boito's advice, and indeed frequently contradicted him, there is not a wisp or a murmur that could be called tetchiness, much less anger.

(Cynics might say that Boito was draining Verdi's blood, but those cynics have not read the book.)

How many of us can say of our closest friends that we have *never* had the smallest spat with them? Well, Verdi and Boito managed it; there is literally not a line in the 300 letters that could take even the form of a fist banging on the table.

You will have noticed that I have been sparse with actual quotations from the letters. The trouble is that it is all but impossible to choose one without the rest of them clamouring to be put in; even the letters that consist of little more than changing a line or two are fascinating. This is a story of how a great composer and his helpmeet worked together, but it is also – and foremost – a story made of genius, fidelity, honour and friendship: and the greatest of these is friendship.

The Times, 1 July 1995

The book is *The Verdi-Boito Correspondence*. Edited by Marcello Conati and Mario Medici. English edition by William Weaver.

A slave state

WOULD YOU LIKE a few dozen slaves for Christmas? Well, not Christmas exactly, because the people selling these goods are very down on Christmas and even more so on Christ. Moreover, the Christians very frequently *are* the slaves, and when they are, they are very likely to be tortured or murdered, and usually both. I should add that the slave-market is filled with men, women and children indiscriminately, and that those taken for slavery are used not only for the normal work of slavery, but for sexual services. Yes, yes, and yes again, I am talking about the horrors of Sudan, which may well at present hold the Blue Riband of savagery. (Christian sufferers are obliged to renounce their Christian names and adopt Muslim ones, but it must be understood that very many Muslims are also suffering at the hands of the savages of Khartoum.)

And when I call them savages, I am not exaggerating, as Abu Adam Abu Bakir Omer would testify if he were in any state to do so:

He was imprisoned for three-and-a-half months . . . while there he was severely tortured. He was hung from the ceiling by his hands and legs and beaten with plastic ropes and sticks many times each day. He was also forced to lie naked in the scorching sun all day long on the roof of the house. While on the roof he was handcuffed with special handcuffs which tightened with movement, and he was forced by beating to keep rolling over, so that the handcuffs became increasingly tight, cutting off blood to the head. At other times he was tied to a table and his legs and feet were beaten so badly that he was unable to stand; they then beat him to make him keep running, saying it "was good for the circulation".

It is important to understand that such mad savagery is not the behaviour of some crazed loner. We are talking of a state – a terrible one, but one that would have to be recognised as such. Nor does that state lack a religion, and with terrible irony it calls itself Islamic although Muslims by the thousand are destroyed by those who have called themselves Muslims. We know, alas, what evil can do in the name of good, and throughout all recognisable time men (and women) have killed to demonstrate their holiness. But what do you do when you get the news of a troop-train which pauses to kill a considerable number of innocent and peaceable people? These visits included raiding villages, killing, capturing and torturing civilians, burning homes and crops, looting and pillaging. And I repeat: these are not runamucks getting what they can until the forces of order arrive, they *are* the forces of order.

Nor does this madness stop or even pause; at least, if it isn't madness it is difficult to say what it is, as this *billet-doux* might show – in the form of a letter (a real one). "In the name of God, the Merciful. Dear Outlaws, Peace be with you. We ask you to be alert for we are coming to you at Nyamell. Our force is 1,800 soldiers strong. We ask you to prepare youselves for we are coming to get you at 3 am – so be prepared. You idiots. If you want peace you should surrender before July, at the latest. Commander P.D.F. Hebeid." The next day, casualties arrived at Nyamell.

But that was nothing to what happened next – and would be expected to happen. It was, of course, the selling and buying of human beings, particularly children. The current average price required to redeem a slave is three cows – with a minimum of two cows. The traders claim that this price is necessary to cover the costs of finding children, abduction (or sometimes negotiating a purchase) and bringing them back. It is estimated by the civil authorities that there are approximately 12,000 children from this area currently enslaved in the North, and that the numbers are growing, for raids are still continuing.

Mind you, there are Good Samaritans (if the words aren't blasphemy), for an Arab trader said (and did) this:

> The slave owners are Arabs of the Zako tribe . . . and almost all of them are Muslim extremists. Since we reached a peace agreement with the Dinkas . . . I have brought back more than 300 children. Just a few days ago I brought back 12 children. Today I brought back 28. Some of the parents of these children will not be able to pay the redemption fee. If the community leaders do not come up with the fee I will not be able to bring back more children. This work of returning slaves is dangerous for me. But I do it because I want the Arabs and the Dinkas to live in peace.

I dare say. And there are many who are working hard to bring them peace, one of them being Baroness Cox, the president of Christian Solidarity International. She has, with a very powerful team, brought to the world's attention the fact that sooner or later – more likely sooner – Sudan will be nothing but a charnel-house, where madness reigns and does not even know that it is mad.

The leaders of many savage places have claimed to be heading an ordered society, even though behind the façade there reigns nothing but anarchy. But in Sudan, conditions are far *worse* than anarchy. This is not the anarchy of a society that has broken into pieces (would that it were), but the anarchy of one bloodthirsty evil that has climbed to the top and cannot be dislodged.

This is not unique. Algeria has for many years now been in the same situation, and the Algerians are still losing huge numbers to the same dreadful fanatics. The fanatics have killed tens of thousands solely in order to create an Islamic state. As I have repeatedly asked: what kind of a religion can it be when its first action is to murder its own people? (I have also asked rather pertinently why the followers of the religions do not stand up and denounce the murdering leaders.)

In the case of Sudan, I am told that one-and-a-half million people have died in this terrible madness, and that five million have been displaced. In the case of Algeria, no one really knows how many have already died at the hands of the mad fanatics. That sea of blood must have drowned countless hordes, but imagine tens of thousands being killed – *not* because the killers want to get even with some real or imagined hated ones, but to bring down the entire Algerian structure so that it can collapse and turn Algeria into a swamp of madness personified.

That is nothing but the plain truth; and it seems the structure that holds up any vestige of sanity in Sudan will hold until – well, I almost said until the mad ones have gone, but I fear that the mad ones will never go, after all, the mad ones in Algeria are still killing and they are still mad.

Madder, perhaps. Baroness Cox's conclusions are very thorough and terrible, and she knows more than anyone in this story. And that story says that what is happening in Sudan is – well, let Baroness Cox speak for herself. Read this, from her conclusions:

The Government's policy towards the people of the South and the Nuba mountains is tantamount to genocide, by means of terror, war, slavery, the mass displacement of the population and the manipulation of aid. In particular, widespread, systematic slavery continues on a large scale in government-controlled areas of Sudan. The raids by government troops and government-backed PDF militia against African towns and villages of the South and Nuba mountains are accompanied by atrocities, torture, rape, looting and destruction of buildings and property. Those not taken into slavery are generally killed and/or tortured.

In normal situations of hunger and violence, the world comes to the rescue or at least tries to do so. War, disease, theft – these are endemic, but by now the ways and means for helping to combat them are obvious. But what if that obvious remedy is deliberately refused – what then? For that, exactly, is what is happening in Sudan. Food and drink are available, but they are deliberately denied. Hunger is used as a weapon, and thousands of victims of the Government's genocidal plan rot and die. The UN itself has only limited access, and soon the Government will have its way entirely: millions are forced into migration and the Government will get its ultimate wish: enslavement with forced labour.

And that is the fate of the people who live and are murdered in Sudan: terror; slavery; at the end, genocide. It all began with human rights, but what can we do against savages who literally do not know the meaning of those words?

The Times, 31 May 1996

The Jews who choose

W HO SAID THIS, and why? "A hundred years ago we had the faith but not the land. Today we have the land, but what has happened to the faith?"

The words come from Dr Jonathan Sacks, Chief Rabbi of Britain. Two days ago he, and all devout Jews, were participating in the most solemn rite of Jewry: Yom Kippur, the Day of Atonement.

I am a Jew, but I was not taking part in the prayers and the rituals. I confess – and Dr Sacks, if he reads these words, will shake his head in sorrow and pain – that I did not even know what special day it was, and I went about all my secular doings, ignorant of the day's significance, until a *Times* colleague – and a Christian, too! – enlightened me.

I am not proud of the words above, but neither do I feel shame. My question is: should I?

I know, of course, that I have lost something precious, or at least beautiful, in abandoning the faith of my forebears. My home was not a religious one; my grandfather read the scriptures to himself silently and struggled through a little English; my grandmother, who could read no language at all, lit a candle on the appropriate days, as did my mother, though for her it was not really a religious sign. My uncles were quite secular (one played the cello in the band of the Savoy Hotel – beat that!), and had hardly anything to do with the religion of their father and grandfathers. My amazing aunt Edith, who died a year or so ago at 95, was a *shikse* (Christian), and thus suspect in the family, but I never heard of her going to any kind of church.

But, as Dr Sacks well knows, he is fighting a losing cause, and I cannot help him in it. I quote:

What has happened to a people that survived longer than any other, in conditions more arduous than any other, that suddenly we have begun to lose the will to live as Jews? . . . Today Jews are free, and accepted, and successful, and above all we have a home. Is it possible that the greatest danger to Jewish survival will turn out to be, God forbid, not Nazi Germany or Soviet Russia but our own indifference?

And, as Rabbi Sacks knows to his grief, the answer is yes. Yes, the Jewish people, living in perfect safety, will die of their indifference. And not, as Rabbi Sacks instantly saw, their differences. But here is a test, I think a grim one.

All round me on my desk as I write are cuttings. They are all about the same thing: the recently discovered huge sums of money, most in Swiss banks, which have been traced to the fallen Jews. It seems that money and valuables were smuggled into Switzerland, the owners' hopes being that one day they would reclaim their own. Alas, there was to be no own, but now there are the offspring of the fallen, and they are claiming their rightful sums.

But the World Jewish Congress and other agencies acting on behalf of Holocaust victims said that the forsaken deposits represented only a fraction of the wealth confiscated from Jewish victims in Eastern Europe that may have been stashed by the Nazis in Swiss banks or safe deposit boxes . . . the Nazi boss Heinrich Himmler for example . . . sent a hoard of paintings, jewellery and money, stolen from Hungarian Jews, to Switzerland towards the end of the war . . .

Yes, but would *you* wish to claim money that had passed through the hands of Heinrich Himmler? And even if you didn't mind, what about the arguments that are breaking out every day now, in which one Swiss banker says that the billions believed to be hidden never existed, and another banker says that even greater sums did exist, and the Swiss demand at least £500 to search for possible treasure, and . . .

Well, I think Rabbi Sacks must have taken the point. Where will he go to find those spotless Jews who reject the very idea of marrying out of the faith? Where will he find the ranks upon ranks to fill his noble endeavour? How will I and so many others reject – gently, I hope – the very idea of going back to our Jewish roots, when we rush to pick over the stolen necklace that once adorned the neck of Goering's wife?

But we Jews aren't the only ones. Solzhenitsyn, after his return to Russia, has found that his voice is heeded by only a few, or at least followed by a few. The world goes round, and will not stop; Russia is crumbling, and the mighty edifice that Solzhenitsyn should by now be erecting has been little more than a whistle-stop journey.

But we don't need to go anywhere near Russia to find such disappointment; how many empty churches of the Church of England are there now, and how many will there be 10 years hence, and how many in another 10 years? The Papacy shivers, believing that any prop that breaks will sooner or later bring down the whole edifice, and yet faithful Roman Catholic priests want to be ordinary people. And why should the Jews be different?

Because, comes the answer, the Jews *are* different. Yes, but one by one, and ten by ten, and thousand by thousand, the Jews are becoming wholly secular, and not Rabbi Sacks nor the Beth Din, nor the memories of Jewry will stop them. We look to the United States, where there are more Jews than there are in Israel, and their numbers are shrinking too. The Rabbi points to the numbers of Jews who marry "out of the faith"; if the numbers in the synagogues are falling, it means the same thing. And if this tide continues there will be no breakwaters. I cheat; there is no *if,* and the tide *will* go on rising.

Over the centuries, whole nations have disappeared, not just by tides and starvation and epidemic; look up and see Tibet, one of the greatest nations the world has ever seen, which in less than a couple of generations will be no more. (True, Tibet will have been destroyed by China's evil and the rest of the world's cowardice, but that doesn't make it any better.)

And here I am, a Jew who doesn't really understand what being a Jew means, and even as I say that, Rabbi Sacks shakes his head again in sorrow. But I *don't* really understand what being a Jew means. Nevertheless, one thing is certain: I am not alone in my bewilderment. And that bewilderment can mean one thing only: that we shall not be coming back to the fold, and nor will our descendants.

Why is the world – well, almost all the world – dispensing with religion? Yes, of course that is a ridiculous thing to say, for very many millions say religion is the most important thing in their lives. Assuredly, Rabbi Sacks does. But overall, the numbers shrink. And it can't *always* be Dr Richard Dawkins who frightens the rest of us off.

Are we to think that the only place in which a religion is taken completely and seriously is the black side of Algeria? Algeria, where more than 30,000 people have been murdered in the last few years, solely to destroy Algeria entirely. And in what name is Algeria to be wiped out? Allah's. For the Muslim fanatics will not cease their murdering until they can rule in Algeria, and a mad, savage and wicked rule it will be. (Presumably, the idea is to make the whole world Muslim, so Rabbi Sacks and apostate Levin will be in the same boat.)

I have come far from the wise, gentle, far-seeing Rabbi Sacks. But what or who will bring back young Jewry to the faith, when young Jewry hardly knows what a Jew is? Perhaps I should say that of myself.

And yet the Rabbi must not despair, for he has a tiny foothold. It is an odd one, but any port in a storm. When I am filling in a form on which there is a space labelled "Religion", I don't hesitate, but put Jew.

So I go back to where we started. Am I a Jew? If I do not pray with the Jews, and sing with the Jews, and cover my head with the Jews, and refuse to eat pork with the Jews, and read books backwards with the Jews, how can I be a Jew? Well, don't forget the form that I filled in.

Rabbi Sacks will not give in, of course, and he makes that clear, saying.

> I am calling for us to reflect, not only on an individual return but a collective return towards a less secular mode of Jewish existence.

Does he believe that can happen? Or does he just wish it would?

The Times, 6 October 1995

Why so obstinate?

L ET US BEGIN with an old friend: neighbours and their fallings-out. How many times have I shaken my old grey head and heard yet again the familiar screams and shouts and in many cases language unfit for young ears? I don't need to look far for the source, for there are only three: hedges, trees and swimming-pools. And before I have taken my pick, I hear for the thousandth time the dreaded words: "I do not enjoy going to the High Court, but . . ." And never, never, never, do I hear the words "I do not enjoy going to the High Court *so I don't go there*".

Yes, yes, somebody says that somebody has ruined somebody's something, and I get to hear of it. I, of course, do not take sides, not least because the writs have begun to flutter, but a brief outline may be useful. The Connor family allege that when they came back from a holiday their beautiful garden had been ruined by the Rudds next door; trees and shrubs and bushes allegedly cut down, and even an alleged chain-saw had been allegedly used. (What a wonderful word is "alleged" don't you think? What would I do without it?)

Mr Connor says that he does ". . . not enjoy going to the High Court" but he then added some words that I have heard approximately seventeen thousand times, every one bringing nothing but misery. The words are: "We can't just let it go, it is the principle as much as anything else."

Oh, Mr Connor, take back those words, alleged or unalleged, and tell yourself, your wife and your cat (though not your neighbours, for obvious reasons), that you *can* let it go, because it is *not* the principle as much as anything else.

Obviously, I don't know exactly what happened and must sit on the garden fence, but surely I can hope that the participants can settle the business without recourse to m'lud, even if only to help starve a lawyer to death.

There is hope. The Connors are not making personal attacks, and indeed they have said of the Rudds that they are "perfectly polite", so fisticuffs are out of the question. But if obstinacy, the greatest curse of the human race, prevails, I predict that everyone in the story will be ruined, and a tide of anger will rise alarmingly.

With which valedictory, I turn to the next bit of obstinacy. (The OED – the big one – has turned alarmingly skittish, and adds to the meaning "Rarely in neutral or good sense." You're telling us.)

This time it is chocolate, but the taste is not the trouble; the trouble is that it is difficult to the point of impossible to believe it. But I must try.

The scene is Woolworths, and before I turn to the matter in hand, I must muse a little about Woolworths. It was truly a cave of Aladdin for little brats like me; indeed, for decades it was the greatest store in the country, perhaps in the world. Even those who aren't old enough to remember that wonderful slogan "Nothing over sixpence" glow when their parents start to talk about Woolies. They were everywhere; indeed, when I came to Marylebone, there was a Woolies in the High Street, but it disappeared many years ago. In those days, shops were not bound hand and foot by hygiene, let alone the horrors of the EU's demands, and I can clearly see the Woolies fitment full of unwrapped sweets, heaped up, which the girl behind the counter shovelled, higgledy-piggledy, into bags.

But what went wrong? Whatever it was, it was bad enough to drive people like me out of the place. Ah, but then came the great change; I don't know who was (and is?) in charge of the Woolworths restorations but assuredly today it has made its new mark. But do they call the Woolies supermarkets now? I hope not. Ah, well; *ehue fugaces*.

To the matter in hand. A Woolworths manager, Roger Newstead, who had been working for the company for 23 years, thought it right and proper that his staff, who had been working their butts off in an exhausting stocktaking session, should have something more substantial than a pat on the back. The pat was not very substantial, but it was something. And the something was eight £1.50 bars of chocolate, one bar each for the team. No, not just bars of chocolate, but bars of broken chocolate. (Such an organisation will inevitably have bits of broken chocolate left over as, I assume, is the case with broken china.)

Some would say (me, for instance) that a few bits of broken chocolate is hardly the Golden Fleece, and that the bounty was miserably small. Still, the staff who worked hard no doubt took the broken chocolate graciously, and knocked off when the whistle went.

Enter Mr Bob Payne, who found the contraband (*broken* chocolate, remember) and says that "Mr Newstead admitted he was aware of the implication in that it could lead to staff damaging merchandise themselves to get it free or reduced". A damned silly idea, but one that might – might, I say – demand a gentle rebuke lasting, say, 10 seconds. But Woolies sacked Mr Newstead.

I do not know where Mr Payne stands on the Woolworths ladder; is he a member of the board of directors, or head of a department, or a sniffer-out of broken chocolate (a very important post in that Woolworths, obviously)? But I hope that it wasn't Mr Payne who fired Mr Newstead.

Without a job, Mr Newstead sought work from two or three hundred places, but it seems that Mr Newstead had been dismissed without a reference. So Mr Newstead went to the appropriate tribunal, and of course won. The compensation from Woolworths has not been decided, but it had better be substantial. As for Mr Payne . . .

And now for the topless beauty. There is a store in Leeds, called Tradex, and a shopper was about to shop there, whereupon the manager said that the shopper could not enter the store. And why not? Because the shopper was naked from the waist up, and the store had a company policy that denied entry to those bare above the waist. Surely, a reasonable denial? Not quite: the topless beauty was 11 months old. The argument went back and forth while presumably the centre of the storm was enjoying it greatly, but the store was adamant. No shirt, no purchase, even though the nakedness (and, after all, it wasn't the lower half of the baby that was on show, but the top) was that of an infant.

I take it that by now my readers have got the message, for I am speaking about obstinacy. It comes in many forms, but it is always instantly spotted, except, of course, by the person who is being obstinate, who will go to the stake, the gallows or the *auto da fe* claiming that he (it is almost always he) was not being obstinate, although everybody around him insisted that he was.

And you will tell me that those who dig in and will never give up are only the short-sighted, the weak, the angry; while of course those with very high brows could never fall into such a trap. Yes?

No.

For this part of the catalogue is about – indeed is made up of – some of the most lofty cognoscenti alive, it has been going for 15 years, and the end is not yet come. Nor, I prophesy, will it come soon.

A psychoanalyst, Mr Masson, was appointed to the job of organising projects from the voluminous papers in the Freud Archives. But he soon began to say that Freud had been a fraud who had twisted his findings for personal gain. He was sacked from the archives, but was paid off. However, a Miss Janet Malcolm wrote about this scandal (if it was a scandal) in the *New Yorker*, and in a book, whereupon Mr Masson sued her and the publishers. The suit began in 1984 and was last heard of in 1993. It is pending, and in my opinion it will pend many more years.

So much for the intelligentsia when it comes to matters of libel and its like; they can be just as bone-headed, implacable, blinkered – in a word, obstinate, as any crier of "I am right, and everybody else is wrong".

Give in! Give in! Nothing is worth all that heartache, time and money, and even if it was worth it, it will dissolve in a fortnight, and sooner or later you will wonder why it didn't disappear within a week.

But none of those whom I am even now trying to pull from the furnace – the furnace, that is, which is made of disillusion and is called obstinacy – will listen. But yet the pity of it, Iago! O! Iago, the pity of it, Iago!

The Times, 1 September 1995

Another bottle, please

I DO NOT usually sing very loudly indeed in the bath before 7.30 in the morning; mindful of the other inhabitants of the building in which I live, I mute my joy, if any, until somewhere around nine o'clock (ten for Wagner). But this time it had to be all stops out. Indeed:

Make me a willow cabin at your gate,
And call upon my soul within the house;
Write loyal cantons of contemned love,
And sing them loud even in the dead of night;
Halloo your name to the reverberate hills,
And make the babbling gossip of the air
Cry out "Dorrell!"

Well, no, it wasn't actually Dorrell who was thus serenaded (imagine serenading a minister!), but he was the next best thing. Anyone who had even glanced at the magnificent and fittingly large headlines that my colleague the Science Editor had rustled up — "Dorrell abandons project to decide nation's diet" — must have cheered, nay, shouted to the heavens.

"Dorrell abandons project to decide nation's diet." I shall repeat that: "Dorrell abandons project to decide nation's diet". And once more — I'm delirious, after all — "Dorrell abandons project to decide nation's diet." (There is a very pitiful addition to the story, before I continue. When the splendid news was given out, the Department of Health "denied any actual change of policy". So deep and ingrained is the norm of mendacity in this Government that even when it does something truly admirable and courageous, it has to lie about it.)

But now for the fun – and what fun! For our fun has left the wowsers not just high and dry, but practically suffocating with rage and self-regard. Surely, we all still rock with laughter when remembering that unimaginably humourless creature Virginia Bottomley advising us to eat "three egg-sized potatoes and three sweets a week"? And who will not cheer three times three at the discomfiture of the leading wowser, Jeanette Longfield. She calls herself "Coordinater of the National Food Alliance", and as if that were not enough she throws in "the Nutrition Task Force". (Have you noticed that these ghastly women – they are practically all women – revel in military nomenclature? Do you suppose that they are dreaming of the day when people like me are taken out and shot for making fun of broccoli and yoghurt?)

Their very language gives the game away: listen to this bit: "The Nutrition Task Force built up a real momentum, and stopping it is bound to set back progress. But there were certain elements in the food industry who dragged their heels and refused to reach a consensus." Just reading such stuff is enough to make me feel the need of a couple of very fat sausages with pickles and of course white bread, preferably accompanied by some decent claret, and if those "certain elements in the food industry who dragged their heels and refused to reach a consensus" will let me know their names and products, I promise to eat a pound or two of every item of your produce three times a week, and urge the same diet upon everyone else.

Come: let us stuff ourselves with saturated fat (and if it isn't sufficiently saturated let us sprinkle even more fat over it), together with huge quantities of salt and sugar. But let me, for a moment, be serious: from my childhood on, I have loved and eaten dishes which demand substantial and regular amounts of salt and sugar. I have thrived on such provender (see my lissom form, the weight of which never moves more than one pound either side on the tell-tale scales), and whatever ailments I may suffer from, none has its roots in my diet.

Oh, but by Alpha and Omega, haven't I told you a thousand thousand times on these very pages that the only truth about eating is the one that is graven on my heart, to say nothing on my gullet: "Nothing you hate eating can be good for you"? With the wowsers, of course, it is the reverse: they are always in wait to reprimand some harmless lover of boiled tripe.

But we have had a great victory, and the wowsers have fled in disorder. It is all very well for me to throw rotten eggs (three a week) at Bottomley, but if the might of the Government had been brought up on the wrong side, my lonely cry in the night would never have been heard, never mind acted upon.

This is the victory; the Government itself has joined in a million cries, and Bottomley herself has been chased off the field. Never mind why or how; the most obvious guess is that the whole rubbishy argument was costing money with no useful return. The wowsers wanted a "pilot scheme" costing some £90,000, and Dorrell can see a haystack in daylight. So the wowsers limped home to paint their bruises, and the £90,000 will be wasted on some other project, some other time.

As it happens, I have another project, and although it is outwardly different from the previous tussle, it is very close indeed to it inwardly. I first put my thumb to my nose at Ms Longfield, because her wowsers were at work telling us what we must eat and what we must not eat. But a bigger and more brutal fight is going on, though the principles are the same.

As I have told you many times, I have never been a smoker, and I shall never be one. But – again, as I have told you many times – I do speak up for the smokers. (After all, there can be no one who is ignorant of the dangers of smoking: my poor grandfather, for instance, started when he was a mere child, and therefore never knew those terrible dangers, so he smoked 40 cigarettes a day for nearly 80 years, and died – doubtless because of his smoking – when he was over 90.)

I am sure that Ralph Harris, now Lord Harris of High Cross, is still standing firm against the wowsers; his particular wowsers are the ones who want him to stop smoking. I should say, incidentally, that Ralph smokes only a pipe, the most harmless and comfortable form of the weed. More to the point, he is still fighting against the most insidious and – the word is not too strong – disreputable forces. His studies have shown that very many non-smokers are perfectly willing to allow one or two carriages for smokers on British Rail. But his studies have also revealed that BR's claims are shamefully bogus. And Ralph, one of our greatest lovers of democracy and fighters against its opposite, has said this:

> Democracy is not served by majorities riding roughshod over minorities, especially when conflicting preferences can be catered for without significant cost or inconvenience to the ruling majority.

Very true. But I still cannot understand why smoking, and only smoking, has been so violently damned. It is, of course, dangerous (see my grandfather's dreadful fate), but unlike "hard" drugs, smoking does not lead to crime.

It is true that pompous people in pompous places are always on the lookout for someone they can bully, but even that would not explain the almost lunatic behaviour of the anti-smokers. It is also true, alas, that the United States, when it gets a good bone in its teeth, will never let it go. To put it less daintily, I would say that the United States, for all its great virtues, suffers from almost incredible domestic cowardice. Our pussy-footing against smoking comes *entirely* from America, so it doesn't count in this argument, but in America the struggle for freedom to smoke collapsed with hardly a word, let alone an action.

This is all the more amazing, given that something similar has happened before, and the results were appalling. Prohibition of alcohol, nationwide, established the gangster mentality which has grown ever since in the United States. The United States, with something like 250,000,000 inhabitants, now clocks up something like 35,000 murders in a year; there is no civilised nation that can touch so dreadful a count, and indeed the citizens of many countries which would not yet be called civilised would be horrified at such numbers. And yet the United States is now getting very close to the total outlawry of nicotine.

But I mustn't end on a gloomy note, or Ralph will wag a finger at me. All we need to brighten the horizon is a novel, but a novel so wonderfully timely, so enchantingly impudent, so witty, so carefree, so gorgeous, so gloriously happy, that – and now I do not exaggerate – it could even bring smoker and smoke-hater together. It is called *Thank you for Smoking*, it is by Christopher Buckley, it is published by Deutsch, and even the most lockjawed food wowser would crack a smile at it. Thank *you*.

The Times, 18 August 1995

Prodnose from Australia

I HAVE MANY times visited Australia, on business or pleasure or both at once (and in Australia the two merge, so open and welcoming are Australia's people), and for many years I noticed that the visitors' entry form was much the same as New Zealand's, both of them being the most simple and homely document. Of course, I realised that the generosity of an entry into Australia mirrored the openness of its peoples; Australians *are* open and immediately friendly. But at some point, something happened that changed the pattern. No, the Australians have not become sour and mean; they are as open and friendly as they have always been. So what has changed? The answer is not the people, it is pieces of paper.

The first change I noticed was that New Zealand's entry form was still roughly the same as it had been, but the Australian one had changed somewhat, and changed considerably for the worse.

To start with, the document needed to enter Australia – and this, you must understand, is only the "Application to visit Australia for tourism or other recreational activities" – is five full large pages, or 10 columns, or 11ft of bumpf.

It starts most charmingly, saying, "Do not buy your tickets or finalise your arrangements before a visa is granted, unless we ask you to provide evidence of confirmed arrangements". That's not even getting into gear; we are idiots from the start, *viz.* "You must answer all questions and write neatly in BLOCK LETTERS" and "You must answer all questions honestly and completely".

Shucks. Try this: "The information provided might also

be disclosed to agencies who are authorised to receive information relating to border control, health assessment, law enforcement, education, payment of pensions and benefits, refugees, taxation, and review of decisions."

Now, it is obvious that few countries want people from other countries who cannot support themselves financially and show no sign of trying to do so. Visitors are welcome – certainly Australia makes them welcome – but not if they make clear that they are going to live off the indigenous, hard-working citizens. (Andrew Symonds the English cricketer had a different problem, but he has decided to go back and become Symonds the Australian cricketer.)

But surely Australia shouldn't get the heebie-jeebies if someone finds that someone else has landed with nothing but fourpence and a lollipop? No, indeed, but we are now not discussing Australia and her great peoples, we are discussing the dreadful Prodnose and his pages and pages of whining. Try this: "The criterion 'adequate funds' may be satisfied by showing personal bank statements, money transfer receipts, pay slips, audited accounts, taxation records or cash in hand, depending on the amount of money represented, the number of persons to support, the type of activities planned and the length of stay sought."

Then sex raises its head – I knew it would. Try this for impudence: "Marital status – select one box which best describes your current situation – Married, Engaged, Divorced, Widowed, Never married [that's me folks], Separated but not divorced."

And then, "Why do you want to visit Australia?" The answer should be "Well, certainly not to meet you, you pimply prat". Next, Dr Goebbels asks: "Do you have any relatives, friends or contacts you will visit in Australia?", and don't believe it when he says that it might be a help if a visitor should be injured or ill, because that bit has already been taken care of.

It hots up now. "Are you currently employed?" Again, it is nothing but impudence, because of course the real questions have been dealt with. But Prodnose wants more, much more, and he snaps: "Your current occupation?", "Name or person of company who employs you?", "Address of employer?", "Employer's telephone number?" (Yes, our little worm demands the telephone number of every person who touches this form – not just those actually visiting.)

And now Prodnose wants to know: "How long have you been employed by this employer?", "How much leave has been approved by your employer for the time you wish to visit Australia?", "Has your employer agreed that you will still have a job when you return from Australia?" I don't know about that, but if the employer is of sturdy form, a punch on the nose would be most fitting. Now you can almost see Prodnose reciting the next bit, which goes like this: "Have you or any children included in this application ever had, or currently have, tuberculosis or any serious disease (including mental illness), condition or disability?", and of course Prodnose has seen to it that the subsidiary question is: "Is the disease likely to be a cost to the Australian community?"

But of course, I am only marking time before the toughest of all the No/Yes questions: "Have you, or any children included in this application

• Been convicted of a crime or any offence in any country?
• Been acquitted of any criminal or other offence on the grounds of mental illness, insanity or unsoundness of mind?
• Been deported from any country?
• Left any country voluntarily prior to the execution of a deportation order?
• Been excluded from or required to leave any country?
• Ever had an application for entry to Australia refused or a visa cancelled?
• Been involved in any activities that would represent a risk to Australian security?
• Ever committed, or been involved in the commission of war crimes or crimes against humanity or human rights?

And finally – you guessed it—
• Any outstanding debts to the Australian Government?

Now as a matter of fact I have to say yes to several of these items. No, I have not been acquitted of any criminal or other offence "on the grounds of mental illness, insanity or unsoundness of mind", but I *have* "been required to leave another country", indeed several times and several countries. And before Prodnose starts to scream the place down, let him know that I am proud of those times when I was ejected. For the first of these chuckings-out were from South Africa, when it was still in the foul days of apartheid when black men were thought of as animals; and the other ejection was from what was then called the Soviet Union, which was then ruled by the hideous criminal called Brezhnev, who presided with savage brutality.

Now *please* understand that these 10 columns of bumpf were not created by any of the Australians I have met or indeed heard of, and I am sure that any decent Australian, shown these papers, would be horrified. The trouble is, that these papers are *not* shown to Australians. Why should they be? After all, these papers concern only the entry to Australia for *non*-Australians, and have nothing to do with Australian rules or orders, and I should think that only one in a thousand native Australians has even seen them.

But that brings me back to those daft and offensive 10 columns of – well, of what? I shall tell you. These words were put together by a committee – no single human being could have devised them. The members of the committee began to put in ideas, whereat other members put in more ideas, whereupon more and more members got more and more ideas, and after a very long time, a *very* long time, the 11ft of bumpf saw the light of darkness.

But this is Australia! Australia, the country I love next only to my own! Australia, the country with its ease and kindness, its bravery and laughter, its beer and its shakehands, its music and its theatre, its generosity and its understanding, its quiet suburbs with their curtains and its marvellous contempt for its MPs, its immense size and incredible landscape, its unique accent, and its glorious seafront with its glorious, thrice glorious Sydney Opera House – assuredly the most striking opera house in the world.

Come, come, Australia. You can do better than this. No, I am not going to say that all frontiers should be abolished, and that anyone should be able to go anywhere, anyhow, with or without money. But I *am* saying that the document which greets non-Australian would-be visitors is a smudge on the great name of Australia. And if you agree, let me help to pile up those shoddy documents into a huge mound, and let me strike the first match. And let Prodnose get the first smudge.

The Times, 13 December 1996

Digging in

WHEN I SEE a headline reading "Man takes lawn into his own hands to bury his bungalow" I prick up my ears. I have seen all sorts of sights in my long life, including a totally plastered Cabinet minister falling down two flights of stairs, and I simply cannot understand how he was doing it. (The bungalow man, not the Cabinet minister.)

So I examined the subject more closely, and when I had fully understood how (to say nothing of why) a man would bury his bungalow, I was rather less amused. Indeed, I made haste to wipe the smile off my face. For this story is far from funny.

Mr Trevor Sedgbeer and his wife Lauretta live in Devon, and Mr Sedgbeer built a bungalow; many do, and in this case did. But he built his bungalow – italic, printers, for the awfulness of what now comes: *he built his bungalow without planning permission*. Now, short of murder, there is nothing so wicked as a man who builds a bungalow without planning permission, or, to be more exact, there is nothing so wicked as a man who builds a bungalow *when the man who deals out permissions has not given his say-so*.

I have said a thousand times that power should be used upside down; the bigger the slice of it the more wary the user should be, and *vice versa*. And when it comes to a Devon bungalow permission-giver, the very tiniest scrap of the heady stuff should be used only with the head immersed in a bowl of very cold water.

It is not clear whether the offence was that the bungalow was in the wrong place, or whether it had not been approved, or both. But after much wrangling, the courts demanded the destruction of Mr Sedgbeer's bungalow.

Mr Sedgbeer complied with the order to destroy his bungalow, which came down flat. Now I have, in my time, done some rum things, but never before have I found myself invited to go about digging holes for bungalows, and I politely demurred. But on inquiring further, I learnt that to bury a bungalow means shifting several hundred tons of earth. It seems that Mr Sedgbeer was in earnest when he said that he would give the authorities their wish with knobs on – several hundred tons of knobs. The battle continued; for a time, any member of the council passing by would have seen nothing but the flatness that had been required. But then, it seems, at least as the council would have it, Mr Sedgbeer's home had risen from the earth – grimy no doubt – and the struggle was renewed: was the earth flat enough, or had Mr Sedgbeer merely repeated his crime? He says: "I have obeyed the court ruling by taking the building down to the original ground level of the site. I have done all they have asked me to do." It is not for me to adjudicate, but what chills my blood is those terrible, those most terrible words, which came from from the lips of someone in the council (they *always* come from the lips of someone in the council): "We cannot allow one person to contravene the law while making others abide by it. We are determined that the building should be removed."

Oh, sing it to the birds, play it on the accordion, whistle it while you work, but it will still be the same ancient rubric: "What if everybody did it?"

What indeed – for Mr Sedgbeer has just been put in prison for a three-month stretch for not destroying his home at the council's behest.

Oh, *what* if everybody did it? I am tempted to answer that the council members would be beside themselves with joy.

But now we must go from Devon to Leicestershire. Here, there is no tinge of amusement, even if there was before. A Mr Pickavant had an 18th-century cottage on his farmland, which he was lovingly restoring. But the council (oh, yes, there *is* always someone from the council) said to Mr Pickavant that there could be only one dwelling on the farm, a bungalow, which Pickavant senior would occupy. But the 18th-century dwelling was for Pickavant junior, who was to live in it with his lady. But if there is a bungalow and an 18th-century cottage on the same farm – well, two ones make two.

Mr Sedgbeer was reasonably young and sprightly. Mr Picakavant is 67, and when *his* struggle began (oh, yes, there was a struggle) he collapsed; he came round just in time to see his world crushed. And crushed is the right word, because the council (oh, yes, yes, yes, there was someone from the council to watch, and for all I know to look smug) had engaged 10 policemen – six of whom were in riot gear – and a giant digger. And the digger was not a toy one. It worked.

And the work of four years (not counting the people in the 18th century who started the cottage) was destroyed.

Yes, yes, yes, the law is the law and must be obeyed. Mr Pickavant had already been fined £500, and a judge had said he was "stubborn and foolish", which indeed he probably was, though it would be a good idea if the judge in question took a 40-year holiday.

But that again is not the point. The point is that someone from the council said – oh, but you know what I am going to say now; the people from the council said: "If we failed to enforce the order, it would open the floodgates for everyone else to build houses without planning permission in the countryside."

Ah, the angels weep; you can hear them clearly if the wind is in the right direction. And their tears speak volumes: "enforce the order", "floodgates", "contravene the law", "if we failed to", "while making others abide by it", "planning permission", "planning permission", "planning permission".

But now we are in the countryside, where things are done differently, but if we pack up and head for the smoky air of the town, do not think that councils have disappeared and we can smile. Because Mr Brian Godfrey of Ilkeston has nothing to smile about.

He is a greengrocer by trade, and he displays his wares on the pavement, as countless greengrocers have done through the ages. Indeed, I am told that that has been the same site in Ilkeston for some 30 years at least. Of course, his boxes are put against the window of his shop, not on the kerb side, and of course he pays rent to the council for a foot and a half of the pavement. But Mr Godfrey has now come up against the same kind of people as those you have just been reading about.

Thirty years have passed with this familiar scene, but now the council (well, of course it was the council – who did you think it was?) has decided to puff out its chest and ruin Mr Godfrey. It claims that his 18 inches of pavement are dangerous, especially for blind or disabled people, though it seems that there has been no accident at all with Mr Godfrey's wares. He says:

> People like to see fresh fruit and vegetables in front of the shop, not through the window. It is something you see in high streets everywhere. It is ridiculous to suggest I have no heed for safety. I have had no complaints, but the council cannot accept that they might be wrong. We have customers who are in wheelchairs. Except for the council, nobody has complained.

When Mr Godfrey stood his ground and ignored the council (hurrah! may there be many more ignorings!), he was taken to court by Derbyshire County Council – there's splendour for you! – *and the wowsers lost!* The magistrates – may the sun shine upon them – ruled that he was not causing an obstruction. The victorious Mr Godfrey, as a handsome token of reconciliation, announced that he was going to halve the space of his display. And what followed? But you know, of course, what followed.

Smarting from the defeat, the council asked the High Court to overturn the magistrates' ruling. And alas, it did. The judge

– may he get chilblains – gave the wrong answer, and you could *hear* the smug smiles on the faces of the county council. And another innocent, useful, happy, hard-working man is ruined. And oh, yes, you will certainly know what comes now in this case. Yes, the bossman did say – these were the very words: "If we had made an exception for Mr Godfrey, a precedent could have been set which could have affected the rights of pavement users throughout the country." That's glory for you!

Remember the rule? The rule that says the smaller the quantity of power, the greater the yearning to exercise it? And have I not just demonstrated that sad truth?

The Times, 14 December 1995

Tiny, but much

S OME PEOPLE ARE never happy if they are not in a fight, or limbering up for one. I know that that is true, because I am myself one of those very people. No, I do not punch heads, far less brandish knives, but if there is a scrap in which words alone are the weapons used, count me in.

I hope he will take this in good part, but I cannot but think that Tiny Rowland fits perfectly the bill of "never quite happy if not in a fight". Even if I am mistaken, Tiny can hardly deny that – whether he started it or joined in or was hit first – he is almost always found donning the gloves, and I don't mean the kind of gloves which keep people warm when it's snowing.

Well, if my readers' appetite has been whetted by the above, it is likely that they will at least want to know more about this remarkable figure (figure indeed, for he stands well over six feet), and it is natural for them to seek more about him from someone who has a *Who's Who*.

Ah, but now for Tiny's greatest trick. We hardened newspapermen watch, heaving with laughter as the trick is unfolded before the eyes of the innocent public; we have seen it many times before, but now bewilderment breaks out in all directions. *For Tiny is not in Who's Who.* And he is not there, because he does not want to be there.

Oh, yes, you won't believe it, and you will borrow a *Who's Who*, or finger one in the nearest public library. We've got him, we cry – Rowland, there is the name in good black print – but you must peer more closely, for the Rowland you nobbled was not Tiny Rowland, but another Rowland, this one Christopher, Professor of the Exegesis

of Holy Scripture, which as a description of Tiny would
be going pretty far.

Nor is there any solace from the next Rowland down,
for he is Rowland, David, Stipendiary Magistrate for Mid
Glamorgan, and no one has ever seen Tiny in Mid Glamorgan.
And Rowland, Geoffrey, QC, Solicitor-General for Guernsey,
no doubt has a lovely, sunny life with hardly a single yearly
murder to deal with. As for Rowland, Air Marshal Sir James,
we have here a brave fighter, so it is fitting, therefore, that he
has been given the honour of being the Governor of New
South Wales.

Then there are Rowland, David, Chairman of Lloyd's since
1993; Rowland, Mark, Social Security and Child Support
Commissioner; and finally Rowland, His Honour Robert
Todd, County Court Judge of Northern Ireland.

As you see, Tiny is an elusive figure. But more to the point,
he is a tough one, and above all a persistent one. Again and
again he goes into a fight (see above) and wins it, even when
the odds are stacked high against him.

Now I have said that I like a fight; but I do not fight at
random. I choose the side which I think is in the right. And
the fight in question here is Lonrho *v* Dieter Bock.

You cannot, of course, have forgotten Lonrho and its
battles. Some of those battles were bloody indeed; when
Alan Bond attempted a challenge to Tiny and his empire,
Bond limped out of the ring and not long after that was
totally ruined. Nobody could call Tiny Rowland a gentle
fighter, and to try to do him down would be appallingly
dangerous; moroever, when he fights he is not necessarily
in the right. And – this is going back into the past – when
he owned the *Observer*, very many at the paper wished Tiny
had never been born.

But this is today, and the adversaries are Tiny Rowland
and Dieter Bock.

I must make clear that Tiny is not fighting to scrape up a
few pounds which would keep him out of the workhouse.
He made his pile, and a high pile it was; experts in these

matters tell me that Tiny for a long time had a yearly salary of a million and a half. But it wasn't the money that caused him to rear up and fight: it was that he had been pushed out of Lonhro, and Dieter Bock had taken his place.

And in this fight, I am on Tiny Rowland's side. (I wanted to start my broadside by saying that Bock is a beastly Kraut, but that might be somewhat embarrassing, true though it is, because Tiny himself has more than a touch of the Krautbrush.)

I am not going to pour statistics over my readers, not least because I would not understand what was being poured. You must understand that this is not to do with mergers or share-holders or conglomerates or rights issues or non-executive directors or a thousand more words that mean something about something else. No doubt that is all very important in the business, but it leaves out one crucial part of the story: the heart.

It is no use telling me that, in the old saw, money has no smell. Tiny Rowland has a fortune that must come to rather more than a hundred million pounds; but he has lost the company that he created, built up, and loved for 34 years. Pause here: when the annual general meeting took place, Tiny was fighting not to bring back his beloved 34-year-old creature, but to be honorary president of the business – not quite, after all, what he had once had, but still something. He had to get 75 per cent of the shareholder votes to become president, and he knew that practically all of those 75 per cent would have to come from small investors, for the other 25 per cent would sniff, wink and make sure that Tiny (by one and a half per cent as it came about) would lose.

And so he did. But as the cheers of the little people rang out, Tiny shouted above the din one very telling sentence. Turning to the members of the board of the company he cried: "I appointed every one of you."

When I was young, and wondering what I might do with my life, I thought of various possibilities. I thought of many, like medicine, or teaching, or the stage, or politics, or art, or even carpentry. But, curiously, business was never even in my mind. Have I wasted my years by not becoming a businessman? Perhaps; who knows how fate throws down the cards? But I have a clue; if a man builds up a huge business and runs it successfully – very successfully – for 34 years, and then is ousted by the very directors he appointed, I think, I do truly think, that I did not make a mistake when I failed to consider business as a career.

Tiny Rowland (incidentally, I have only met him a couple of times and those briefly, and I have never had any favours from him) is the epitome of the man who will not give in. Remember his colossal and enormously expensive fight against the al Fayeds? In the end, they kissed and made up, but something tells me that this time it will be a fight to the finish. I have already had countless column inches from him, and if I know Tiny he won't stop there. One very Tinyish statement from him suggests that he will certainly not stop anywhere. It says: "Let there be no doubt, Mr Bock won't have the time to do property deals in Germany or anywhere else. He'll be too busy facing me in court."

Tiny has a forest of Big Berthas, but he can be subtle when he wants. He has put together a fascinating sideways attack on Dieter Bock in a somewhat rarefied form. With no shouting (much less shooting) Tiny tells investors who are thinking of taking shares in – well, let Tiny speak for himself:

The Board of Lonrho proposes a merger of its platinum assets with a competitor, the Impala platinum mines . . . These terms are not good enough, when it is realised that as formulated they result in: a price far less than that envisaged . . . loss of ultimate control of Lonrho's biggest asset . . . loss of Lonrho's central attraction for outside investors . . . loss of direction at Lonrho . . . exclusion worldwide from any further platinum dealing or mining by Lonrho . . . It is my firm belief that this is the wrong deal and should be voted down in the interest of Lonrho and its share-holders.

Not bad for a man who shouts down an entire board, eh?

At the moment, Tiny is out of the ring, and can only wield Tiny's Curse. But I found in this tale much to think about. For 34 years he cultivated that company, and now he sees it in other hands. Was I not right, all those years ago, to shun business?

The Times, 8 December 1995

Clumsy crooks go barefoot

I WOULD NEVER make a criminal. For one thing, I would leave huge numbers of fingerprints all over the place, to say nothing of my spectacles, and for another thing, if I spotted one of my own books on a shelf in the sitting-room that I had come to rob, I would take it down, settle myself comfortably on the sofa and wonder why nobody was bringing me a pot of tea. But did you read about the real criminal (this is going to seem like an Irish joke, but the man actually *was* an Irishman) who phoned the police to tantalise them by giving them the address that he had burgled, and was still holding the receiver when the cops arrived at the phone-box?

With which I return to my infinite fascination with those great and wise figures, those captains of High Finance (oh, yes, the capital letters must remain), those mighty brains which can understand the most intricate and detailed matters of money while we poor mortals are groping in the fog to understand even the first word the great ones speak, those cool and smiling ones (the smiles denote that the smiler has just made a deal involving not millions but billions) who are the very figures who the following week are obliged to admit that they got a few noughts in the wrong place so that the great deal has vanished, leaving no trace except a red face and some mumbled apologies, while we little ones, ignorant from our heads to our feet in money matters, have got another half per cent on our modest savings, and are very pleased to get it.

Do you remember Queens Moat Houses? The chairman made a speech. I have it. "Growth, expansion and increased earnings are our clear philosophy, and we have two billion pounds of property on our books," he said, adding that at the next shareholders' meeting there would be £80 million of profit to share. Unfortunately, at the next shareholders' meeting it turned out that the company was £1.3 billion in debt, and the shares had been suspended. And no one in QMH was on the take; it was pure, unsullied, truthful, honest incompetence. (They came back later.)

As for IBM . . .

But what about the crooked ones? Once when I was writing about honest old QMH and honest old IBM, I signed off with these somewhat prophetic words: "One of Germany's most powerful and distinguished business figures, a Herr Schneider, has disappeared, and so has some £3.2 billion from the Deutsche Bank. I rest my case."

But now I have to open my case again, because Herr Schneider has been found. Not in Germany, which would be *de trop*, but in Miami, a much pleasanter retirement spot. And he settled down so comfortably that he and his wife stayed for a year and a bit. Alas, someone who recognised him blew the whistle, and Herr Schneider is therefore awaiting extradition to Germany.

But he is not awaiting it quietly. According to Mr Henry Hamman of the *FT*, Herr Schneider, so far from exhibiting contrition, is spitting rage, and is denouncing the Deutsche Bank (I said that he had gone off with £3.2 billion, but the final tally was £5.2 billion) as scoundrels, oath-breakers, and – well, let him speak, or rather shout, himself:

> Economically, with regard to me and my wife, the bank criminalised me. They accused me of being a criminal . . . They involved the media and through an unjustified filing for a bankruptcy petition that totally destroyed the good reputation we had enjoyed . . .

And when he saw the bank's reaction to his "refinancing proposals":

> I knew there was no point in returning home because

they basically destroyed my empire in a few days . . . I
knew exactly how banks operate and that doesn't always
mean business as usual . . . the banks knew where my
liquid funds were located, but they had no quick direct
access . . .

As for the Deutsche Bank, it said: "Mr Schneider's comments
lie between the nonsensical and the outrageous".

And those who know me, will know that of course I am
on Herr Schneider's side.

Yes, that is a shocking statement. After all, what if everybody started to cheer the crooks? Well, let me make my
true confession. I would never admire or smile upon those
whose depredations would or might touch the poor. My
eyes go bright only when the really stinking billionaires are
in question, and even they take the back seat when it is a
matter of banks and such.

Banks and such; what a delightful phrase! Over the years, I
have flown that flag – the flag, that is, of making fools of the
banks and such. In those years, I have not just catalogued the
imbecilities, but have taken it up as a hobby.

The clue is that the giant bloopers are always made from the
top, and my studies in this recondite but important field show
it. The truth is that when billions upon billions are on the
table, they cease to be real, and even cease to be visible.

I lick my lips at a headline reading "Tokyo regulators knew
of huge loss run up by Daiwa". For those even more ignorant
than I am in these matters, I should say that "Daiwa" is not
the name of some sweetie-pie who persuades a humble clerk
to shift a few noughts so he can buy her a diamond necklace,
but the name of the very bank in question.

But the first words of the story told it all: "The Japanese
Government acknowledged on Monday that it knew of a
$1.1 billion loss by a rogue trader at the Daiwa Bank six
weeks before American regulators were informed." But it
gets much better: "In that period the Japanese Ministry of

Finance did not act on the information, nor did it inform their American counterparts, officials said. When the loss was finally announced, in late September, it rattled the world financial community and raised new questions about the solidity of the Japanese banking system."

But it gets funnier yet, because a Japanese Cabinet minister, Tomoharu Tazawara, who has somehow got himself into this murky business, is the Justice Minister, no less. Nor does the merriment end here; the whole business, it seems, pivots on something called a "secret deal"; Mr Tazawara called a press conference and said: "Swearing by my conscience, I have never done such a secret deal" – but immediately resigned.

Meanwhile, did *you* know that in the Japanese Parliament there is a party called the Clean Government Party, which is also mixed up with the now famous secret deal?

Yes, I have fun among the millions, but I don't just laugh and go home. Remember what I said earlier: "The truth is that when billions upon billions are on the table, they cease to be real, and even cease to be visible." Take the man who first spotted the Daiwa scam; what did he think as the truth rolled out in the Daiwa Bank's New York office? Consider; Toshihide Iguchi had been at his amazing task for 11 years, years in which he lost for the Daiwa Bank more than *$1 billion*, and forged no fewer than 30,000 documents to keep his giant scam afloat.

I deceived you: there was no "man who first spotted the Daiwa scam", because Mr Iguchi himself felt that it was time to confess, and confess he did. But if he hadn't confessed, he would presumably be doing the same thing until he died, and no one would have pointed out that there was a substantial hole in the accounts.

And please don't raise an eyebrow and wink, murmuring that the Japanese are a very different race. They are, but however different is their diet, the colour of their hair, and their quaint habit of sticking scimitars into their stomachs (and often other people's) they know the price of a loaf of bread.

But just like us, they don't know the price of a billion dollars. Just look at the similarities in what happened in the Daiwa Bank. A crook had embedded himself in the bank; that happens regularly in Britain. They try to hush it up; so do we. They fail to; ditto. They put up a sacrifice and boot him out; we do exactly the same. They lie as long as they can; oh, so do we! They say that their shareholders are in no danger, whereupon the shares immediately collapse; the very same.

You still deny? Well, then, how about the Prime Minister of France, M Juppé, who is now said to be rather bent, and the Secretary-General of Nato, M Claes, who seems to have been rather more so. Beat that.

Stop Press: Sweden's Deputy Prime Minister has been caught fiddling credit cards. Alas, we shall never see Gummer's hand in the till.

The Times, 3 November 1995

Scream? Yell!

I HAVE BEEN quite enchanted with the story of the stolen *Scream*, and so I should be. But I say that not just because it is a fascinating story, but because in Marylebone High Street, not 50 paces from my palatial abode, there is a somewhat puzzling shop, the owners of which have seen fit to adorn the window with not just one version of Edvard Munch's most famous picture, *The Scream*, but a dozen or more. (I bet you don't know what *The Scream* is called in its own language. Give up? It is *Skriket*, and the first person to say "That's not scricket" will incur my most severe displeasure.)

Munch's *Scream* was his most famous picture, and surely Norway's most famous one. It has been copied, disliked, admired, caricatured (see Marylebone High Street), instantly recognised, even made people shudder. Indeed, they *should* shudder, for the scream is obviously a scream of pain, or more exactly of despair. It has been said, most unkindly, that Norway is the most boring country in the world, but that cannot be true; anyone who has seen the Frogner Sculpture Park in Oslo will never be bored again – all the seeker need do is summon up the sight of what the visitor saw the first time. Nevertheless, Frogner Park or no Frogner Park, *The Scream* is truly Norway's emblem.

Munch himself tried to elucidate the picture, saying: "I was crossing a bridge by a fiord under the sunset – I sensed a scream passing through nature. I seemed to hear the scream. I painted the clouds as actual blood."

You wouldn't believe it, but in his early work he was much influenced by van Gogh and Gauguin, but they were far too bright and colourful for his gloom, and no doubt his work fitted Ibsen much better than Grieg. I am not sure, but I think he must have painted *The Scream* not in Norway but in Germany; he lived in Germany most of the time from 1892 to 1908, but had a nervous breakdown (no wonder he painted *The Scream*), and came home. His *Girls at the Bridge* at first sight suggests sunshine and happiness, but the alarming giant cabbage (or whatever it is supposed to be) spoils the harmony. Before that, though, he had had a clash with the Berlin Artists' Union. He was ordered to take down 50 of his pictures – they could hardly have been too naughty in 1893 and Berlin, so I suppose they must have been too gloomy. (Munch *too* gloomy? Come, come!) Anyway, the uproar got so wild that Max Liebermann – a forgotten figure today, but then a considerable power in these matters – marched his people out and put them together again, which is why it is called the *Sezession*. It is also said that German Expressionism started from that clash; would that it had never started at all.

But I mustn't wander any more; I must now discuss the theft of Norway's greatest picture.

I have often thought about the business of theft in art, and I have never succumbed to the widely held belief that vast numbers of great pictures and even massive sculptures are always being stolen for the delectation of wicked but enormously rich men, who own beautifully lit impregnable cellars in which they loll in comfort, sipping Krug, and admiring their latest criminal acquisitions. I say that I have never believed the picture I have painted, but I am now not so sure; I am told by Professor Michael Levi, a professor of criminology, that there is a considerable traffic in stolen art, and another voice says that there is a billion dollars a year in the artistic criminal trade.

The Scream was stolen from the National Gallery of Oslo on February 12, 1994.

Even my waverings about art theft will not stretch far enough to believe that a *very* rich wicked man had got *The Scream* and was perhaps inviting other wicked men, almost as rich, to come over and see it close up. (Come to think of it, he wouldn't, because the other jealous wicked rich men would shop the one who had landed such a prize.)

Well then, if the robbery was not for art but money, it could only be as a ransom; instead of the youngest child of the multimillionaire being kidnapped for ransom, the most famous picture had been kidnapped instead. Yes, and if the Norwegian State kept its nerve, the thief could always fall back on saying that he would destroy the picture if the State didn't pay up; here we have an example of Russian roulette.

Happily, it ended with the famous picture intact. But the story of its rescue is a story in itself.

As you may suppose, when *The Scream* went missing there were many white faces, starting with the guardians of the treasure. How had the precious jewel escaped in the first place? It seems that two men (presumably at night, because the Oslo Gallery cannot be *that* lax, surely) put a stepladder against the wall, climbed thus into the gallery and went down as they had come up, leaving no address. It was immediately obvious that the thieves knew what they were doing; this was no smash and grab, but the purloining of one of the world's most famous pictures. And that picture was now in very dangerous hands.

The picture had been valued at £30 million, though such figures can hardly have any real meaning: its notoriety was its fame, not its cost. But, as you may expect, a flood of chancers poured into the game, claiming to know where the booty was to be found, and that all would be revealed for a very substantial sum. But then a British criminal contacted a (respectable) British solicitor who had been given a tip-off, and from him it seemed that a genuine line had been thrown. The Norwegians asked for help, and got it. The head of Scotland Yard's arts and antiques squad, Detective Chief Inspector John Butler, sent out two of his men, following the hint. These two were given aliases – Chuck Roberts and Sidney Walker – and were supposed to be representatives of the Paul Getty Museum in California. The idea was that they would be taken to where the treasure was to be found, at the price of £315,000. But something went wrong; the two men somehow became separated, and back at HQ Chief Inspector Butler was getting alarmed for his men – after all, they were facing criminals, and criminals who were armed and were known to be violent.

Chuck Roberts went into the lion's den – he was taken to a hotel near the sea, not far from Oslo. There, the villains took him down to the cellar, and there he saw something wrapped in a blue bedsheet. Unwrapped, it was instantly obvious that the prize was glittering before Chuck's eyes. He was, of course, still the Getty Museum's man, and they drove back to the Oslo hotel. There, they discussed the money, first at the bar, and over breakfast the next day. The crooks wanted £300,000 for the treasure, and another £15,000 for expenses (*ah, messieurs, quelle delicatesse!*)

By now, the other undercover agent – alias Sidney Walker – had returned. The deal was that there would be two bags, one holding £200,000, the other holding £115,000. The crooks examined the money, and presumably gave it the thumbs-up. Then one of our intrepid pair went with the men for the bags of moolah, while our other hero rewrapped the picture, climbed up the hotel fire-escape (he thought it better than walking through the hotel foyer in these circumstances), and then waited patiently, but not for long, for the Oslo Force.

But alas, the villains were not men of culture or taste; indeed, they used words that should not be spoken before the young or the delicate, much less both. When the deal was slowing down, the head crook said that if the money didn't appear soon he would "eat the picture, shit it out, and send it to the Minister of Culture". Coarse and vulgar persons, indeed, but nobody could fail to understand what they meant.

All's well that ends well. But there is a wonderful image

in this story, apart of course from the splendid success that the rescuers of *The Scream* had. It is the image of a British policeman, clutching a huge bag in which there was £500,000 in real money, and which he guarded with his life every moment of his travels, *though he did not know why*. He was asked, later, whether it was ever explained to him why British, rather than Norwegian, policemen should have supplied the money. "I don't know, sir," he replied, "I was given my instructions and I conveyed the money to Oslo. It was not an unusual request."

And that, dear readers, is British *sang froid* even if it is in French.

The Times, 27 December 1995

Pride before death

I HAVE TO start with poetry, and I shall end with poetry. You will find that the poetry is not at all the light and merry kind, but neither is it simply the dark and awful kind. There is heroism in this story, and there is also folly, but of wickedness there is not the slightest sign. And yet for all the heroism and folly, the greatest characteristic of this story is its pain.

Pain and poetry have frequently come together and in this case those two hold hands from beginning to end. Heroism and folly and pain; one more attribute was needed, and that is persistence. And persistence these innocent people got – got in such quantities that in the end they cursed the very word.

> We wise, who with a thought besmirch
> Blood over all our soul,
> How should we see our task
> But through his blunt and lashless eyes?

These words are for a man called Timothy Ley. He was 45 years old when our story begins, and he was (mark the "was") a most respectable gentleman; he was married with grown-up children, and I am quite sure that he was on the most perfectly pleasant terms with his neighbours; and if he ever were (mark the "were") called to settle an argument, he would do it in the most delicate manner, so that nobody would be unhappy, let alone angry.

Now, when I said "was" and "were", you must not think that what he was doing was anything wrong, anything that concerned dishonesty, for Timothy Ley was the very soul of uprightness. At the very thought of breaking the law – even the tiniest law – he would, I am certain, shiver and change the subject. And to top all that, guess what his job was? Yes, he was a clerical officer in the Inland Revenue, and you can't get any more respectable than that. And so, the members of the family Ley went on their ordinary, harmonious, leisurely, way, for years and years and years.

Well now, Timothy Ley went off every morning – no doubt after giving his wife the happy usual morning kiss – and rain and shine, shine and rain, he went to his office to do his work, no doubt perfectly. He did this exactly the same for years on end; off he went, his briefcase swinging, with that briefcase full of files. Nor was he the kind of man who, after doing the same job for many years, wanted to bang his head on the wall: no, Timothy Ley was quite content to go on with the same work until retirement, a couple of dozen years away. There are many such people in this reasonably calm land; I could not live like that, and many others could not either, but there are certainly many who not only do the work dutifully, but enjoy doing it. Timothy Ley, it seems, was just such a man. At least, he seemed just such a man. But that man's seeming turned out to be something very different, something extraordinarily, something incredibly different.

Because, one day, without telling anyone what he was going to do, Timothy Ley took a flammable liquid, and poured it over himself, and then struck a match. And so complete was the burning of his body that he could only be recognised from dental records.

What can be said? Nothing, of course. We are entirely bewildered, indeed we cannot understand anything at all. Suicide, and a specially dreadful kind of suicide, would be unimaginable for Timothy Ley. But he did it, without warning and without any kind of reason – or at least any reason that any reasonable person could discover. And death shall have no dominion.

Well, there was – is – an answer. An answer, that is, for

a placid, honest, decent man called Timothy Ley. But for the rest of us, if your head is still spinning with horror, the answer is more terrible than the match he struck.

Timothy Ley had lost his job. No, it was not for any kind of wrongdoing – Timothy Ley lived and died a respectable, honourable man, who would not pick up a penny from the pavement unless he was certain that it was his own. So what had happened to make such a man kill himself? It is that *he had been made redundant.*

No, no, no; he had been made redundant, but *not* because of any fault of his. It was just because the Inland Revenue, no doubt under orders, had to start cutting its cloth; everything had to be squeezed because there is less money for anything, from furniture to train-tickets, and from midday cups of tea to human beings.

To human beings.

A blow. A considerable blow. Anyone would go a little pale at the news that his or her work was not needed now; even though it is not because his or her work has become less thorough. Picture the moment; the head of the department calls in the man who is to be made redundant, and tries to cushion the blow. He repeats that the redundant man is not losing his job because his work has become slipshod or dishonest. Certainly not – perish the thought. But then there are shake-hands all round the room. And he goes home to tell his wife the bad news.

Correction: he goes home, but he does *not* tell his wife the bad news. And he does not tell his wife the bad news for two years.

But how, you ask? Take a deep breath. For two years, *two years*, that poor devil, that heroic devil, that pitiable devil, that incredible devil, that great and unique devil, left his home at the exact time as he had always done in all those years (no doubt never forgetting to kiss his wife) and stayed away from his home until, swinging his briefcase – that briefcase that had held so many files – it was time to return . . .

*   *   *

There are many aspects to this almost unbelievable but true story. For one thing, what did he do when he left his home to kick his heels for about six hours five days a week? Let his wife answer.

> He told me in August that he was starting a new job with an insurance company and would be going on a training course. Until then I had no reason to suspect anything other than that he was employed by the Inland Revenue. He insisted that all the paperwork would come through after he had been working there a month.

That won't do, surely. Where did he remain all through the hundreds and hundreds of hours? Where did he sit, where did he stand, where did he eat or drink, for hours and hours and hours? It is likely that, when he began this terrible march to oblivion, he wavered and thought he would own up (though God Almighty himself would have told him that he had nothing to own up to), but there comes a moment when the coin is spun and comes down heads or tails, but alas, not both.

Pride. We all have it, one way or another. But to pretend that a man is working at his desk five days a week, when he is not working at all, and indeed is doing nothing at all, would surely kill a man. And indeed it did kill him. I repeat – that pitiful man was not being sacked for laziness or stealing or incompetence. He was being sacked because and *only* because the Inland Revenue had had orders to cut the number of the employees. And Timothy Ley picked the short straw.

Very well: he did. Pride, we are told, goes before a fall. But in this case the pride went *after* the fall. And not only did that pride refuse to follow: it stood like a ramrod. For two granite years he stood, and he ended his life by himself.

But we are missing the point, the terrible, dreadful point. A man, bowed down with the pride he should have abandoned long ago, decided that he would give up the heroic and pitiful waste of life. And so he lit a match and gave himself to the flames. If that is pride – and it is – let us pray, and pray fiercely, for humility.

This infinitely tragic story has no simple answer, and indeed hardly any kind of answer. The very heart of it cries out to say there is nothing to say. There is a grieving widow and there are two grown-up offspring and a tombstone. Not enough. Not enough.

> Alive, he is not vital overmuch;
> Dying, not mortal overmuch;
> Nor sad, nor proud,
> Nor curious at all
> He cannot tell
> Old men's placidity from his.

All the lines I have quoted are from Wilfred Owen. Did I not tell you that I would start and finish with poetry?

The Times, 8 November 1996

Internet – boon or ruin?

WELL, I NEVER thought to see a huge, five-column, top-of-the-page story headlined "Porn as a guide to business potential" in the *Financial Times*. But there it was, with Tim Jackson's byline. What's the world coming to?

I shall answer the question in good time, but before I do so, let me jot down something else of interest. "Police said yesterday that the Internet global computer network was teaching children how to commit serious crimes, after six boys from an independent school admitted using the system to organise a sophisticated credit card fraud against mail-order firms."

Still on the same subject: "Bomb-making recipes and formulae for making napalm and the drug Ecstasy can all be found on the Internet, along with price lists for illegal drugs and limitless supplies of free, hardcore pornography."

No, I'm still at it, and will be for a very considerable time yet: "The Internet is absolute dynamite and it is without any form of quality control." (I have about 30 pages of this: perhaps you should sit down after all.)

Because "the Internet is giving extremists a previously undreamed of possibility for spreading racist and anti-Semitic propaganda. Bomb-making instructions and computer games such as *Achtung Nazi*, in which the aim is to gas as many Jews as possible, are being posted on the worldwide computer link. Denials that the Holocaust took place, glorification of the Third Reich, and hate articles about prominent Jewish families are readily available."

Had enough? No, you haven't had enough. I'll tell you when you have had enough.

"Armed with a computer, modem and telephone line, they use the global Internet computer network to organise illegal meetings and disseminate racist propaganda. Austrian authorities admit they are powerless to stop the spread of the computer underground: the cyber-Nazis use an unbreakable code when sending messages."

Thirty pages, I said, and I think it was an understatement. "More important than the opening of physical space is access to the enormous several-trillion-dollar pool of money that sloshes around in supranational cyberspace, moving by computer in and out of offshore banks and chasing profits in 24-hour markets, all largely beyond the reach of governments' control. This space without rules is made to order for those who co-operate without them."

Let's have a breather; I need one, and I imagine you want one even more. Like most people, I do not understand what cyberspace is, nor do I understand what the Internet is and does. But before I spread my ignorance at your feet, let me bring in that startling *Financial Times* headline, "Porn as a guide to business potential".

Is it true? Well, Mr Jackson has clearly studied the subject, and is sufficiently knowledgeable to state what he calls Jackson's Laws of Media Futures. These are: "If pornographers are among the early adopters of the new technology, then it has definite commercial possibilities", and "If there is a public backlash against pornographic use of the new use of the new technology, then its future is assured".

We smile; but one day we shall have the smiles wiped off our faces. Because, of course, what I am saying in roughly 1,500 words is that, in the words of the old proverb, "I have caught a bear, but he won't let me go". We don't need to know what animal an Internet is; we need only listen to, or read about, the catastrophes that the Internet has *begun* to cause. I shuddered when I read that people in America involved in the Internet were being charged with crimes and being punished for those crimes; how very right and proper – those American lawmen are on the trail, night and morning. So why did I shudder? Because I am quite certain that very soon those lawmen will have been swamped by the new crimes, committed by the new criminals – fanatics, madmen, cheats – and when they are asked how they did their wickednesses, they will say – the coolest first – "we did it on the Internet". And then it will not matter whether the Internet is a physical object or just a series of words.

The "porn for business" notion is being strenuously attacked by an American Senator, James Exon, who is drafting legislation against such things, but he is making very heavy weather of it. But heavy or light will soon not matter, and this is why. There is a comparison between pornography in the form of magazines and videos and in the form of what the Internet provides; physical pornography is illegal in the United States, and sooner or later non-physical pornography will also be outlawed. Oh, yes? And is there any city in the United States, in which illegal pornography cannot be acquired with a few more dollars? Of course not; and so it will be with the Internet.

Though it seems otherwise, I am not simply putting the case against the Internet; my scope is very much wider. I argue that just as television has corrupted and poisoned the world, so the computer will, in its time, destroy the world entire. Mad, am I? True, today we can almost literally put the whole works of Shakespeare on the end of a pin, and thousands upon thousands of things have shrunk to vanishing point. But I read not long ago that if all the heads-on-pins we have today were blown up to their original size, we would need thousands of Albert Halls.

In many places in the world there are people – it is their job – who are working on the dangers of nuclear fission. Should they be worrying not about nuclear weapons in the hands of savages or madmen, but in the hands of those who can manipulate the Internet and break open its mysteries? We shall be told – indeed, we have already been told – that there are strong defences against these dangers. Oh, yes? And how long did it take the skilful thief to get money from the out-of-hours bank cash machine? Stop for a moment to think about a group – a horde – of the most fanatical fanatics. Then think about the same, when armed with the Internet's "weapons".

Most of us who move amid computers have had more than one "crash"; the machine on which I am writing has had several. They do no harm, other than making me rewrite something that the crash wiped out. But think of such a crash in the Bank of England, then think of a crash that would ground all the major airlines at once, and then think of such a crash in half a dozen countries.

The problem is the interdependence of so many computers. For the most significant fact of my crazy picture is indeed its inextricability. Remember, "I have caught a bear, but he won't let me go". But we cannot turn the clock back. The dangers are here to stay. We have all seen the photograph of the first "road locomotive" with the man walking in front carrying a red flag. We look at the picture and smile. I wonder, if the man was still there with his flag and his stately marching in front, how much less happiness would there be in the world? Do I dare to say that there might be *more* happiness?

Absurd! But you must remember what we were told about the wonderful new nuclear fuel. It would be perfectly clean, it would be absurdly cheap, it would be amazingly undangerous. One of the claims made for the new wonder fuel has stuck in my mind through all the years; they said that the *Queen Mary* could sail right round the world without stopping on a piece of fuel no larger than a tennis-ball. And in the end it was a ludicrous waste of money and dirty to boot.

Our society lives by one precept: if it can be done, let us do it. And I regret to say that noble science herself follows too often that evil star. Did you read the story of the scientists who changed the sex of an insect? That is surely a "first", and indeed the boffins must have taken many hours of selfless labour to achieve their miniature goal. But I don't believe they paused to recite "And God made the beast of the earth after his kind, and cattle after their kind, and every thing that creepeth upon the earth after his kind: and God saw that it was good." For the scientists saw that it was even better.

The Times, 22 September 1995

Still the evil waters flow

D O YOU REMEMBER Mr Butz? Perhaps I should say, did
you ever hear of Mr Butz? Mind you, it is not all that
long ago that he died – hardly 20 years, if that. But of one
thing we can be absolutely certain: it is that the last words
he spoke would have been a denunciation of the thing he
passionately denied – no winks or ahems – the gigantic fraud
called the Holocaust.

He was an American, and I don't think he ever came to
Britain, but to my astonishment he did reply (in a letter to *The
Times*) to a mention of him in my column. I cannot remember
the details of the exchange, but he must have been holding up
the banner of "no Holocaust" in some way or other, and I
recall that he was not raving but quite civil. Then there was
that French lunatic – Faurisson, I think he was called – who
beats Butz easily, for it was he who said of Hitler and Hitler's
end that the Führer's downfall was because "He was too pure,
too honourable". And he, too, believed, with no making it
up, that this had indeed been the cause of his hero's demise.

But why do I bring up the shades of these dead crazies?
For good reasons, I think, because yet another group of
neo-Nazis has raised its pitiful (and usually shaven) head,
not so much to denounce the Holocaust as to take up where
it left off – smashing windows and painting vilenesses on
walls. And when window-smashing palls, something more
elevating takes the stage. Butz is dead, but others aren't: step
forward Gary Lauck, an American gentleman who publishes
and disseminates neo-Nazi materials, and *has been doing so for
more than 20 years.*

I am sorry, and I know it will give offence when I say it, but I cannot but admire a man – even a man who sells (or gives away) hatred and evil – who sticks to his filthy guns for two decades, when he must know that his product is made of lies. He is 42 years old, and he claims that he became a Hitlerite at the age of 13, after reading *Mein Kampf*. (Ah, there is the first crack in the fabric of truth, for, he did *not* read *Mein Kampf* at the age of 13 or any other age, because no one, not even me, has read it; a few pages here or there, yes, but in full, it is utterly unreadable.)

I said that I could admire him, and I fear that my admiration grows when I discover that he has grown a moustache in the shape of Hitler's, so profound is his love of his great leader. Nor does the love stop there; when he speaks to people in English he changes his native American accent for a German one. But at this point I abruptly stop admiring him for the rigidity of his beliefs, for it is very difficult indeed to admire a man who says: "In my opinion the Jews were treated too humanely. We must never make this mistake again."

Mr Lauck was arrested in Denmark, which has laws against inciting racial hatred, and Lauck will soon be extradited to Germany, where he had first been distributing his muck; he will be tried there, where he faces a minimum of five years in prison. (His original base is in the United States, which means that there he could not be prosecuted; American law does not prohibit – indeed protects – such activities, which is how he can distribute his stuff round the world.)

Had enough? Have just a bit more. Does the name Ewald Althans strike a bell? Well, for him, the bell certainly does toll, for he has just been sentenced to three-and-a-half years; he is a German citizen, and his sentence is for breaking the German law which prohibits any public claim that the Holocaust did not happen. Mr Althans makes clear – very clear – that he at least denies the Holocaust, for when groups of people were going to see, understand and face the numbed truth of Auschwitz, he used to hang about that terrible place and tell the visitors it didn't happen. Later on, he was on television in a programme about the Holocaust, and when his turn came to discuss Auschwitz he cried: "What is happening here is a giant farce". Nor did he stop at that, saying: "We didn't kill them. They all survived and now they're taking money from Germany." No wonder the judge in his case called him "a mental arsonist".

Now we turn to something tragic; indeed, only the Holocaust can bring more tears. It is happening in an ancient mansion in Germany, and it is crammed from cellar to ceiling with files. Tread lightly, visitor, because you are treading on the greatest crime in all history, for the 1.6 million files in that mansion have been assembled to sieve out – and this must be the last dredgings – the remaining war criminals.

"The remaining war criminals." What words! Are they worth it? I have argued that the remaining criminals are not worth the effort of finding them, and the greater waste is that so many decades lie between the crimes and vengeance that no verdict of guilty could be safe. Those tireless searchers after the blood of innocents think otherwise, and yet they know that with every year, every month, every day, the prospect of seeking, finding, accusing and prosecuting the criminals becomes more and more chimerical. But one of the seekers said words that struck home with great force. She said: "I believe no culprit should be allowed to climb into his grave without being unmasked." It is true and right, but every time the clock ticks, it ticks for another murderer who is now beyond the power of punishment. And so little time remains, that Efraim Zuroff, one of the most powerful of the searchers-out of villainy, says: "Now I find myself in the almost unconscionable position of praying for the good health of the criminals, because I want them to come to trial."

But there is one more category of wickedness in my schedule, and that is the one – the only one, as we have seen – which harbours criminals not in their nineties but in some cases almost in their prime. It is in this search, not the one for the last tottering Jew-killer (who anyway cannot be found), that we should be ticking off our targets. For we seek

out the men who shot down innocents, innocents who had
no weapons, who had their babies in their arms, who had no
secrets to give away, who only wanted to leave their homes
for other homes, and died by the hands of men who are at
this very moment saying "I was only obeying orders". Have
you forgotten the Berlin Wall?

So far, those who have been punished are the mere border
guards, who would indeed themselves have been shot if they
had disobeyed their orders; that is why they were prosecuted
for manslaughter, not murder. But now it is the turn of the
generals, all of them steeped bloody in murder, and the vilest
kind too. Let me name a few: Helmut Borufka, Wolfgang
Rheinhold, Heinz Handke, Wilhelm Elm, Horst Steckbarth.
These were not "only obeying orders", they were *giving* the
orders, as a revealing paragraph in their own minutes makes
clear: "Border violators should be destroyed and all attempts
to breach the defences should be prevented." And as if that
isn't enough, try this: "The number of one-shot kills should
be raised to the maximum."

I was there. I remember the huge billboards that told us we
were approaching the danger zone, but my first view of the
Wall itself is etched on my mind, and that first glimpse was
of dirt. That wall was dirty, high and wicked, and for night
after night after my visit I tossed and turned in the almost
incredible knowledge that the Wall had been put up not
because otherwise people would get in, but because otherwise
people would get out.

I remember, too, my first drive *through* the Wall. My
driver looked over his shoulder and tossed a West Germany
newspaper, of course prohibited, *onto* a rubbish bin, not into
it. I asked what he was doing; he said somebody would pick it
up and read it, and give it to others. But isn't that dangerous,
I said? He wound down the window and spat, eloquently.

I hope those generals will go to prison and spend the rest
of their lives there, but I wouldn't bet on it. Everything
is different now, apart from those generals. Unfortunately,

death does not stop to sort out the good and the bad; let us hope that in another, better world, things will be different. For a start, I would like to continue my chat with that brave German taxi-driver.

The Times, 27 October 1995

Growing up as killers

I HAVE ALWAYS admired the Labour MP Frank Field. His work is sensible and honest, and he helps those who need help. A while ago, he wrote an article in the *Daily Mail* which – but let him speak for himself:

> They are the new barbarians; a growing army of louts and thugs who make life hell for my most vulnerable constituents. The biggest change I have seen in my Birkenhead constituency since I was elected in 1979 is the seemingly unstoppable rise of this underclass of brutish and almost unemployable young males who "mature" into anti-social, often criminal, adults.

I said that I admire Field, and I do, but I have to add that if he has just discovered these barbarians, he must have been asleep for a considerable time. Let us begin with three photographs. The first is a man in middle age; he is one of three brothers. He lives rough, but doesn't seem to mind, and he can always be found on a park bench. He is a known and friendly figure. The second photograph shows a young boy, aged 13. He looks a nice lad, with a pleasing smile. The third character is the same age, but he looks a nasty little runt. He is. So was the other boy – his smile was untrue.

The two boys – remember they were both 13 – tortured the homeless man to death. He was robbed, hit, kicked, covered by poured molten plastic, and finally set alight. His burns were such that he was in agony for three weeks before he died.

I repeat that the two boys were 13 years of age; in plain English they killed a human being for fun. Now, what I want to know is – how did little children in Britain become killers?

Pass.

But try this. Peter Moore, 50, the homosexual owner of a cinema chain killed four men for the pleasure he derived from the act of murder. The men he killed were complete strangers, none of whom had done anything to annoy or aggravate him. Moore's first victim was Henry Roberts, a retired railwayman who lived as a recluse near Anglesey. The second victim was Edward Carthy, who was stabbed to death with a combat knife, and of whom Moore said, "I think he was a bit frightened, actually". The third was Tony Davies. His fourth victim was Keith Randles, and Moore said this about the way his victim died: "There was a certain enjoyment from it but the enjoyment certainly wasn't sexual. Like everything, it was a job well done. You know, the job was done." When a victim asked why he was going to be killed, Moore replied "For fun".

Now we turn to the old man (truly old – he was 84), Kenneth Speakman, who was a member of a shooting club in Ramsgate; he was murdered for his guns. He was a highly respected resident of Ramsgate. He was very sprightly. He had been interested in guns all his life. He was a very conscientious person and he was a firm believer in keeping his guns locked away securely. But when the thieves broke in, the guns were not just stolen: Speakman was beaten and strangled, for no comprehensible reason.

We have all read of the dreadful killing of Louise Allen. Again, one of the killers was 13, and the other was 12. The innocent child was kicked to death.

Are you feeling sick? You will be much, much sicker. Try this headline: "Widow, 94, raped by youth in graveyard". Harken to the widow:

I decided to take a walk down to the graveyard. I wanted to go to see the flowers of my neighbour's husband's grave. I thought I would go through the grass. I was walking towards the grave and I passed my husband's plaque when someone from behind pushed me and I fell to the ground. He seemed amused and was laughing. I was screaming and yelling as loud as I could. I said to him "Why don't you get a younger woman? I am in my nineties." He said "It doesn't make any difference." I was helpless and there was nothing I could do.

The young man who did that, Steven Barton, has been caught, tried, convicted and has started a 12-year sentence.

Now do please believe me when I say that this hideous catalogue of dreadfulness is not compiled just to cause nausea, though there is plenty of nausea to come. All these terrible things have a meaning, and a particular meaning.

But there is more. A wandering man, whom none would harm, found himself harmed to death, and a very terrible one it was. But that is not the point: killers abound and always have. More to the point, the shocking Bulger case was not only a "one-off", but something quite different: it is clear that the boys who did the deed had no conception of murder or indeed any kind of evil.

But the two who killed Alan Whittle, and killed him in the most dreadful manner imaginable, were only 13 years old *and should have known exactly what they were doing*. As should those children who killed Louise Allen.

These are not scraps from my album, and if they were, there would be a clue. When the Louise Allen case was in court, someone murmured these words: "It is another shocking example of schoolage gang violence sweeping the country." And what did Frank Field say? "They are the new barbarians; a growing army of louts and thugs who make life hell for my most vulnerable constituents."

True, but it is only the edge. Louts and thugs, new barbarians, stone-throwers, yes, but this is not adequate to describe the world we are now sinking into. I want to know why that hideous killing of Alan Whittle took place, and I must know why a little child did it.

And again, I turn to the terrible impossible. Hear the prosecutor for the case saying, "There is no doubt the defendants knew that what they were doing was wrong". Then in the name of God, how did such children know what it is to kill another human being, and even how it is done?

I say it again. There are, in our civilised Great Britain, children who are hardly out of their swaddling-clothes who know how to kill human beings, and some of them have already actually killed human beings, and some of those have killed human beings *for fun*.

And the father of the dead child said: "We have tried to bring our children up correctly, but law and order is a joke when you have got gangs running around wild. We never hit Louise even once, we didn't have to. You only had to shout at her and she would burst into tears." And the father of the dead child added: "I brought her up the way I was brought up myself – respect your elders, be polite and have good manners."

When did the rope break? How did Peter Moore manage to murder four separate men, none of them known to any of the others? And when one of his victims was in his grasp, and he was ready for murder, how did he feel? He tells us, plainly – though it is scarcely credible – that he did it for fun.

And the 94-year-old lady who was raped in a graveyard, and whose assailant laughed as he did so? And the 84-year-old gun-expert whose guns were stolen, while the owner was strangled?

My *pot-pourri* of horror is not, I assure you, just to make your blood freeze. I chose these horrors – and especially those involving children – because Frank Field and myself are now living in an era that we cannot understand. In the time of Dickens it would not be strange to find child criminals of 13 or younger. But we are not in the time of Dickens, we are in the time of the millennium. And he would be a remarkably optimistic man who, surveying such horrors, would pat a head or two and say that lads will be lads and indeed lasses will be lasses, particularly if he is having his head broken and his throat cut at the same time.

Once upon a time, a naughty little boy might throw an apple-core out of the speeding train, and all the other people would be shocked. But now, a headline in *The Times* cries out "Soaring vandalism threatens murder on railway" and all the other people are *not* shocked.

The Times, 20 December 1996

Those nasty critics

IT COMES ROUND once a year, strictly speaking once a year and a half. I myself must have watched the show for something like 30 years, until I could take no more and gave in for ever. The pattern never changes, but the speaker does, very frequently, for it is felt that the tremendous burden would break the back, nay, the very soul, of so treasured a figure.

Some fainthearts have said that surely it will be stowed away for ever soon (some scoundrels have even said that it should never have started), but I knew better, and I was right. The bell rang once more only a week or two ago, so it is fully fresh – or would be fully fresh if it were not steeped fathoms deep in the stink.

What, you ask, is all this about? If you keep quite still when the wind is in the west, you will know, because faintly, then less faintly, then loudly and then tremendously loudly, you will hear the complaints.

Which complaints, and who is complaining about what? Why, of course, it is the Luvvies who are doing the complaining – it is *always* the Luvvies who are complaining. And why are they always complaining? Why, because they think they have not got their true and complete deserts.

The Luvvies are coming! The Luvvies are coming! How many times, over how many years, have I heard that cry? And the cry is, was, and will ever be: "We are actors, we are directors, we are people of the theatre, so we must be treated and fêted to show the world how important we are

– so important that we, rather than the author, really should be taking the bows."

I tell you, and I tell you true, that there can be no trade or work or business or craft or vocation – not even a Member of Parliament or a newspaper columnist – that can beat the stage for vanity.

I suppose we all know by now about the new *New Statesman*. The rescuer of that dying magazine is Geoffrey Robinson, MP, who has put considerable sums into the *New Statesman*, in the hope – a good hope I would guess – of reviving the old mag under the editorship of Ian Hargreaves and turning it into a new one. Anyhow, browsing through the *New Statesman*, I found an article by one Michael Bogdanov, of whom I had never heard, but who from now on is to be called Old Boggars, for I discovered that Old Boggars was the immensely important and indeed absolutely necessary theatre director, who directs and directs and directs, day and night, and even chucks in a bit of designing for the designs.

Very well, very well, get on with it. I do get on with it, for the whining begins almost immediately.

The whining starts here? But why should there be any whining? Stop and think – who is the enemy? The whiners think well of themselves, but that is true of most of us. Where's the difference? Step forward those dreadful, evil, disgusting, loathsome and absolutely appalling people called critics. Ladies and gentlemen, the famous director Old Boggars has got a bad notice and the world must stop immediately and then go round the other way.

Now I have been a theatre critic three times, and each time I swore I would never do it again. (It took the third go to make it certain.) The first time was in the then *Daily Express*, and I was so young then that I thought I had died and gone to Heaven. For a time, my dear friend Robert Muller was the critic of the *Mail*, while I was at the *Express*, and at curtainfall we pounded down to Fleet Street arm in arm, each to our respective desk, to beat the chopper, sometimes by only a few seconds. (Some wit called Bob and me "The Kosher butchers".) Robert quit early, but I went on to become a columnist as well as a critic. The *last* time I was a critic was very many years ago; I was the critic for the *Sunday Times*. I remained a columnist but handed on the baton, and now John Peter has it, poor devil.

I have digressed, but for a purpose. The purpose is to demonstrate to puffed-up, ignorant, whining Old Boggars that critics not only don't go about to ruin the lives of brilliant, immensely clever theatre directors, but actually have an entirely different job to do. When I started on Old Boggars's ghastly wailings, I said to myself – I should have put money on it – that Old Boggars would, somewhere in his dreadful prose, tell us that

> I would like our critics to undergo a course of practical theatre, the graft and grind of directing, to give them a better understanding of how theatre happens and who is responsible for what.

And he truly believes that what is necessary for the critics is for them to see behind the curtain, *when the exact opposite is called for.*

Doesn't he even understand that what comes over the footlights (and yes, I do know that we don't have footlights now) has nothing to do with the backstage mechanics, however important those mechanics are?

The people who have paid money to see the play do not want to know what goes on behind the scenes, indeed most would shun an invitation – almost as much as they would shun Old Boggars's showing off with words and names like *Unterhaltungstheater* and Aristotle and Schlegel and Schopenhauer and even Robert Lepage, who is told off for "textual ineptitude". But Old Boggars truly makes himself an ass and an absurdity – it really is an absurdity – when he goes so far as to tell us that Peter Brook's immortal *Dream* was all rubbish. (Did he even see it?)

Now it is said that Old Boggars is a very good director. I would be the last to deny it, particularly as I am not at all certain what directoring actors is. Do they run about shouting "director that man this instant" or "you're getting your directoring in a twist"? But a man who can – and does – write this gibberish should go to his proper place in the theatre and stay there, *viz.*, behind the curtain, preferably a very thick curtain. Hark:

> Life-art criticism is not a straight line but a triangle, with the critic at one apex, life and art in the others. If we were to draw an authorial triangle, the writer would occupy the same position in relation to life and art.

Now if you look at the page in any newspaper's theatre listings, and examine the list closely, you will see that roughly half the theatres are filled with musicals, and a considerable number of the non-musical plays have been in the same places for years on end – yes, and not just *The Mousetrap*. For instance, *Dial M for Murder, Don't Dress for Dinner, The Woman in Black, Blood Brothers*. And many of the plays that don't stay for years are themselves oldies. For instance, at the moment, we can see *The Cherry Orchard, Who's Afraid of Virginia Woolf, An Inspector Calls, An Ideal Husband, A Doll's House* and *When We Are Married*.

What does this mean? It means, at least to me, that the British theatre is in an appalling state, and Old Boggars should address himself to that state, rather than poncing around and beating his breast and implying that he is the greatest director of plays in the entire history of the world, bar none.

But let us apply ourselves to a rather different theme. There are, at the moment, a tiny, a very tiny, number of first-class new plays in London, where, after all, most of our theatre goes. Actually, at the moment, there is only one new truly first-class play going – the teasingly named *Art*, which is a stunningly brilliant and funny three-man story, which turns into something very tragically unfunny.

Let's have more good plays, eh, folks? But Old Boggars would say – scream, actually – that the excretory critics (I forgot to say that Old Boggars is one of those who think excretorily) would ruin the plays.

Well, they might. But would it matter very much? I do greatly enjoy the theatre, but I would not throw myself over a cliff if the theatre in Britain shrivelled up and died. After all, there is precious little left of it now, and there will be even less in a few more years. I said that our theatre is in an appalling state, and so it is, but the world will not stop spinning.

Sometimes I wake shuddering, and think that I am a theatre critic again, but I shake my locks and think of Old Boggars and I smile. And – I shall let you into the secret – I smile because Old Boggars doesn't.

The Times, 22 November 1996

And frankincense

G OLD. JUST SAY the word. Say "gold" and nothing else. Say it again: gold. Try it against silver, against iron, steel, uranium, platinum, and anything that could be metal. Gold.

Gold. Look at the index of the *Oxford Dictionary of Quotations*: there are 61 references to gold, together with 32 for gol*den*, but there are only 24 references to silver. Say gold.

I thought that the world's resources of gold had been extinguished, but immediately another giant poked its head out of the gleam. This goldmine is going to be a giant; it is to be found on Lihir Island in Papua New Guinea, and it will have to wait until the huge volcanos that have just erupted have settled down. (Though there is no reason to believe that even greater ones may not burst out at any time.)

Lihir is a very long way away, and the amenities are unlikely to be those of Knightsbridge, but one intrepid explorer, Kenneth Gooding, has gone there and brought back the news that gold, gold, gold is to be found.

And all through the ages, 6,000 years of those ages, men have dug for gold, prayed for gold, begged for gold, robbed for gold, died for gold, killed for gold, gone mad for gold, and wasted their lives for gold.

And still they come, while I shudder because the headline of Mr Gooding's article is "Gold lures miners into the shadow of the volcano" and is followed up with "There is so much gold at Lihir, one of the biggest undeveloped deposits in the world, that the miners cannot resist having a go, in spite of the daunting problems presented by the site." (And one of the least daunting problems is the fact that the mining atmosphere will reach a temperature of 140 C, or 284 F.)

Curiously, although gold fascinates almost everyone, the encyclopaedias are almost silent on the subject, leaving it to things like gold being a good conductor of heat and electricity. But I found a book with the title *The World of Gold*, by Timothy Green, and it was written for the layman, *viz.* me. And when the first paragraph of the first page of a book about gold contains a speech by Disraeli saying "more men have been knocked off balance by gold than by love", and the second contains a message to King Ferdinand of Spain in 1511 saying "Get gold – humane if you can, but at all hazards get gold", it behoves me to read on.

Why is gold the greatest of metals? Not only because it cannot be tarnished, not only because it shines with a glow that no other metal does, not only because Schliemann, when he opened the golden treasures of Troy, said, "I have looked upon the face of Agamemnon" (he was wrong, as it happens), not because one ounce of gold can be beaten into a sheet covering 100 sq ft, not because one ounce of gold can be drawn into 50 miles of thin gold wire, not because any of those things, but only because gold is the one metal that all mankind bows down to. (And I forgot: Schliemann made his money in the California gold rush.)

The serious early alchemists failed just as the manifestly dishonest did (and there were countless fraudulent ones), but many went on trying, particularly Bernard of Treves who, in the year 1450, mixed 2,000 egg yolks with equal parts of olive oil and vitriol, then cooked this goulash on a slow fire for two weeks. All it did was poison his pigs.

But eventually the real Californian goldrushes started; there is a photograph which shows a snow-covered mountain; when you look at the picture more closely, it seems that a thick black line had been drawn from the base of the mountain to the top. When you look even more closely, you can see that that black stripe is a line of hundreds of men and women, all striving towards the top, because they believed that gold was there for the taking.

Down on the plain, the diggers dug; at one time there were some 40,000 diggers at work, and not many got much gold for their sieving. Nor were the diggers all American or British; at one time there were 25,000 French diggers and 20,000 Chinese. But there were tragedies; from the little town of Dawson a great flood of hopefuls began; but of the 100,000 who embarked, 30,000 arrived, and only 5,000 even got a chance to dig.

But there were, and are, more suave ways of coming close to great quantities of gold. Once, in New York, I was allowed to see all – all – of the Federal Reserve Bank's gold, which is considerably more than there is in Fort Knox. I descended into a cave that Aladdin would be proud of, and a huge steel door, 3ft thick, swung silently. Around me, was gold, gold, gold.

My chaperone swung a giant pair of scales eight feet high. "Watch", he said, taking from his pocket a crisp one-dollar bill, he threw it on to the gigantic scales. They moved at *three hundredths of an ounce*. "Watch", said my guide, taking out another dollar bill out of his pocket and showing it to me. "This one's dirty," he said, and threw it on the scales. The scales shifted at *four hundredths of an ounce*. Those mighty scales had turned by a speck of dirt.

The gold gleamed out at me; the gleam was soft, the place was silent, though silence was not required. At the end of this magical roundabout I had to go through what I suppose is the standard joke; my leader motioned to me to pick up a bar of gold that now lay at my feet. Clearly, it was screwed to the floor, but why? The smiles around me said that I was having a leg pulled; it took *two* men to heave the bar off the floor, and there was no screwing down. You see, gold is very heavy.

But the Federal Reserve Bank does not just sit around watching the gold tarnish (it doesn't). It moves the gold around. The mighty blocks of gold are stacked, as you would expect, neatly in their wire cages. These cages have numbers on them – not names, so that only in the holy of holies can an outsider tell which golden stack is from Britain, or France, or China.

And I suddenly realised that what I was seeing was nothing but madness. For when any country that needs to sell or buy gold – perhaps there has been a stream of strikes, or clamour for lower prices – it does not sell or buy that country's gold on the open market, or even in the dark of night; no, but far away at the Federal Reserve Bank, some gold blocks are solemnly shifted out of one of the cages and put in another.

You must believe me, though you won't. For there are sturdy men whose only work – and they do it in shifts all the year round – is to move blocks of gold from one place to another, even though the moving is only going three or four paces. They move around blocks that will never see the sky, or anything else for that matter. Did I add that the movers, on an ordinary day, can hump up to 2,000 blocks?

I come back to *The World of Gold*. In some countries – and Britain is one – it is illegal to hoard gold. But in many countries, whether or not hoarding is legal, there is an enormous traffic in hoarded, stolen, cheated or smuggled gold. And the ingenuity with which the wrongdoers do their wrongs is amazing. One version was to paint gold pellets so that they looked like date-stones. In another case, a great traveller was known for trundling about on his bicycle, until, that is, he was caught filling his bicycle-frame with gold pellets. Then again, the endless folds of Indian saris could cover many a sheet of gold. And the ingenuity of these splendid rogues goes even further: one smuggled the booty into Hong Kong by sticking it on his skin with 2,642 strips of adhesive plaster. Indeed, journalists have carried typewriters with solid gold space-bars. (Some of these rogues must be distinguished from others; these are mostly Indian holy men, who remain beggars, and ask that the gold fillings in their mouths be used to pay for their funerals.)

Gold is the child of Zeus, said Pindar; on the other hand

Benvenuto Cellini had a golden salt-cellar so large that he could have had a bath in it. Gold has been the downfall of millions, and the yearning of many millions more. And to think that it is, and always has been, and always will be, absolutely – *absolutely and entirely* – useless.

The Times, 4 October 1996

Darkness and devils

A FRICA AND THE heart of darkness; how did the two get so terribly entwined? Yes, there are places in that continent which are as democratic as we are, and one or two which shame us, at least when we examine the yelling and sneering and finger-pointing that goes for argument in our democracy (particularly, of course, in the House of Commons). Yet, after all, we do not throw our opponents into jail without trial, let alone *with* trial by judges as corrupt as the throwers.

Some would say, some *do* say, it is because of the colour of the skin, a *non sequitur* if ever there was one. Others say "give them time"; perhaps, but many have already had plenty. Others again say that us whities have no right to denounce African brutality while every scrap of Yugoslavia is steadily being reduced to rubble, blood and insanity – a view it is very difficult to contest. Well, then, let us abandon comparisons entirely, and start with a clean plate. Never mind what is going on in other continents, dreadful things are happening in Africa. Robert Mugabe is one of the most sophisticated (or perhaps I should say wily) of African leaders; moreover, he is almost certainly not financially corrupt, and not even corrupted with power. But woe betide any Zimbabwean who thinks he could run the country better and even shows signs of trying to effect the change. (In some ways, he resembles Lee Kuan Yew, and I wish I knew which of them would be the more affronted by the comparison, if either.) Mugabe's recent hysterical denunciation of homosexuality (as if he cares!)

suggests that although his throne is of course nowhere near to crumbling, it is not quite as firm as it might be, and he exhibits the usual stigmata of a rocky leader: "Go out and hit somebody."

But Mugabe, whatever his faults, keeps to a considerable amount of decency and even democracy, neither of which fits Moi. Moi, indeed, is almost the picture of the stock savage, who marks differences by sending groups of thugs (of which he has an ample supply) to beat up any remaining dissident. Very recently, that great man Richard Leakey, who not only tells the truth about Moi, but stands against him with whatever scraps of real election remain, was, with his team, ferociously attacked by Moi's brutes with an iron bar, heedless of the fact that Dr Leakey is confined to a wheelchair because he has lost both his legs.

And to top all that, there is a movement to bring back Idi Amin from his Saudi Arabian exile, which has now endured for 16 years. The idea came from the Ugandan Defence Minister, and was approved by Lieutenant-General Yorewi Kaguta, the present President of Uganda, who has thus extended the hand of reconciliation. Those who are old enough to remember Idi Amin will first smile, then laugh out loud, but then fall silent, struck by horror. For Amin was indeed first a buffoon, and then an irritant, but finally a mass-murderer. Laugh *that* off.

Mind you, the Ugandan President is no fool; he has fitted a tripwire which might give Idi Amin pause for thought, because although the Ugandans who had acted hideously have been given immunity from pursuit of their crimes, that act of mercy does not extend to the crimes Amin himself committed, which were very numerous.

This has become something of an African catalogue, but the rest concerns only one more country. It would be almost a waste of time to try to make a ladder of African nations, from the worst at the bottom to the best at the top, if only because there are always coups that break out and mess up the list. But however frail the ladder, and however far those who

climb it may see, there will be a place for that one tormented
land: Nigeria.

The only time I have gone there, very many years ago,
was to partake in Nigerian independence, for it was at the
moment that Nigeria had at last been given her complete
autonomy: the Brits had gone. Etched on my memory is
a tall and handsome man, laughing and dancing and crying
out over and over, "We got time, we got time, we got all
de time in de world".

I wonder if that man is still alive. If he is, on which side
is he? Perhaps he is one of the persecuted, the brutalised, the
cheated. But then, it is just as possible that he is one of the
persecutors, the brutalisers, the cheats. For all I know, that
man could now be General Sani Abacha. I hope not.

I have written before about Abacha's coup: he carelessly
allowed genuine elections and was heavily beaten, so he
cancelled the elections and he now rules the country with
just himself and his cronies.

But time has passed; the stolen elections are gathering
dust, and General Abacha faces new enemies, and now
very powerful ones. They are the United States, and I have
rarely, if ever, seen such a statement from a democracy to
a tyranny. The usual niceties were thrown aside and the
American State Department said this: "Nigeria is riddled with
corruption, insincere in its promise to curb heroin trafficking,
and engaged in systematic abuses of human rights."

A perfect summing-up; but President Clinton is more than
usually disturbed, for Abacha holds a group who are supposed
to have organised a coup against him. There is no way to test
the claim, because Abacha claims that the plotters have been
arrested and indeed already tried and convicted, all in secret;
a brisk fellow is our Abacha.

Brutality, imprisonment without trial, the fat of the land
stolen, infinite corruption, theft and trickstering; no wonder
that madness itself gets in: someone in Nigeria has been
practising a tremendous scam, and been very successful at

it. I received one of the come-ons myself, and had a few
minutes amusing myself. (The trick is simple: huge sums
of money are promised, but the first tranche has to be sent
before the heavens rain cash. Believe it or not, hundreds
were hooked.) So a magnificent advertisement appeared in
the *Financial Times*, thoroughly disclaiming any part of the
scam, in these terms:

> Given the frequency with which some gullible people
> still fall victim to the business scams, the Central Bank
> of Nigeria deems it necessary once again to . . . alert
> the international business community of the increasing
> spate of attempts by international syndicates to defraud
> them . . . the authors of the circular letters who bear
> Nigerian names are part of an international scam . . . out
> to dupe gullible overseas recipients who are themselves
> both villains and victims in the bogus "business" deals.

Well? Even ignoring the corruption, would *you* do serious
business with such people? And could such people be trusted
with others' lives? Abacha says that there was a conspiracy,
but if so, hurrah, for it must have been directed at him and
his satraps, and gives hope; there are brave men and women
in every country. One day the Abachas and their like will be
thrown down, but that is not the end – it is the beginning.
For more important is the question of how and when will the
tormented people of Nigeria get a decent life? Hang Abacha
as high as you will, the ground-down people of Nigeria will
take years to get an even half-decent life.

I ask again, and again, and yet again: how did Abacha and
his like, and Idi Amin and *his* like and Moi and *his* like (which
includes hitting a cripple over the head with an iron bar) get
into power and stay there? The white supremacist has his
answer ready: he will say the darkies haven't yet come down
from the trees. But apart from the dreadful things he says and
even believes, the answer *cannot* be that; indeed, there is a grim
way of testing it – Abacha is as black as coal, but he is certainly
clever enough to take hold of an entire country and put it in

his back pocket. And for that matter, there are some shadowy figures in Nigeria whose entire fortune hangs on there being a sufficiency of whities, thousands of miles away, so stupid that they will give their last pound to a black man they haven't heard of, let alone talked to.

There are bad people and good ones, and it is sometimes very difficult to distinguish which is which. And that is why I end my column for today with these words:

> The Central Bank of Nigeria wishes to warn all recipients of fraudulent letters that they should exercise caution and immediately contact their local law enforcement agencies or Interpol to help track down the international crooks and swindlers. The Bank will not bear any responsibility for any loss sustained by any person or corporation that fails to heed this warning.

The Times, 8 September 1995

They need a hiding

THERE'S NOWT SO queer as folk. But when the queerness turns into something truly terrible, we wonder yet again that human beings can do things that we believed could not be done.

Imagine it is 1966, just 30 years ago. The war in Vietnam was raging, the Berlin Wall had not long been put up, drugs were just about to start their rampant progress, Albert Speer had got out of prison, the Moors murders were in everyone's mind, Lowry had had his first big exhibition, Harold Wilson was Prime Minister, Lurcat's tapestries were seen in Britain for the first time, we had won the World Cup and everyone was in love with Twiggy.

And then there was Desmond Lockwood. And then there was Karen Morgan. I shall begin with Desmond Lockwood.

The boy was a very ordinary boy; the only picture of him shows a charming smile. No one would or could have guessed what might follow.

Desmond Lockwood was a young building worker; he was 19. His pleasant attitude and demeanour suggest that he worked well. But he lost his job. It is unlikely that he lost it because of bad work or behaviour; in those days employers sacked and took on workers very casually.

So it was not a very remarkable thing to happen. But in Desmond Lockwood it caused a kind of rage, and he took the rejection as a personal slight from society. "Damn it," he said to his older brother, "if that is the way they treat people, I'm not working any more." Nor did he, ever.

Now we turn to Karen Morgan.

She was a bright young woman, winning a place at Bexley Grammar School. But there was darkness in her, and she, like Desmond Lockwood, had decided that the darkness was where she wanted to be. So she, like Desmond Lockwood, rolled down the blinds. She was 16 years old when she went into her last stopping place, and she lived in the darkness for 13 years, and died in it.

The word that obviously comes to the surface, is of course "mad". It is much too easily spoken. Take first, Desmond Lockwood, when he decided to lock himself away. Did he think that he would remain self-immured for the rest of his life? Or was he just trying it on – making fools of the family? Remember his last words before he went into the cave: "Damn it, if that is the way they treat people, I'm not working." How many hundreds of annoyed family members have thrown the milk-jug across the room and shouted "I'm never coming back?" And how many *didn't* come back? One in a hundred? One in a thousand?

Well, we know one now. Desmond Lockwood said he was not coming back, nor did he. So what did he do in the darkness, for *years?* Well, he had television, but in those days – remember we are in 1966 – the fare would have been pretty thin and repetitive. Pause, reader, at that thought. We can collect bits and pieces from the hermit and his relatives; after all, he had to eat. It is said that he ate nothing but ice-cream and drank nothing but tea; surely he would have died from such a regimen? But it seems otherwise: the bonny lad who started this turned into a 15-stoner, but didn't die until he was 49. Mind you, his hair grew so long that it reached his waist, and he eventually sported a 2ft beard.

Yet there is no evidence that he yearned for the outside world; indeed when anyone came near him, he vanished immediately. Mad or sane, he lived as he wanted to live, and who should rebuke him?

The story of Karen Morgan is somewhat parallel, but in this case there is tragedy, very dark tragedy. Desmond Lockwood liked his strange home, but the girl's home was a hell. Not a hell thrust upon her, but one that she had taken to her bosom for herself. For 13 years she lived – if it could be called living – in her bedroom, and never came out, until the pitiful child came out dead.

There is no point in going over the details of the people who lived cheek by jowl with her and apparently did not notice the dreadful dying of Karen Morgan; suffice it to say that they must have been blind, deaf and stupid, until they noticed that she was dead.

But what about her relatives? Why did they not notice? The answer is a terrible one, but one also that can be understood. The girl came from a working-class background: when their daughter became unhinged they did not immediately get in touch with the appropriate organisations, indeed they got in touch with nobody. Why? I said it was a working-class area; when their daughter became mentally ill, their immediate response was, in effect, "What will the neighbours say?" – and for 16 years Karen Morgan's parents hid the terrible truth, because "they were too ashamed to talk about it to anyone".

Oh, great Heaven, when will such shame die out? The girl might – almost certainly could – have been saved. Saved, that is, from this:

> She had been hidden from the world, suffering her own
> extreme personal torment in a bare first-floor bedroom.
> She slept on the floorboards with a bucket for a lavatory
> and her food was left on a tray outside the door.

Her brother mirrored her; he was also psychiatrically ill; he too did not venture out into the world for 10 years, and when Karen Morgan died, he tried to kill himself.

There's nowt so queer as folk. Karen Morgan suffered as far as suffering can go, and was overlooked. Would you swear that Mr X, whom I see frequently in my neighbourhood, is not burning in dreadful torment? Ridiculous! Is it? How do you know? And if you are certain that there are no chalk-marks on the blackboard, well, what about those people whom I pass without a glance? How do we – you and I – know that perfect outsides can be hell insides?

Where does the line run? And how far? A cheerful boy loses his job (but at a time when jobs are easily found) and walks into the darkness and stays there for the rest of his life. Nor does he chafe at the darkness; indeed, he lives with the darkness, and it is his lifeline, for what would he have been without television?

Where does the line run? And how far? It does not run, apparently, with Karen Morgan, though it does run, happily, with Desmond Lockwood. A neighbour says: "It's a shame he chose to live like that. He missed out on such a lot." But did he? There is no sign of any newspaper in Desmond Lockwood's cave; can it be that he scorned not just the light and ordinary food, but everything that was going on in the real world? (Or what *he* would call the unreal world.)

And the girl with the terrible fate? Was that ordained? For that matter, did Desmond Lockwood ever see or hear of Karen Morgan? And reciprocally, did Karen Morgan ever cross the path of Desmond Lockwood? Does it matter? It might have mattered, if the two of them had been in the right place with the right words. For surely, if Desmond Lockwood had known the torments that Karen Morgan was suffering, he would have tumbled out of his strange cage to help.

The word "hermit" is a somewhat odd one. It is used, obviously, for someone who puts his head in the sand, but if we turn to the real meaning of the word, we find that it is almost always spoken warmly and with reverence. It is not surprising, because we have the image of a hermit in our minds: the cloak, the hat, the sandals, particularly the sandals – and of course those hermits who went on their Christian way barefoot.

Surely there are hermits today – real ones? I wouldn't like to find them buzzing about in very small motorcars. But today I imagine that they keep their vows and do their good works (for who ever heard of a hermit who was a bully?). Would such a hermit clash with Desmond Lockwood and his strange hermitage? Or would our modern-day hermit turn immediately to do what he can for the tragic Karen Morgan? The latter, assuredly.

There's nowt so queer as folk. (Not least when I recall that the word "queer" used to mean homosexual.) We come back to where we started: we cannot know what triggered off Desmond Lockwood into a true hermit, and I wish I could bring back to proper life the pitiful Karen Morgan. One thing we may be assured of: there will be more hermits, odd ones and terrible ones, and we shall never quite know which is which. Oh, yes, indeed; there's definitely nowt so queer as folk.

The Times, 6 September 1996

That sinking feeling

L ONDON BRIDGE IS falling down, falling down, falling down, London Bridge is falling down, my fair lady. I don't want to worry you, but whoever coined that jingle wasn't far off the mark, particularly because the nursery rhyme has another, even gloomier, version, *viz.*, that *Westminster* Bridge is *broken* down; it has been worked on for a long time, and I don't know if they have got it right. Earth hath little to show more depressing than those eternal roadworks. Oh yes, London's bridges are falling down, falling down, falling down, London's bridges are falling down, my fair lady.

Worse; there is considerable evidence that Tower Bridge itself will shortly slide quietly into the Thames, which would certainly bring sorrow to lifelong Londoners like me and all those visitors who never got here. (No, dear, Madame Tussaud's would *not* be an adequate substitute.)

I am not joking now. Tower Bridge is one of the most ridiculous but splendid buildings ever put up in London or anywhere else (it is exactly 101 years old) and the traffic on it is shaking it to pieces. For some time, there has been a good lot of patching and stitching, but a firm of engineering works has been called in to give it the once-over, and heads have been shaking gloomily. (There has also been a lot of pie-in-the-sky; who started the rumour that there was going to be a wonderful area around Tower Bridge, filled with brand new playhouses and concert-halls?)

Who (I wouldn't be surprised if it was Ted Heath) gave the whistle for the giant 12-wheel lorries that have destroyed most of our great cities' roads? And that is no exaggeration, for I have proof; I never learnt to drive, and I suffocate in the Tube, so the London taxi-men feast on me, and once upon a time I could read the newspapers as I went. No more.

I come back to Tower Bridge. The expert engineers say that if the volume of traffic thundering over that mighty but loony edifice continues, the great bridge will last only 10 years, or 15 at best. And the same experts tell us that the Rotherhithe Tunnel (which is getting on for the same age as the Bridge) will die just as the Bridge does. How could it be otherwise when there are 35,000 vehicles going over the Bridge every day and 30,000 similarly going through the Tunnel? The grim truth is what the Road Federation man says it is:

> . . . the findings clearly show that structures designed for another age cannot meet the needs of a modern capital. This situation only serves to highlight a London-wide problem of growing demand being placed on increasingly decrepit infrastructure. It is a situation which will worsen in the future if remedial action is not taken. It is impossible to plan either for the long or short term with a transport infrastructure that is in an unreliable or even dangerous condition . . . it has been discovered that as the tide rises and falls and river-bed materials shift, the centre of the Rotherhithe tunnel is constantly lifting and settling while its ends remain in fixed positions. Though heavy protective pads have been sunk over the tunnel, the stresses threaten to rupture the ageing tubing, which dates from 1908.

Dear reader – would *you* be *quite* happy going regularly through a tunnel beneath the water which is constantly lifting and settling *and which dates from 1908*?

That's nothing. The grim truth is that the entire infrastructure upon which we live is sinking. When last measured, it was found that the entire Palace of Westminster is two millimetres lower than before; true, two millimetres are hardly enough to get John Major drowned, but beloved

Big Ben himself has sunk three millimetres deeper. But "Daftest Bugger of the Month Rosette" must, surely, go to the London Underground spokesman who said, "The problem we are finding is that the historic buildings in Westminster just aren't as well-built as the modern ones."

Ah, but what about the Leaning Tower of Pisa, eh? We have all seen pictures of it, and many of us have been there. Those who go there are invariably cornered, most genially, by the sellers of guide-books and nuts for the birds, but for a few more lire they can enjoy the Great Tower Joke. This takes the visitor a specified distance from the Tower; the visitor stands as if beside the Tower with hand outstretched; the vendor steps back and clicks his camera; when the visitor sees the picture it looks exactly as though he had been holding up the Tower.

But *someone* will have to hold up the Tower.

It is one of the oldest monuments in Italy. Charlemagne came here, to what was a truly great city. It began in the 11th century, and the Pisans continued to add to their prize with great mosaics and bronze doors, frescoes, a beautiful baptistery, a cathedral, a *Campó Santo,* a cemetery. And then, the very last item was built – a bell tower. And that bell tower is the Leaning Tower of Pisa.

Galileo was born in Pisa, but almost all the stories of him are apocryphal; he didn't say *"Eppur si muove"*, though he certainly thought it; he didn't throw stones off the Leaning Tower to demonstrate his theories. But you see, the Leaning Tower began to lean early in its life. Fall or no fall, the Pisans' great monument has already stood for more than 700 years, and if it falls now, it can be proud of itself.

I must have been one of the last to climb that wonderful tower, because in 1990 it was closed to the public – the danger was too great. Mind you, when I did climb that staircase I came down trembling; the famous tilt has an extraordinarily powerful pull; going towards the outside (there is nothing to hang on to) I thought I would be thrown over the edge. Incidentally, is it true, as I have heard, that no one has committed suicide by throwing himself off the Leaning Tower, by contrast with the substantial number of suicides from the Eiffel Tower?

But hark! Yet again, a bevy of scientists has galloped to the rescue of the wonderful tower; this time it is one Paolo Heiniger with his idea. There is talk of giant electrodes planted deep into the earth beneath the Tower, and 750 tonnes of lead have been put in.

But that is not the only tower with troubles. When the Venetians' greatest tower, the Campanile in San Marco, collapsed at the start of this century, it had endured for a thousand years, easily beating the Pisans', but of course Venetians can never leave well alone. There was a thunderous argument as to whether it should be rebuilt as it had looked for a millennium or whether the space should be left clear, opening more of the piazza, or even whether to rebuild it in another place. The *dov'era, com'era* army ("where it was, as it was") won easily.

There are more leaning towers than you might think; in Venice itself there are dozens that are at least a bit wonky, and one – S Giorgio dei Grechi – that really makes newcomers hurry away. (But as J.G. Links puts it: "It started to lean as soon as it was built in 1592, and has always been a source of anxiety.")

We don't have many leaning towers ourselves, but we have a good few figures that we would like to see roll off a cliff. Over the years, we have managed to come to terms with the Albert Memorial, only to find that it is now entirely shrouded in hideous coverings for ever. It was supposed to be cleaned and made safe, but I have not seen or heard anybody at work there. (Here, I used to play my Albert Memorial trick; if you studied the figure you could see that Albert holds a book in the crook of his arm. The trick was to ask: what is the book? No, it is not the Bible – too obvious. Nor Queen Victoria's Diaries. I would offer a clue: it is most apposite. Even then, very few got the answer.)

And now, I learn that the Admiralty Arch is up for sale; like everybody else, I thought it was a joke, and it isn't. Why can't these pests be sent to Edinburgh and made to live for the rest of their lives on the steps of the Scott Monument? And how goes the rescue of the Taj Mahal? When last I heard, the battle to clear from the sky the dreadful poisons which are rotting that great monument was under way; any news?

(And Albert's book? It is, of course, the catalogue to the Great Exhibition of 1851.)

The Times, 19 July 1996

Leave them to God

I STARE AT what I see lying beside my keyboard, as though someone had put it there while I was not looking. It is not so; I know perfectly well what it is, and my problem is to believe my eyes. It is one of the myriad learned journals that scholarship produces: *The Journal of Contemporary History*, *The Journal of Common Market Studies*, *The Journal of Public Policy*, *The Journal of Business Finance and Accounting*, *The Journal of the International Phonetic Association*, *The Journal of Law and Society*.

And *The British Journal of Holocaust Education*.

Did *you* know that there was such a haunting volume rubbing shoulders with *The Journal of Narrative Technique* and *The Journal of Musicological Research*? I didn't. Well, the best thing is to open it and study it. So we do. It is no hoax, but as serious as its title, and indeed it displays the mark of a serious subject: footnotes. The first item in this issue of *The Journal of Holocaust Education* is entitled "The Murder of One and a Half Million Jewish Children by the Nazis in Europe 1940-45", and it has 47 footnotes. Idly, I doodle, to stop myself thinking about what those words mean. I go so far as to say that the figures reveal a slaughter of 32,000 children per footnote.

Rage swims to the surface; how the people who run *The Journal of Holocaust Education* (issues twice a year) can stand it, I cannot imagine. It is all very well to say that they are academics, and therefore must put feelings aside, but how do you put aside the feelings of a million and a half murdered children?

The title chosen for the journal is an interesting one;

not "The Journal of the Holocaust", but "The Journal of Holocaust *Education*". Presumably, it wants to teach those who need teaching on the subject. But who are they? Not children, I take it; certainly, the Holocaust should be taught in schools when children reach the right age, but this admirable journal can hardly offer the kind of Holocaust studies that the young would understand.

For a moment, I wondered whether there *should* be a *Journal of Holocaust Education*; if, in ages to come, the Holocaust is forgotten, or at least shuffled off as something in the past which has nothing to do with the present, we shall have failed to keep the flame burning, and then it matters not whether learned journals publish interesting matter on the subject which perhaps only scholars will read.

These thoughts did not come to me by accident. The bandages are being torn off once again. When, in 1991, the War Crimes Act was going through Parliament I took no side; partly, I have to admit, because I was convinced that it would never be used. Well, it is now about to be used, and the signs are going up again, and the arguments are being refurbished.

Now, I must tread warily. None of my family or friends died in the Holocaust, but I know people whose relations did, and they have a right to feel things that I can only feel from a distance. For those who have come to the argument even later than me, I must give an outline of what will soon be a deeply painful episode.

At the end of the war, there were many monstrous criminals who had committed terrible crimes – crimes that no era before had seen. These criminals ranged from the little man who turned the switch at the gas chambers to the big men who were indicted in the Nuremberg trials, who were tried, judged and punished. But of course not all were captured, and many lived long and died in their beds. (Many of these took shelter in the French churches, where they were safe and warm because the murderers of Jews would naturally be well looked after. Charming, don't you think?)

Some of these fugitives managed to make it to Britain, and in the chaotic aftermath of war there would inevitably be some who were never unmasked, and who lived and died as British citizens. I must remind you that I am talking about people and matters from half a century ago, so details, as you may realise, can hardly be exact. But – perhaps it should be so – the criminals who had escaped justice in Britain were not the only figures in this terrible story; there were also those who escaped death from the Nazis and who came to Britain with families dreadfully decimated.

Two plus two makes four. If the murderers have lived in Britain unrevealed (and there is evidence that they have), should they, even after this length of time, be revealed and punished? This argument was fought out in both Houses of Parliament, and the result was the War Crimes Act, 1991. And now the terrible chickens are coming home to the terrible roost, for those who demand an eye for an eye – and why should they not? – are waiting for the War Crimes Act to be put into effect, while others shake their heads and say let the dead bury the dead.

Because, you see, since the War Crimes Act came into force, people have begun to name names. And not only names, but numbers; there are seven men over whom there lies a terrible shadow. If the seven are murderers, what do we do with them? But if the seven are spotless, how can they show their innocence?

In our judicial system we do not have a statute of limitations, and the twin shadows have stretched themselves to an infinite length. Now we must settle that which cannot be settled, for though the law does not hasten, neither does it forget.

The Attorney-General, Sir Nicholas Lyell, has to decide in each case whether prosecutions should be set in hand.

But should the cases go forward at all? I believe they should not.

Here, I am on difficult ground; as I have said, no one from

my family suffered, and it is impossible for those who left behind others who died not to think of vengeance. (Though I believe that some who did suffer nevertheless reject the option of punishment.)

The truth is that those who did not suffer at the hands of the Nazis cannot fully understand that suffering. And yet I must make my plea, and it has two strands. First, how can we be sure, after half a century, that we have got the right men? One of these has already been "indicted", and will soon stand trial. He is 83 years old; they are all old men. The passage of time puts lines on men; their hair falls out or changes colour, marks on their bodies may be innocent or may be the tell–tale scars.

It is a terrible thing to make a mistake that kills a man or imprisons him till death. I believe that after many centuries of hanging in Britain we abolished the practice not because it was barbarous (though it was), but because anyone with any conscience would shiver at the thought that a man or woman might be hanged by mistake. Nor is that fanciful; in my own lifetime men and women have been hanged who, years later, were found innocent, posthumously. But alas, a posthumous apology is not much use.

You may say that even if the seven men are plainly guilty, they will not be hanged. No, but they will remain in prison for the tiny remainder of their lives. And will that bring back to life those who died so abominably? I say, leave them to history; or better still, leave them to God. We can be sure that if it is the latter, there will be no mistakes.

Vengeance, true vengeance, the kind that justifies itself, is necessary. But forgiveness is far greater. Seven old men, who will anyway soon be dead, may or may not have committed terrible crimes. Will a trial end the pain? Will it roll back the years? Will – I have to look down at my shoes as I write the words – will the dead come back to life?

And when your own time to die comes, will death be more easy because your last days were filled with hate? Oh, yes, fully justified hate, but whoever found hate a satisfactory meal? Better far to forget, or at least forgive. Easily said, by me, but not by the survivors. So the only words left must be these: Be merciful.

The Times, 25 July 1995

Run for a bun

IN ALL THE world's countries – certainly in all the very many countries I have visited or even heard of – there are people who are significantly different from the rest. Of course there are vast numbers of "differents" everywhere, from those who love broccoli and yoghurt to those who shin up drainpipes, climb through windows and steal jewellery. But I am not talking about that kind of difference; I am talking about those who – in the vulgar – are so different that passers-by are tempted to tap their foreheads as they hurry past. And for reasons I cannot fathom, and I think are not fathomable, almost all of these are to be found in the United States.

Do you remember the tragedy of Jim Jones – "Jonestown" – when this savage madman told his followers to drink poison and that they would therefore go to heaven, whereupon they drank it? Do you remember the similar horror at Waco, when another nut and his followers burnt themselves to death? Do you know that there was another of these sieges at Ruby Ridge, Idaho? What inspires American people – and people in significant numbers – to believe that they can be made immortal if they follow an obvious lunatic?

I have recently come back from America, where I found myself watching from the wings another of these self-immolations, though happily this one gave up without bloodshed. Happily, yes, but when I tell you that the group had been holding out for 81 days, and every day could have been a massacre, surely you will agree that there is something about the United States which is not to be found elsewhere. (No, I have not forgotten Dunblane, but that was greatly different from the American blood-lettings.)

Mind you, when the men and women of the stand-off had filed out peaceably, there was much more to come, because the filers, it turned out, had filed out with millions of dollars in bogus cheques, and when the judge started proceedings, the filers threatened to kill him. So if you were thinking that the Freemen (that is what they call themselves) should be patted on the head, you should take care that they don't bite you. For those amazing people who held out for 81 days were, in blunt British terms, a pack of more or less dotty libertarian extremists. Outside, the loonies and semi-loonies were having a high old time; the publisher of the far-right (and *how* far-right!) magazine *Free American* was saying "It's just another small part of how the Government keeps America divided."

Now I started by saying that the United States has peculiar ideas and is not shy of exhibiting them. But that is the terrible side of our friendly cousins. There is, of course, a side to America which exhibits no violence. But I am not just measuring the violent side and the peaceful side, I want to examine another extraordinary facet of the United States. It comes under the heading of intensity. And I know no other country that uses enormous intensity not just on its dark side but on the bright side as well. (I once listed countries by the number of murders by handguns a year – the list read: Britain 33; Sweden 36; Switzerland 97; Canada 128; Australia 13; Japan 60, and the United States 13,220. I doubt if there has been any substantial change.)

But return to the matter of intensity. Of course, we would classify murder under the flag of intensity – what else could it be called? But the very strange thing is that American intensity is just as strong when it is contemplating murder as when it is contemplating a McDonald's, and I say that not as a grim gibe. For I shall now put the two together, and tell me whether there is a not a clear and distinct similarity between them.

Between the two? Between a passion of men out of control with savage violence and others mildly asking for their fondest bun to be improved? Yes, and you might note that each of these two items from the newspapers – the story of the mad savages and the story of the popular comestible – took up the same number of pages: five.

Now for McDonald's and the precious – apparently very precious – bun. I have to admit immediately that I have never eaten a McDonald's meal, or indeed entered one of its speckless eateries, and this goes for Burger King as well, to say nothing about Wimpy (surely the man who invented it?); but before the McDonald's lawyers – I bet they have thousands and thousands of them – descend upon me, saying that I have said wicked things about their immaculate foodstuff, I must say that I do not propose to say anything at all about the nature or taste or quality of this no doubt delicious sweetmeat. All I propose to do is to discuss the almost incredible lengths that McDonald's will go to to promote a new burger.

I said five pages, and I meant it. True, we are talking about what happens in the United States, but the very new American McDonald's kick-off itself is enough to make your head swim: many ordinary goods and services are helped into the market by a simple giveaway, but what would you say when you discovered (as I did) that as a promotion – promotion! – McDonald's has given away, free, *50 million dollars-worth* of burgers?

The new burger (nobody has as yet discussed the possibility of throwing in an ingot of pure gold to go with the burger, but give them time) is called the Arch Deluxe, and although it has gone off pretty well, in the McDonald's boardroom there is apparently a frown or two. Hence the headlines (oh yes, in America burgers are frequently to be found in the headlines) saying "Consumers not exactly flipping for new burger", "Arch may not be much of a triumph" and "No one really knows if this sandwich will have legs".

So, solemnly, McDonald's called up the infantry: the Arch Deluxe has got its polling firm, Louis Harris and Associates, and we now have seen what we have seen. For the pollsters have announced that one quarter of the American adult population have eaten a McDonald's Arch Deluxe. But that means (because many will have eaten more than one, and very many children have eaten lots and lots) that we must, even more solemnly, say that McDonald's Arch Deluxe has been eaten by not less than 80 million people, and the end is not yet in sight.

Then the figures begin to make me reel: 69 per cent said they might eat another; 90 per cent said they would not go to McDonald's more often just because of the Arch Deluxe; 60 per cent prefer the Big Mac to the Arch Deluxe. And do you remember that incredible figure – 50 million dollars-worth free to promote Arch Deluxe? Well, stop remembering the 50 million dollars, because McDonald's has announced that it is going to spend *two hundred million dollars* to promote the Arch Deluxe.

And this, dear readers, is nothing but a bun. A bun, moreover, that is not something amazingly new; it is, after all, what oldies like me call a hamburger, *viz.*, chopped steak, a bit of salad and two buns to hold the steak. In even more familiar language, it is a sandwich. I have nothing against a sandwich, but surely nobody would buy one because of its startling newness. Well you and I wouldn't, but 80 million have already done so.

And at last I come round from where I started. Well-cooked steak, I grant you, is hardly a subject to discuss when murder has just been making the running, but please go back to where I started. My theme was intensity, which I think – no, I am sure – is woven into all or most countries, but most deeply and darkly into the fabric of America.

Terrible things happen in almost all countries. But the United States takes the prize. It is not just Waco, Ruby Ridge, Jonestown and the vast numbers more. It is something – as I call it – like intensity. And, as I say, it has also a sunlit side. I repeat: all countries have their eccentricities, even if only in their religion. But the United States, I firmly believe, is absolutely *sui generis* in this matter. And when you think that the matter in hand includes not only hamburgers, but ghastly multiple murderings, surely it is that unique intensity which makes vast pools of blood, and simultaneously makes chopped steak.

The Times, 26 July 1996

Gentility? What's that?

THAT INDEFATIGABLE MAN Digby Anderson, together with his cohorts, has recently put out a substantial volume with the remarkable title *Gentility Recalled*, and the subtitle *Mere Manners and the Making of Social Order*. But perhaps I should say a word or two for those who do not know Digby and his splendid army. He is the head of a group called, most mellifluously, the Social Affairs Unit and the Acton Institute For the Study of Religion and Liberty, and the previous book in the series is called *The Loss of Virtue: Moral Confusion and Social Disorder in Britain and America*.

Gentility Recalled has work by 11 pairs of hands, plus a foreword, and the names and essay titles make very clear what kind of book this is. Here they are:

Digby Anderson. The Little Things that Matter: Trivia and the Maintenance of Social Order.

Caroline Moore. Being a Gentleman: Manners, Independence and Integrity.

Rachel Trickett. Being a Lady: The Protection of Courtesy.

George Martin. Speaking Properly: The Need for a Shared Vocabulary.

Anthony O'Hear. Knowing Your Place: Manners between the Generations.

Athena S. Leoussi. Keeping up Appearances: Clothes as a Public Matter.

Simon Green. Playing the Game: Sport and the
Learning of Manners.

John Shelton Reed. Flirting and Deferring: Southern
Manners.

Robert Grant. Respecting the Truth: Manners in
the Academy.

Bruce Charlton. Keeping Your Distance: Manners
in the Surgery.

Michael D. Aeschliman. Running a Respectable
Household: Habits of the Home and Social Order.

H. Tristram Engelhardt, Jr. Why Do It? Because
That's What We Do: Manners in the Ruins of Community.

Now a mere glance down that list will show that the authors
are all unhappy, and indeed much more than unhappy, about
the way the world is going, at least in the areas of decency,
honesty, courtesy, law and order, cleanliness, and – I steel
myself to say the word, knowing that vast numbers of people
do not know what it means – manners.

This book, *Gentility Recalled*, speaks of a time in which
gentility not only existed but – and throughout all the lay-
ers of society – behaved as though gentility was something
to go by. Manifestly, that has disappeared in its entirety, and
the authors are not so foolish as to think that that world
will come again, but they want to discover *why* it died,
and they also want to study what it has been replaced by.
I also want to know why the world has changed so much
and so dreadfully, and I sought the answer from *Gentility
Recalled*.

At that point, I was going to start my investigation,
but I was stopped not so much in my tracks as in my
stupefaction, for my eye had caught a tiny "cut" in
the *Sunday Telegraph*: a child had called out "My dad
couldn't get into his flat: they said they'd smash his head
in if he tried," and that threat had also been made by
children.

Now, *Gentility Recalled* is not made only of disappointments, it has to face – and I also must face – a world in which the children are criminals. So I went on reading about these children of 14, who steal, smash cars, smoke drugs openly, and cannot be apprehended.

Well, well, we all know about crime, and we are sufficiently grown-up to shrug when *Gentility* is under discussion. But we must look at the word *Recalled* as well as *Gentility*; why, and how, did our world turn into something in which "An average of one secondary school head is assaulted every week by the father or mother of a pupil . . . One Hampshire teacher whose face was gashed by the mother of a 13-year-old boy said: 'Despite the fact that this woman was fined £50 by the local magistrates for the attack, her son is still at the school. She stormed into my classroom, shouting hysterically. Then she flew at me, clawing at me with her fingernails for two or three minutes, and I saw blood all over my shirt.'"

Very well; just *how* is *Gentility Recalled*? Well, take me and my coevals. In a train, for us not to offer a lady a seat – indeed our own seat – would be quite impossible. Similarly, it would be impossible not to stand when a lady comes into the room. The same goes for a lady and gentleman walking on the pavement together; the gentleman would instantly take the outer side. Oh, and therefore it is obvious that a lady *always* goes first.

Now I know that that last paragraph will be regarded as lunacy. Indeed, in some quarters it is now regarded as impudent and offensive. I cannot help it; that is what I learnt as a child, and I cannot, and will not, unlearn it until I die.

Call it my generation, call it respect, call it duty or whatever you like, but when, only a year or two ago, a lady to whom I was speaking casually said that that very morning she was travelling in the Underground, and not only did a man fail to offer her a plainly vacant seat but pushed her roughly out of the way to get to the seat for himself, I found it almost impossible to believe that such a thing could happen.

Yet, for some – I am one – gentility *is* recalled. What is more, we are not talking about something in far-off days; the thing has happened within just a few years. The writers of *Gentility Recalled* all knew that their cause was lost before they started to recall it; indeed, they quite realise that in another few years nobody reading *Gentility Recalled* will understand it.

Take the very first section. The question is: whence comes the demoralisation of society in the modern era? That it has happened no one can possibly deny. Very well; but why did it happen? Yes, the diminution of culpability has done it, but I ask again, where did the diminution come from?

Was it money? Kingsley's marvellous riposte would be very faint today: "Let the rich be as rich as they will, I, and those like me, covet not money but manners." Anthony O'Hear puts it plainly when he says "Acting one's age: better a young fogey than an ageing trendy," and goes on to say:

> . . . far more foolish, and far more dangerous to society as a whole, is it when the middle-aged – who, after all, should have the experience and wisdom to know better – comport themselves as if they were young: when they dye their hair, have their faces lifted and wear baseball caps back to front (or even the right way round) and shell-suits and trainers; when they buy exercise bicycles, jog in public and go ten-pin bowling and listen to pop on Walkmans; when they go to wine bars and discos with their secretaries; when they talk to the young as if they, too, were young.

Some time ago, when I was among a group of friends, the talk turned to clothing, and then specifically to jeans, their usefulness or clumsiness or cheapness. From a pause in the chatter, a friend murmured: "I don't think we shall ever see Bernard wearing jeans." The friend was right, but why was she right? The chapter on dress in *Gentility Recalled* is quite startling in its meaningfulness; dress *is* important – not for showing off, nor to be one of the boys. I always don a dinner jacket and stiff shirt for Covent Garden, but that has always been because it gives me extra pleasure through the opera. But Athena Leoussi (her chapter in *Gentility Recalled*) makes it much more than that.

And Simon Green goes further; his contribution is about cricket, and if you think that cricket is not sufficiently important or significant, what do you think the phrase "It's not cricket" means? For that matter, why do you think Robert Mugabe, the Prime Minister of Zimbabwe, says: "Cricket civilises people and creates good gentlemen. I want everyone to play cricket in Zimbabwe; I want ours to be a nation of gentlemen." (If I may stir the pot, let me remind you that Mugabe is savagely hostile to homosexuality.)

Reading this catalogue of *Gentility Recalled*, I find it impossible not to mourn. Again and again, I turn the pages for this wonderfully full story – a story that has died. Digby Anderson is as tough as they come, but such a gentle title is enough to bring tears to Digby's eyes, and for that matter mine.

Everything changes; I am not such a fool as to think that gentility was likely to stay for ever, but I rage when I read such words as Digby's: "When a later generation abandoned manners as 'repressive' or 'bad faith' it gave itself up to selfishness unlimited by thought for others. That sort of selfishness, in fact, makes everyone less free." Gentility, thy name is besmirched.

The Times, 7 June 1996

Gentility Recalled *can be ordered through bookshops, or directly from the publishers at the following address:*

Social Affairs Unit,
2, Spey Close,
Altringham,
Cheshire,
WA14 4UG

The book costs £15.95 plus £2 postage and packing.

A grubby housekeeper

IT IS SAID that there is honour among thieves. Perhaps. But it is quite certain that there are thieves among honour, as the Prince of Wales has recently discovered, to his dismay.

The name of Wendy Berry is unlikely to make a stir among the chancelleries of Europe; indeed, until a few weeks ago, it would have been known to only a handful of people, and practically all of those would be merely her family and friends. Now, however, she steps into the limelight, and a pretty garish limelight too. For Wendy Berry used to be the housekeeper at Highgrove, the residence of the Prince and Princess of Wales. Well, you say; a housekeeper is a very useful person, but not, surely, one to make the headlines. In the ordinary way, I would agree with you, but you see, Wendy Berry is, among other things, a cheat, a breaker of sworn – literally sworn – promises, and one who dare not set foot in this, her native country, because the might of the law would fall upon her.

And what has she done to provoke such anger? Has she stabbed a policeman, robbed a bank at the point of a gun, been found behaving indecently in Hyde Park after sunset? No such luck – no such luck, that is, for Prince Charles.

For Wendy Berry has struck gold, and perhaps lots of gold, and that eternally sought-after substance drags her from solemn promises and dips her into such a mire that she will never again be clean.

Mrs Berry, it seems, not only did the housekeeping at Highgrove, she did the eavesdropping as well. She claims (though there is no obligation to believe anything she says) that she has written a book about the lives of the Prince and Princess of Wales, which, she says, is filled with the most private intimacies of the Prince and his consort. With this, she thought, rightly as it happens, she could make money. (The "book" is called *The Housekeeper's Diary*.)

But there was first a hitch, in the form of the law. Mrs Berry, when she was housekeeper for the royal pair, signed a confidentiality agreement (I believe that all staff taken on royal payroll have to make such a promise), and the Prince duly went to the High Court for an injunction and got it. Mrs Berry, it seemed, was stymied. Then someone in the United States surmised that money could be made out of this housekeeper's reminiscences, and in no time they were selling like hot, but rancid, cakes. Whence the heap of gold in Mrs Berry's apron. And whence, also, Mrs Berry's flight from these shores. For if she had tried to publish what she was trying to sell in Britain, she would have found herself in contempt of court.

As I write, Mrs Berry is in Toronto, presumably whipping up sales for that market, having done the same in the United States. And you can hear her licking her lips as (presumably) the money comes rolling in. For instance (I borrow from the *Mail*'s George Gordon):

> I expected them to go after me and I knew it would get rough. They will stop my pension and they will probably seize my house. They will go after everything I have, but they won't get my money from the book. I'll hide it offshore. I have got to be very careful, even here, because I think the Royal Family and the British courts would like to put me in jail. I know they want to get me for contempt. They want to make an example of me so no one else will dare speak out about the real life of the royals. I am not greedy or grasping [the book could earn her £150,000], I just want enough money to live in relative comfort for the rest of my life.

So do we, dearie, so do we. But most of us get it

by working hard, not by cheating and breaking promises.

But before I change the subject, I have to give the Prince bad tidings. He is said to be "utterly determined" to prevent Mrs Berry profiting. Quite right, and I cheer him on. But it won't work, I'm afraid; just cast your mind back, Highness, to the *Spycatcher* absurdity, in which practically every country in the world was printing, publishing and selling the book, while Britain was supposed to be ignorant of its contents. The whole thing became a joke; people were playing a game of "I brought back four copies from America", "Ah, but I brought back *six*". And, more to the point, the very prohibition made it certain that people who had little or no interest in the matter were sufficiently intrigued to change their minds. And so, I regret to say, it will be with the Prince.

But I want to widen this argument. Mrs Berry is a shoddy breaker of promises who breaks her oath for money; but once upon a time she wasn't. I said that it was the pull of gold that turned her into what she has become, but it does not need money to do the dirty; there are plenty of oath-breakers, and a vast number of ways of doing the breaking. I believe, in short, that yet another bastion has fallen, and honour has begun to be a joke.

Obviously, the decline and fall began in politics, but I do not say that politics was rotten from the start. In my days in the Parliamentary Press Gallery, I made mock of the politicians below, but I very rarely thought any of them dishonourable. Oh, I never thought that they were angels utterly different from us – there was enough indiscriminate fornication to put that idea aside. But there is a great distinction between the weak flesh and the grubby deal. As I recall, two MPs were expelled in those days, and one of them wept audibly and visibly as he went; today, when two MPs were found whose shame was parallel to those who went before, it took three months to find a way of *keeping* them in the House, and it was finally settled by a ludicrous apology.

Of course, what I am talking about is by no means confined to politics. I do believe that honour has been not just sidelined, but turned into a weak and ghostly shadow of itself. Take a very trivial but very meaningful signal; I haven't travelled by the Tube for many years, but I have recently been astounded to learn (from someone who does) that not only do men no longer stand up to give their seats to women, but they now shove women aside to get to the seats; and as if that isn't enough, I am assured that it is commonplace for an obviously pregnant woman to be standing up until another *woman* comes to the rescue. (And if any woman says that I am a sexist pig who doesn't know that giving up his seat is a disgusting thing to do, I shall throw my lifelong chivalry out of the window and set her knickers on fire.)

And what about today's crime? I leave murder and attempted murder alone, so extraordinary is the thought of it for me, and I look at less terrible actions. I know I am repeating what thousands have been saying for years, but I must say it again. I have friends who live in a country village. How few years ago was it that they could go out and leave their home unlocked, unguarded, unthreatened? Ten years? Not more, I think. And now they would be thought mad if they were to go out for half an hour without locking up and putting the Neighbourhood Watch sign on the door.

There is another side to money-grabbing, and it doesn't involve crime. Remember those women soldiers who got themselves pregnant, were naturally discharged, and then scooped hundreds of thousands of pounds? And every day many more thousands are mopped up by other scams; a grazed knee can call down enough to buy a new house; a trivial word can be puffed up to half a million in the libel courts; tribunals abound, distributing thousands as they go. The very word "benefits", spoken aloud, is enough to start a stampede to the trough.

I come back to Mrs Berry. What of her now? Is perpetual banishment from her native land worth the bawbees – even thousands of bawbees? And when the money has run out –

and be very sure that it will – when those who paid for her treachery have no longer any use for her, what then?

Ah, but by then the slide towards the mire will be so fast that Mrs Berry will be forgotten, and cheats and oath-breakers will be ten a penny. I earnestly hope that by then I shall be dead.

The Times, 8 August 1995

Homo sapiens for ever

I AM NOTORIOUSLY GULLIBLE when it comes to science, but there are limits to my credulity. When I saw a headline – a small headline, to be sure, but a headline nevertheless – reading "Water is found on the Sun", I took out my trusty credule, ready to hit someone with it. Our science editor tells me that the surface of the Sun has a temperature of approximately 6,000°C ("Who hath measured the ground?"), so I decided that any boffins who wish to slake their thirst on the Sun should also wear light clothing.

I jest, but that is only to annoy the sillier scientists, and you wouldn't believe how silly those can be. They sometimes write to me, and can hardly hold the pen with rage to see me with thumb to nose (hardly scientific behaviour, don't you think?).

But, as I say, that is only to cause annoyance. No one, surely, can contemplate the wonders of the heavens and of the deeps without feeling awe; well, so it is with science. Many people make the mistake of believing that some of the more weird experiments that scientists carry out are not only otiose but absurd. As a matter of fact, that is true, and many a taxpayer gets hot under the collar (though not quite 6,000°C) when he sees a man in a white coat, presumably sane, measuring the length of the average cat's whiskers. I sometimes wonder whether, if Professor Doll had never come upon his truly epoch-making discovery – that smoking is dangerous – the world might be just as well off, or even – perish the thought – very slightly better.

There is a dark side to science, and many scientists

acknowledge that darkness, which takes the form of "If it can be done, it must be done". When Professor Christiaan Barnard did the first heart transplant in 1967, the world was stunned, and he was hailed as not only one of the greatest scientists in all history, but almost as a man who had found the way to abolish death. His first patient, Louis Washkansky, lived only 18 days, but by then the sluice gates had been flung open. As I recall, the only voice raised against the hero was that of Malcolm Muggeridge; who will now say that Muggeridge was wrong? How much knowledge, effort, money and bed-space was – still is – being wasted on the glamorous successes of science, instead of the dozens of unglamorous hip-replacements that knowledge, effort, money and bed-space need? This is the red rag of sense to the bull of science, but it still rankles, and it is still true.

But pause for a moment with those words, "Barnard had found the way to abolish death". They are not nearly as ridiculous as they should be. Deep down in the thoughts of millions, and not only in the thoughts of the old, there lingers a belief – not spoken, of course – that the abolition of death is coming closer, and many are found looking over that non-existent horizon to see the Sun rise over eternal life. Well, Barnard has shown the way, hasn't he? So the next step must be living for ever, mustn't it? No matter that the only thing every human creature without exception must endure (and every animal for that matter, though they don't make such a fuss about it) is death. Say it again: "If it can be done, it must be done."

But it *has* been done; it was done some 300 years ago, in the ingenious mind of Jonathan Swift. Swift called up a people, the Struldbrugs, who did indeed live for ever, but there was a catch in it (of course there always is), for the Struldbrugs had to live with all the infirmities of body and mind, which went on getting worse, becoming more and more terrible, so terrible that they prayed for death, and were refused it.

There are real Struldbrugs. Two Chinese refugees, who

had escaped to America, testified that the Chinese Government removes organs from executed prisoners and sells them for use in medical transplants, which of course is nothing compared with the more recent revelations of the Chinese "dying rooms" in which superfluous babies are left unfed and unattended in their filth until they die.

I feel a little queasy; doctors, of course, are trained not to be queasy, but before I come back to the best in science, may I pause for a moment and ask the scientists what they think about that slogan "If it can be done . . ." What proportion of our scientists live by that rubric? Do these applaud the Chinese spare parts system? After all, these people are dead, and now have no need of bodies.

I know it is tiresome, but I must ask: where does science stop, and "If it can be done, it must be done" begin? More tiresomely still, if the scientists say that there can be no such division, how does it come about that ordinary people, with no scientific knowledge, can quite easily understand the question?

Enough of interrogations: let us look at the bright side of science, and as it happens, we have a shaft of light so powerful that it would illuminate most of the dark side. Did you read the story of Professer Cano of California and the bacteria, patient creatures that they are? Patient indeed, because if Professor Cano is right, the bacteria – *live bacteria* – have been asleep for upwards to 30 million years, and this is the hour in which the doors are flung open, and the bacteria, shaking their heads and stretching, emerge.

Thirty million years. To make the story even more marvellous, we learn that the little creatures slept through the centuries in tropical amber. Amber itself is a mysterious thing; mysterious enough, anyway, to find that a ball of amber (perhaps in a bracelet or necklace) has turned the tables, and trapped a fly or even a bee.

Already, Professor Cano has been under attack; he is not denounced as a fraud, but those scientists who cannot believe the Professor's *trouvaille* argue that some modern bacteria must have got into his, by contamination. The Prof denies that, and insists that he was working in the most meticulous conditions. I hope he is proved right, and I think most people hope with me.

Why? Why do people – very much including me – want to believe that the Prof is right? It is, I am sure, the feeling of awe, a sensation that has been withering away for a good many years now, and will die entirely unless there is something or someone to breathe life into it. Professor Cano has done precisely that; he may put it in different words, but I am certain that he walks with a spring, his eyes glow, and he sings in the bath. Not because if he is right he will get into the science books, even the encyclopaedias (though it seems that these are disappearing fast), but because he has tasted awe, and that taste lasts for ever.

With the warmth of Professor Cano wrapped round me, I am almost willing to believe that there is water on the Sun, but I don't need to, because once again, science has come up with something I can understand, or can almost understand. There is a tussle in the undergrowth; it seems that scientists have been trying to discover when the first "men" walked the Earth. The boffins worked with chromosomes, which are beyond me, but it seems that we are all descended from African ancestors (one in the eye for whitey) who lived between 100,000 and 200,000 years ago, which rules out *Homo erectus*.

Again, we do not need to be experts in these matters; all we need is awe, and those thousands roll out to greet us. Never mind the brontosaurus and his cousins; something that we can recognise has been examined by science, and however primitive those ancestors of ours, we are assured that our forebears were not fishes or snakes or, for that matter, platypuses; we, however rudimentary we were, had somewhere in us, *Homo sapiens*.

Most of us are ignorant of science, but that is not entirely our fault; in their hearts the scientists despise us. Not just because *we* are ignorant, but because *they* are arrogant. When I wrote, earlier in this column, about the priorities we think vital, you brushed us away as though we were idiots. Come – where is there a leading scientist who will say clearly that it would have been better for the world if Christiaan Barnard had never been born, and his invention never thought of?

We cannot leave it there; happily we do not need to. A last item catches my eye, and the scientists are lining up. It seems that bees existed before flowers, but how can that be? Well, if you give us the answer, we shall give you the awe.

The Times, 20 October 1995

The Nazi legacy

Y ET AGAIN, THE shadow of the Holocaust throws its
darkness upon the dead and the living. Once again the
earth stirs, hell breathes its poisons, goodness shines, and the
Times headline tells it all: "Daughter hunts for painting of
father who died under Nazis". Here is the story:

> Lilly Gill, 73, was 15 when she made a dramatic escape
> from Czechoslovakia to Britain with her younger sister.
> Their father, who went into hiding after helping his
> daughters to flee, was dragged from his bed in the early
> hours by Nazi troops rounding up Jews.
>
> Mrs Gill says: "My father, unable to escape from
> Prague where my parents had fled from Germany,
> died in a concentration camp. I believe it was at
> Theresienstadt." Her mother, who was not Jewish,
> was arrested for trying to protect her husband, but was
> eventually released. Later she received a curt official
> note: "Your husband died in 1940."

You can feel the chill, can you not? Five words of unimaginable evil, and look at it how you will, it says that evil
rules the world, does it not, and there is nothing else?
Nothing? *Nothing?* But there was something, wasn't there?

> We made a miraculous escape by train. It was a precari-
> ous journey. The train stopped on the way. Nazi officials
> searched everything. We hadn't got proper passports.
> Our documents were invalid. Tessa talked to the Nazi
> official. One of the officials looked at the passports and

disappeared with them. He looked grim. We thought we would be arrested. But he returned them. Nothing was said. I think he did it as an act of mercy.

And the picture? Mrs Gill now seeks it high and low, and well she might, for it is a picture of a child prodigy – which Mrs Gill's father was – at the piano. This was in 1891, when Nazis did not exist and Mrs Gill's father had glowing write-ups, such as "The boy gave an outstanding performance of his skill on the piano. The audience was captivated and gave him tremendous applause."

Little did the infant Levin know, when he weekly haunted the Albert Hall and from the very top gallery (one shilling) heard again and again that great violinist Bronislav Hubermann, *accompanied by Leopold Spielmann, the man who was to be Mrs Gill's father, and who died in the Holocaust.* Repeat those words: "Your husband died in 1940", and if you want to cross yourself don't be shy.

Now come with me to Oxford; surely, a mere glance at the dreaming spires will show that no such memories could be found, nor such horrors dug up there. But wait; what stir do I see and hear; can it be something connected with the most terrible evil mankind has yet produced? And at *Oxford*? Alas, yes.

The stir begins like this. A new chair has been brought into Oxford, the Flick Chair of European Thought, and the first holder of the Chair is Professor John W. Burrow. The Chair was made possible by a very substantial gift to the University: some £350,000. But the ice, it seems, was very thin – very thin indeed. Because, you see, the bare words "Flick Chair" are enough to have the dreaming spires collapsing, and even collapsing over the £350,000; for Friedrich Flick was one of the most evil men in the horror of the Holocaust.

Friedrich Flick was a giant maker of things, but when Hitler called, Flick came to the salute and put his evil genius at the feet of Hitler. Nor was he reluctant to do so; he used hundreds of thousands of slave labourers and Himmler relied on him. Indeed after the war he was indicted at the Nuremberg trials, and served time in prison.

And, you see, it would be somewhat embarrassing if Oxford had a Chair of Murderous Evil – nor, of course, would Oxford do such a thing. So what is to be done? Oxford is a delicate place, is it not? Well, its delicacy came to the rescue in this case. No longer will anyone call the Chair of European Thought the Flick Chair; from now on, it will be called the Dr Gert-Rudolph Flick Chair. And if you think that a mere trading of names would send all the participants home, you must realise that there is something more to come. The evil Flick must be very clearly distinguished from Dr Gert-Rudolph Flick, because, you see, Dr Gert-Rudolph Flick is the grandson of the evil Flick.

And we are back yet again to the terrible truth: good men can come from the loins of bad ones, and frequently do. Now do you know why I say – and say with pain, anger, weariness and unbelief – that I have repeatedly asked (but heard no answer) my question: "Great God, when will that tap stop dripping?"

Because I must now offend. These tiny embarrassments of Oxford are not particularly amusing, and for some the wounds have yet to close. In the delicate argument that went on, Ben Helfgott, who survived the Theresienstadt concentration camp, said wisely that the Flick money was soaked in blood but Dr Flick bore no personal guilt. Of course not; but as the Oxford argument went on, it was plain that some could not come to terms with the present, so terrible was the past. Mr Helfgott says that "There are still people today who will not listen to Wagner and who are bitterly opposed to anything tarnished by Nazism. Others feel you have to get on with things as they are."

Now I am not such a fool or knave as to wave away those people who say that they will not listen to Wagner. Here, I am walking on hot coals, but I cannot and will not run away from the argument.

Yes, Richard Wagner was an anti-Semite. So was Dostoevsky. And many more noble figures in the arts. What is the difference? Why is the difference so great that some music-lovers will not listen to his work?

To start with, I heard *Tristan and Isolde* a few days ago, at the ENO. It is one of the greatest works of art ever made. It was made by an anti-Semite, but if you had never discovered who wrote it – better still, never discovered that the writer was an anti-Semite – you would agree that it is a masterpiece of music, unless, of course, you don't like it.

But even then your dislike would not be *because* of anti-Semitism, for that evil would have never contaminated your feelings. Some people claim that they can hear anti-Semitism in the music; that is nonsense. No, Beckmesser is *not* an anti-Semite, and if you heard *The Mastersingers* for the first time, without any background, you would never think of anti-Semitism. So where does this strange and terrible mystery break out?

First, Hitler was a devoted Wagnerian. Second, Hitler murdered the Jews. It therefore follows that I, being a devoted Wagnerian, am also a murderer of Jews. So are most of the leading conductors, who are not only murderers but Jewish murderers, these being presumably murderers ready to deal with any Jews left over. I plead not guilty, and so do the conductors. We must, we *must*, we MUST distinguish between a bad man doing bad things, and a bad man doing ordinary things.

It is true that almost all of the family of Richard Wagner, from his birth (probably illegitimate – the argument continues) to the youngest member of the clan, are, and always have been, such as to bring a shudder through any ordinary person's body. As if that were not sufficient, they are always quarrelling – to such an extent that it is a miracle that nobody in that gang has yet been murdered. (They make up for it with regular and frequent banishments.) But if you knew nothing at all of that, and just went into an opera house with a programme, a translation and a surtitle, you would never guess either that the Wagners are awful, or that that wonderful music was written by an awful man.

In my daydreams I sometimes wonder what Mozart would make of Wagner. I believe that he would shake his head and get on with his work. But what would Beethoven say? I think he would listen, and even say that in years to come this music will hold the world in amazement.

I have wandered, but if I have to defend Wagner (Wagner's music I mean — no one could actually defend Wagner the man), I would argue — I *do* argue — that there is nothing evil in Wagner's music, and there is nothing evil in Hitler's listening to music.

For those who suffered at the hands of evil, and thus cannot bear to hear Wagner's music, I ask pardon. Remember, though, that one day Wagner will be a forgotten name, but his music is eternal.

The Times, 15 March 1996

Hitler's martial Jews

WHEN WILL THE Holocaust be the Holocaust, in all its terrible meaning and no more? When will professors stop finding a new "angle" on something that can never have an angle? When will the dreadful fools and madmen who prove that there was no Holocaust (I have just got another pamphlet saying as much), stop hating and even stop being mad?

Never, I fear, but I have long ago given up trying to convince fools and professors that my nose is of standard British length and width and no more. Wearily, I shrug, and say, yes, I am a Jew, and no, no member of my family died in the Holocaust. And, just to clinch it, no – my name has always been Levin, and never Featherstonhaugh-Golightly.

Now then. What would you say if Adolf Hitler were on his throne and the Holocaust was in full blast, but German Jews were not only serving in Hitler's ranks, but personally enlisting in those ranks. Not just to find a place that the Nazis might not spot, but with full intent to take part in the war on Hitler's side? It sounds lunatic, and in a sense it was. But read this:

It seems that those Jewish Germans who enlisted voluntarily and made efforts to remain in uniform even after their Jewish origins came under scrutiny by the authorities were allowed to do so. Indeed, some rose to high rank and several won the *Ritterkreuz*, the Knight's Cross of the Iron Cross, Germany's highest military decoration, awarded to fighter aces, U-boat captains and tank destroyers. They performed their feats of bravery at the height of the war, when the Nazi state was murdering German Jews in hundreds of thousands and the Jews of Eastern Europe in millions.

Only they can explain why they chose the path they did, and all are now old or already dead.

These almost unbelievable facts were dug up by a young American student, Bryan Rigg, who, in a chance meeting, was to reveal some of the most extraordinary true stories of the Second World War. Rigg did not even know, before he began his studies in this fascinating story, that he was of German-Jewish ancestry, but believed his family was of the Protestant Bible-belt, and among his amazements were the members of his family who had stayed in Germany and died in the Holocaust.

And now, with this extraordinary story at our elbows, we are tempted to believe that the whole thing is, and must be, a hoax. But it isn't. It is not only true, from top to bottom, it is terrible. Terrible, you say? Just glance at one headline (the story broke in the *Daily Telegraph*), reading "Why men of Jewish blood shed it for Adolf Hitler". Answer that.

I can't. Nor can anybody else. I am a Jew, and thus to be hated by Nazis; very well, I understand that, and shrug. But Mr Rigg has not just found a cache of almost unbelievable matter about Hitler's Reich and its evil madness, he has pointed a dagger at some of the newly known facts of the Holocaust, and – well, let me say it again: "Why men of Jewish blood shed it for Adolf Hitler". For they did, they did, they did.

Have you ever heard of Major Robert Borchardt? No? Nor had I until very recently. He was a half-Jew, and a very brave man, and a very great fighter on Hitler's side. He did not commit atrocities, nor did he allow them in his units. He fought in Russia, in Rommel's Afrika Korps, and he was strewn with medals. Not long before he died, he spoke to the children of his old school, and this is what he said: "Many German Jews and half-Jews who fought in the First World War and even in the Second World War believed that they should honour their Fatherland by serving in the military." And many of them did.

But what I want to know, and I imagine many others want to know, is *what did Jews think they were doing when they were fighting for Hitler?* Take the remarkable story – a perfectly true story – of the way Rabbi Schneerson was saved from the Nazis. The rabbi was the leader of the most ultra-orthodox Jews, and when the war broke he was trapped, and very likely to be killed by Hitler. There was a plea from the United States to let the Rabbi Schneerson go. It was touch and go; but then another German Jew, fighting in the war on the side of Hitler, took a hand: he was a very high officer, Ernst Bloch, who had fought in the First World War, and Schneerson was saved.

And saved in the most macabre manner imaginable. Admiral Canaris recruited Bloch, and then Hitler made the world go round the other way; with a half-Jew staring him in his face, Hitler read the appropriate document: "I, Adolf Hitler, leader of the German nation, approve Major Ernst Bloch to be of German blood. However, after the war, Ernst Bloch will be re-evaluated to see if he is still worthy to have such a title." (Who said Hitler was sane?)

But still the question must be asked and answered, why men of Jewish blood shed it for Adolf Hitler.

Most of those men are now dead, and the dead cannot speak. If they could speak, what might they say? There would be many who would say "I didn't know – how could I know? The whole world was there, and nobody knew – nobody knew what that man called Hitler would do to the world and millions upon millions."

Not enough. Not enough. You, the ones who were there, could see. Oh no, very few indeed could have guessed the whole of the madness (though even that could have been spotted and *was* by the tiny number who could read *Mein Kampf* from beginning to end), but that was not enough.

Very well, not enough. What next? We must try to think into the minds of the survivors, and what they did and what lies they told. There is a very old man, 82 and failing, who has asked for anonymity; he shall have it. But he says that he served six and a half years in Hitler's military, and became a captain. Presumably he drew the curtains when a Nazi went by.

That's small fry. What about a real field marshal, a good friend of Goering and indeed a very important figure in the Nazi camp, for it was he who made the Luftwaffe the tremendous thing it became. That was Field Marshal Milch, and he was a Jew. But a field marshal, surely, should know better. And so should a Jew.

Surely should? Did. *Did.* We come back to where we started. But not quite. For we now know the massive quantities of horror that poured out of Bryan Rigg's find. (It was luck, of a kind: he had just come out of a cinema and started to chat to another cinema-goer, a German, whereupon they began to speak, and the other man spoke of his life, whereupon "they talked until dawn". I bet they did.)

We come back to where we started yet again. What were real Jews or even half-Jews (and there were many of these) doing with Adolf Hitler? True, there were people who saw through Hitler very quickly, but were sure that he would be a busted flush in no time. Well, he wasn't, and in the end the blood poured copiously. And there was no shortage of important people; Helmut Schmidt, who became the Chancellor of West Germany for eight years, had when somewhat younger been very much in the wrong place.

This is yet another question that cannot be answered unless the dead rise from the grave to give the answers. It would be dreadful to say that the dead deserved what they got, because they didn't. Again, we hear the terrible words – how could we have known?

Perhaps the most pitiful or most deserved – you can take it either way – is that of Milch, the one who was "a personal friend of Hermann Goering". And instantly the thunder rolls; how does a Jew become a personal friend of Hermann Goering, and more to the point, why is he prepared to be one in the first place?

Milch was tried and convicted in the Nuremberg war trials; his Jewishness did not help him, and he was imprisoned for 10 years. But again and again, we ask the question, the question that cannot be answered. What was a Jew, or a half-Jew, doing with Adolf Hitler? God forbid that I should take sides in such a dreadful argument. It is enough that almost all the people concerned are now dead. But if they came to life, would they not instantly go back into the shades?

The Times, 6 December 1996

Odd volumes of stuff

I HAVE NEVER been a collector of books just for their covers and their dates of publication, much less for their bindings. As far as I am concerned, a book is something to read, and nothing else. Of course, I can and do admire a beautiful book as an object, as I would a picture or a jewel; I have had copies of my own 15 books beautifully bound, and I am not above running my fingertips over the lovely leather (tactile pleasures are just as worthy as the others). Moreover, I am a lifelong book sniffer – many an odd look I have had from many a bookseller.

But all of a sudden there came through my letter-box a booklet, handsomely put together, its beautiful pages hungry for sniffing, carefully illustrated, and a pleasure to handle. This, I realised, was a bookseller's catalogue, but it was in the category of rare books – and rare they must be, when some of them are priced in thousands, and indeed one would set you back no less than £28,000 (credit cards not accepted).

But you must remember that I am not looking at these books for their contents. Or that was what I thought as I flipped the pages, but in only a few moments I found myself steeped in the most fascinating and *recherché* matter, from which I could hardly extricate myself, and did not want to.

The very first item that caught my eye – and well it might – was labelled plainly "Lunacy", and the title reads: *Observations on the Nature, Kinds, Causes and Preventions of Insanity, Lunacy or Madness*. I assumed that it was some crude and meaningless item – the date was 1782 – and the author, Thomas Arnold, meant nothing to me. But then I looked at the bookseller's commentary.

> One of the seminal works in the history of psychiatry. Arnold ran a private mad-house in Leicester, and from 1794 was head of the Leicester Lunatic Asylum . . . He made two main divisions . . . hallucinatory and delusion insanity, with numerous subdivisions supported by case histories gathered from the literature and his own practice, some of which read like descriptions in modern textbooks . . .

Now who would think that such a treasure trove was lurking in the calm recesses of Mr J.F.T. Rodgers's "100 Rare Books on 100 Different Subjects"? Not I. Nor did I think that I would have found myself in the middle of an argument between a leading astronomer and Voltaire, and even if I had, I would not have imagined that Mr Rodgers would sign off so coolly – referring to the astronomer – with "He was executed in 1793".

What about Edward Barlow with his *Meteorological Essays, Concerning the Origin of Springs, Generation of Rain, and Production of Wind. With a Rational and Historical Account of the Causes and Course of the Tide: Its propagation thro' the Great Ocean?* Charming, you would say, and so it is. But Mr Rodgers is so profligate with his knowledge that when he has finished with the wind and the rain, he tells us that Barlow ". . . had earlier achieved some fame as the inventor of repeating clocks and watches".

Then there was a Casanova – not the one we know about, but the one who founded a new school of writing which was dominant for 150 years. That in itself may seem uninteresting, but Casanova II changed entirely the style of legal documents, so that it was based on simplicity. (What I want to know is who changed it all back again?)

But some things don't change at all. In 1737 we could read an edict that ran: *Abstracts of Several Laws and Rules*

That are now in Force, relating to the Importation of Wines into and out of Great Britain.

What astonished me most in my peeps into the past is the extraordinary number of ventures into the unknown. A German landed on Greenland in 1746 (and made fine engravings of birds of prey, whales, narwhals, as well as kayaks). From Hamburg to Iceland is not a great distance, nor, presumably, did Johann Anderson think it was when he landed. But what about those truly intrepid voyagers who went, in the 17th century, too, and what befell them?

What befell them was that they were captured and in time ransomed, but not before the sharp-eyed Emanual d'Aranda had made copious notes.

> Of all 17th-century travellers, Aranda is without doubt the one who had with least sophistication depicted the misery of slavery in Algeria . . . one of the most interesting and dramatic voyages of the 17th century.

But the next figure to leave a presumably comfortable home (in Mannheim) must have had a special pull, and indeed he had. He was a Jesuit, and his call took him to California, of all places. He lived for 16 years in the Mission, and left only when the Jesuits were driven out. Our bookman says: "Like most of the German Jesuits he found conditions in the Missions insufferable, and his book amply expresses this disenchantment." I am beginning to think that our splendid Mr Rodgers is a cynic.

But he *must* be cynical about the next item, because it is almost certainly a fake. That is, the travels that are recounted are probably fraudulent, but as a story – and a story in 1670 – they can certainly delight in the Münchhausen-like boasting, and the boasting is certainly powerful:

> The Late Travels of S. Giacomo Baratti An Italian Gentleman. Into the remote Countries of The Abassins, or Ethiopia Interior . . . An exact account of the Laws, Governments, Religion . . . With many Observations

which some may improve to the advantage and increase
of Trade with them . . . Together with a Confirmation
of this Relation drawn from the Writings of Damianus
de Goes. and Jo. Scaliger, who agree with the Author
in many particulars.

But there can be no mistake with the next story. First, it
emphasises the extraordinary wanderlust that has over the
centuries dragged so many men from their beds, to seek
– to seek what? Not necessarily gold, and in the case of
Captain Philip Beaver, certainly not. His title-page reads
like this:

> African Memoranda: relative to an attempt to establish
> a British Settlement on the Island of Buluma, on the
> Western Coast of Africa, in the year 1792, with a brief
> notice of the Neighbouring Tribes, Soil, Productions,
> and some observations on the Facility of Colonizing
> that part of Africa, with a view to Cultivation: and
> the Introduction of Letters and Religion to its Inhab-
> itants: but more particularly as the means of gradually
> abolishing African Slavery.

In 1792? Yes indeed, if you have a captain like Beaver. For
he said that the slave trade could be curtailed, if not ended,
by the growing of sugar cane. To prove it, he bought the
island from its king – King Niobana of Ghinala – and got
started. (Our intrepid explorer paid for the island with a
variety of goods, including an 18-gallon cask of brandy, five
handkerchiefs and six hats.)

Nor did the voyagers stop there. William Bruton sailed
to Bengal (or Beng alia as it was then called) in 1638, and
the first thing he did was to describe the indigenes and their
customs. "Also their detestable Religion, mad and foppish
rites and Ceremonies, and wicked Sacrifices and impious
Customes used in those parts". He too bartered successfully,
this time for trading concessions, for which he paid "Twenty
pounds of Cloves. Twenty pounds of Mace. Twenty pounds

of Nutmegs, two bolts of Damaske, one faire Looking-Glasse, one Fouling-piece, with two Locks, and one double Pistoll". (Ah, but that "faire Looking-Glasse"!)

I was on the verge of asking "But where were the pirates that these intrepid voyagers had to deal with?" when I turned the page and remembered that in those days the line between pirates and voyagers — and there were some famous names on the list — was very thin. What about this?

> Bucaniers of America: Or, a true Account of the Most Assaults committed of late years upon the Coast of The West Indies, by the Bucaniers of Jamaica and Tortuga . . . both English and French

And all of a sudden there comes a new Dictionary — but not a dictionary such as the OED. This one goes like this:

> A New Dictionary of the Terms Ancient and Modern of the Canting Crew, in its several Tribes, of Gypsies, Beggars, Thieves, Cheats. Useful for all sorts of People (especially Foreigners to secure their Money and preserve their Lives), besides very Diverting and Entertaining being wholly New.

But I think we should finish as we started — that is to say, among the curiosities of the world, and particularly Mr Rodgers's generous supply of those curiosities, with this:

> The Book of Feet. A History of Boots and Shoes, also Hints to Last Makers and Remedies for Corns.

Yours for £180.

The Times, 26 April 1996

A very ruddy duck

I BET I know more about the Ruddy Duck than you do. Bet? You'd lose your money, I can tell you. In fact, I'm so cocksure that I can say I know more about the Ruddy Duck than anyone you have ever met. Indeed, apart from the people who actually breed Ruddy Ducks, together with a very few ornithologists who specialise in the creatures, I am pretty sure that there is no one anywhere who could beat me at Ruddy Ducks, and Magnus Magnusson has booked me for *Mastermind* next season, special subject: Ruddy Ducks. (Between you and me, I think I know more about Ruddy Ducks than the Ruddy Ducks do themselves.)

Now you obviously want to know why I am so interested in Ruddy Ducks, and – more to the point – why I have become an expert in the subject all of a sudden. You must agree that I am much more at home with a Ruddy Duck that has been trussed, cooked and put upon my plate than one that has not yet stopped quacking. Yes, of course, but you must understand that when I tell you that the real subject of this grave matter is not actually the Ruddy Duck, but the White-Headed Duck, you will immediately realise that it is going not by its familiar name, but its real name, *Oxyura leucocephala*. (The real name of the Ruddy Duck is of course *Oxyura jamacicensis*. I take it that you understand.)

By now, however, you must have realised that some kind of document has got into my hands, and I am about to make fun of somebody or something with it. But before you get worried about the fate of the Ruddy Ducks and the White-Headed Ducks (and any other ducks that are going about) I must introduce the Ruddy Duck Working Group, and the first thing I wish to say on the subject is that I never knew it was there. The second thing I must say is that not only was I ignorant of the existence of the Ruddy Duck Working Group, but I was ignorant *a fortiori* of the fact that the Ruddy Duck Working Group comes under the aegis of the Vertebrate Ecology & Conservation Branch. The third thing I must say is that I am not at all sure that I want to know all that.

But cannot these creatures go about their business without help? Or have all webs become loose through some strange malfunction? No, the problem is, I am sorry to say, one that human beings are prone to; for when the White-Headed Duck is waddling about, doing no harm and behaving perfectly, the Ruddy one, eyes gleaming, leaps upon the poor whitehead *and eats it!*

Well, there should be no problem there, because the UK branch of the Ruddy Duck Working Group was formed in 1993 "to provide advice to the Government and others on the threat posed to the White-Headed Duck". What's the problem?

Now I don't want to dash anybody's hopes, but I must be blunt: not only has the Government got more on its hands than it can hold, but even if it had a spare weekend the problems of the White-Headed Duck would be a very long way down the schedule. Just imagine the Cabinet in session. Gummer is making a nuisance of himself as usual; Heseltine beats his chest; Portillo tries to beat his chest but misses; the latest MORI looks like a graveyard, and then Bottomley says: "What about the White-Headed Duck and – more to the point – the Ruddy one?" There would, at the least, be something of a silence, would there not?

But the problem will not go away, government or no government, and somebody had better hurry, because "the White-Headed Duck is globally threatened, with a world population of only about 19,000 individuals". Nor is that the worst, for "it is the only member of the stifftail tribe of ducks native to the Palearctic". (Has anybody ever heard of the Palearctic? I haven't, and neither have several encyclopaedias I consulted.)

It gets worse. Not only does the Ruddy Duck gobble up the White-Heads, it – er – has sexual connection with them. No wonder; the female Ruddy Duck lays seven large white eggs at a go, and believe it or not the Ruddies have the nerve to lay eggs in the nests of other birds, particularly *Aythya fuligula*. (No doubt it sings *fuligulee, fuligula* as it goes.)

There is no chance of seeing the Ruddies done in, because in the Americas alone there are some 600,000 of them, and worse still they are now sending their black sheep to Europe, where they breed (well, obviously, black sheep like nothing better than breeding), so the poor Whities are even more in danger.

Moreover, the Ruddies have invaded Britain. There are about 3,500 already, and the population is growing at a rate of 10 per cent a year, so if nothing is done about it, in a few years there will be more Ruddy Ducks than people – a fine state of affairs.

For a time, it seemed that there would be a truce, that the Ruddies and Whities would hybridise; but it didn't last, and soon the Ruddies were at their usual business, for "male Ruddy Ducks compete aggressively with male White-Headed Ducks for mates and have been successful in fertilising female White-Headed Ducks".

And if you think that *that* is disgusting enough, try this:

It is not known whether male Ruddy Ducks would continue to mate with White-Headed Ducks if more female Ruddy Ducks were present on White-Headed Duck breeding grounds [of course they would, the dirty brutes]. It is possible that the two would interbreed less [not likely, with these randy buggers around], although experiments with captive ducks suggest that male Ruddy Ducks would still attempt to mate with female White-Headed Ducks [and succeed, if I'm any judge].

Nor does the savagery of the Ruddies stop here. Not content with strewing the grass with the bones of many a White-Headed Duck (just think about the poor fledgelings waiting for a mother who will now never come), the grim reaper has turned his wicked eyes not only on *Tachybaptus ruficollis* but also *Podiceps nigricollis*.

But this is the bit you won't believe. There is, as you will know, protection for a wide range of wild animals, birds, fish and even flowers, I think. (But not human beings, as yet.) Even I, with my suspicion of any kind of decree, and even more suspicion of the rustle of wigs and gowns, find myself applauding the laws that keep nature going. Then I winked at the nearest White-Headed Duck, those shockingly persecuted creatures, and what did I find?

The European Commission has advised that, as an introduced species, the Ruddy Duck is not protected under EU Directive 70/409 on the Conservation of Wild Birds. *It is, however, protected under national legislation in the UK.*

We must have our fun. We can get it easily and free, if we will only write to "The Secretary, UK Ruddy Duck Working Group, Monkstone House, Peterborough, PE1 IJY, UK." If you follow the instructions you too could have the Information Note (as it is called) of the UK Ruddy Duck Working Group. And we have had our fun.

Yes, we have had our fun, and I hope that the UK Ruddy Duck Working Group has not been upset because I have been making fun of their work. For you see, I do *not* look down on those whose days (and nights, I wouldn't wonder) are filled with the work in hand, and indeed I truly admire them. For consider: if their work was not done, we would have lost something precious, something rare, and above all something irreplaceable. I am a townee from the top of my head to the soles of my feet, but I know that the countryside is not only where we get our food; it is also where we get our beauty, our richness, our understanding of the soil we stand upon.

That richness and beauty is in great danger. It is not only the pesticides and their ilk which are destroying the countryside. Sometimes, the countryside comes to the town. Not long ago, a peaceable man was looking out of his window at a long bed of flowers on the other side of the road, put there by the local council to further brighten the town. As he looked at beauty, he saw a gang tearing up the flowers and smashing the fitments. He came out of his house, crossed the road, and remonstrated with the brutes. They kicked him to death.

Yes, there are people who actually hate beauty, and in particular the beauty that comes not from man's hand. I applaud with all my heart the UK Ruddy Duck Working Group. May they flourish.

The Times, 5 September 1995

But are there blue men?

L ET US START with an odd but just possibly significant
bit of trivia. When the conversation turns to the subject
of extra-terrestrial figures, whether it takes the form of
ridiculing the very idea of such things or whether they
are truly believed in − even to a claim that one of the
party has actually seen such a figure − there is complete
agreement that the Things, real or chimerical, *are always
little green men.*

Why little, why green and why men? I do not know. For
a moment I thought the idea came from the truly green little
man in the shape of E.T., but a moment's thought showed
that the idea had been deeply embedded in our culture long
before E.T. arrived, and I leave the puzzle where it was born
− if, that is, I can discover who started the thing.

Now, I have repeatedly asked why the notion of creatures
from another planet should be treated with mirth and contempt,
though we know from the scientists that there are countless
billions of other worlds, some of these being thousands of
times bigger than the size of our speck in the universe, and
thousands of degrees hotter to boot. If you just think for a
moment about those vast numbers of other worlds you should
be rocking with laughter if anyone suggests that the universe
is peopled only by us. How we get in touch with them is
another story, but no doubt in the course of the centuries we
shall find a way to shake their little green hands.

But that terror − for terror it truly is for those who cannot
accept that our world and its inhabitants may be duplicated
millions of times over − holds a far greater terror. It is

the terror of believing that the universe is *not* random, and that there is a hand which guides us. And we call the hand God.

Ah, but when the word "God" is spoken in the hearing of Dr Richard Dawkins, something like hysteria breaks out. Here is a scientist of very great knowledge and understanding, but the very thought of God, indeed the very word, puts him in such great rage and fear that he all but foams at the mouth.

I do not exaggerate. When a man with Dr Dawkins's mind and knowledge sinks to such childish vulgarity as he is capable of, the only explanation must be that he is not as sure of himself as he would like us to think. He says of a certain Christian polemicist that "he can have no independent mind, because he is told what to think by an elderly Pole [*viz.* the Pope] who has no qualifications and is moreover a dangerous world-damaging dictator. What an ignominious, contemptible, retarded basis for holding the deepest beliefs of one's life." And to top it, Dr Dawkins says that theology is no longer a respectable subject for universities to teach. Mind, Dr Dawkins is sufficiently silly to insist that he is not an agnostic but an atheist; he *knows*, you see. But if you ask him where and how the universe came into being, he would be just as flummoxed as any of us, though he would pretend to understand it, so we might as well say right out, "God moves in a mysterious way, his wonders to perform," which at least is couched in beautiful language, which is more than can be said for Dr Dawkins's.

But, though you may think otherwise, I did not come here to try to make Dr Dawkins burst with rage; actually, when I started out, Dr Dawkins was not even in my mind. I was, once again, shaking my head at people who cannot believe that there are other beings in other places in the universe. That, surely, is the clue to the argument over the little green men; if there are beings like us, but far, far ahead in wisdom, understanding, peace and love, we shall be shamed. The little green men, are, in our subconscious, there to make fun of the dangers.

But what, you ask, is the danger? After all there *aren't* little green men around, are there? No, but there is a much more powerful danger, and it is that I want to discuss.

It begins in America (where else?) and in Harvard (where else?) with Dr John Mack. This man is a very distinguished psychiatrist; he is a Pulitzer prizewinner, his papers are accepted by *The American Journal of Medicine* and he shared with one other such teacher the honour of founding the university's school of psychiatry. Nor does he confine himself to his psychiatric work; he has written a biography of Lawrence of Arabia. But he has had to go through a disciplinary hearing, from which he has only just emerged. Moreover, it was touch and go whether he would be dismissed from his position. (William Langley had the story, and it was splashed in the *Sunday Telegraph*.)

Very well; what has he done? Has he harassed female students? Of course not. Has he been drunk on the lecture podium? Perish the thought. Were his pockets a-jingle when the petty-cash had just disappeared? Ridiculous. Professor Mack's crime is to believe many of his patients when they say that they have been taken from their homes by space aliens and subsequently brought back to Earth.

Professor Mack is, of course, familiar with the sight of a patient lying on the couch, and pouring out his or her troubles or pains or even madnesses to him. But this is something very different; very different indeed:

> . . . "Jerry", a 32-year-old Massachusetts clerical worker . . . believes she has been kidnapped more than 50 times since she was a toddler. Now married, with three children of her own, Jerry says she knows when the terror is about to begin from a ringing in her ears and a strange crackling energy that straightens her hair. "I am awakened by a tap," she says. "I feel paralysed but awake. They invade you entirely. Then they float you out."

We have four, and only four, responses. The first is that the "subject" is deluded or even insane. The second is that the doctor has deluded himself. The third is that the doctor is making money with a giant fraud. The fourth is that both the patients and the doctor are right.

Naturally, the other doctors and the Harvard high-ups instantly discarded the fourth response. All universities are cowardly, and the cowardice grows greater with the prestige of the university. Better, far better, to sack an eccentric professor than to risk being laughed at. But there is a difficulty in sacking the prof: he broke no Harvard rule, and *a fortiori* no law. Nor does he want for friends, as witness Professor Alan Dershowitz:

> John has been doing this work, quietly and diligently, for years. And the moment he gets any recognition for it, the university freaks out. The kangaroo court they have set up will damage Harvard's reputation more than anything John is ever likely to do.

Nervously, grudgingly and cowardlily, the Harvard University kangaroo court let Professor Mack alone, and he continued with his work, a mere hundred thousand dollars lighter for legal fees and having wasted countless hours defending himself.

Now then. I am obviously in no position to adjudicate or even have an opinion on the story. Possibly, Professor Mack and his "patients" are mad, or have discovered a gigantic hole in the universe. Others would say that the prof has got very much the wrong end of all of the sticks in this business. And so on. But that brings me back to another academic, Dr Dawkins. What would he say if he were confronted with Professor Mack's dilemma? We already know that Dr Dawkins can throw a fit with the best of us; he might, having looked at the Mack business, have gone pale and backed out of the room. But to do him credit, Dawkins is not one for backing out of anybody's room. A lurid picture can be seen through the mist. Prof Mack shows his materials to Doc Dawkins;

Doc Dawkins examines the evidence, and announces that Prof Mack is – how should we put it? – a good few coupons short of a pop-up toaster. Trouble breaks out.

Perhaps both men would listen to me for a moment (I fear that Doc Dawkins will not listen to me, or perhaps anybody, whereas Prof Mack seems a most mild figure), because I think I have an answer. There is no chance that Doc Dawkins will have anything to do with God, whereas Prof Mack is clearly attuned to the sounds of mystery. Well then, have them change places for a week; Prof Mack will calm down Doc Dawkins, and Doc Dawkins will be so bemused that he will find himself muttering: "God moves in a mysterious way, his wonders to perform".

We can but try.

The Times, 22 August 1995

From Elysium

SOME SAY THAT Beethoven is taken for granted, and that it is only Mozart who makes us gasp with every note. Some go further and say that Beethoven is old hat. I smile at their impudence, but if Beethoven is old hat, pray give me any hat, however old and battered, and I shall genuflect before it.

Let me assure you that I have not come here to announce the news that Beethoven was a rather good composer. It is that I have been to the Coliseum – the English National Opera, and ENO for short – to hear and see *Fidelio*, and I have much to say on the subject. (I must, of course, ask pardon of all those music-lovers, and particularly Beethoven-lovers, who live too far from London and St Martin's Lane to be there in the flesh, though once upon a time – unless I dreamt it – the ENO thought nothing of taking an entire performance around the country. And are we not even going to hear this one on radio?)

Now then. We know that Beethoven wrote only one opera, and the devil of a job he – and his helpers – had to get it right, throughout all the changes and quarrels. Did, then, Beethoven dislike the very idea of opera and have to be cajoled into *Fidelio* with a cry of "never again"? Well, it *was* never again, but no one could claim that Beethoven would shudder at the thought of doing it again, because his papers reveal an astonishing gallimaufry of operas he toyed with, including *Romeo and Juliet, Alexander the Great, Macbeth, Bradamante, Romulus and Remus, Dragomira, Faust, Alfred the Great, The Founding of Pennsylvania, Melusine, The Return of Ulysses, Bacchus* and *The Ruins of Babylon*.

Yet he chose only *Leonora*, or *Conjugal Love*, and even that changed, into *Fidelio*. And thus it was, and is.

No one could claim that the libretto and the plot are masterpieces; that matters very little. Nor do we need to smile at the heroine when she is disguised as a man – the number of operatic cross-dressings is countless. But for all that, *Fidelio* clutches at the heart and the mind even without the music.

That, if you stop and think about it, is a remarkable statement. It must mean that Beethoven, for all the clumsinesses of the libretto, had infused the words – very few of them his – with something far more than telling a story. It means, surely, that *Fidelio* has yet another layer that we must heed. The late William Mann was entirely steeped in music, and when he surveyed *Fidelio*, he said this:

> The greatness, the undiminishable impact of *Fidelio* ... flouts all the rules of successful opera, but it strikes hard at the spot which a real opera must strike. In cold blood, and on the libretto's printed page, the characters may appear to be puppets ... But connect any of them to Beethoven's music and each one comes to life; the two dimensions turn into at least four. For ... the point about *Fidelio* is not that a man falsely imprisoned is saved from murder ... by his wife's plucky intervention; nor even that she cleverly persuades the jailer's daughter into fancying her a marriageable young man; but that all over the world, at any time in history, injustice is being perpetrated and it can be prevented by the convinced, individual action of anybody on earth who sufficiently believes in the human moralities, and above all the sanctity of human life.

Now Beethoven was no churchgoer, though as the old *Grove* puts it:

"Beethoven's was a deeply religious nature: of this the Mass itself is witness ... unsustained by canonical doctrine, he strove to reach and encompass a God whom he knew existed but could not comprehend."

But I have not come to give a lecture on *Fidelio*; or rather, I *have* come to give a lecture on *Fidelio*, but of a different kind. Anyone who has followed the work of Graham Vick (as I have) will know that he has directed countless operas, in Britain and elsewhere. More to the point, the man is steeped for life in unwavering integrity.

You do not have to think in terms of profundity; anyone who saw Vick's production of *Eugene Onegin* will know with what delicacy, pain and even humour this man can bring an old work to life. Put it beside the dreary bilge of Covent Garden's current *Ring* (particularly the idiotic toy aeroplane wiggling across the backdrop with no conceivable meaning) and you will instantly know the difference between Vick and thingummyjig. So I went, in high heart, to the ENO for the new Vick-made *Fidelio*.

My companion had never heard *Fidelio* – an astonishing admission – for she is far too young to have heard the great Klemperer's triumph and the most recent London attempts were wretched and didn't stay long.

I confess that my palms were clammy through the overture; even my hero Vick might have come a purler. Shame on me, shame to doubt him, for what we saw at the beginning of the work was a huge tarpaulin, almost filling the stage, and as the cloth was peeled away, the entire audience could hear my sigh of relief. For, you see, Beethoven really did not need to be told how to do his work, and Graham Vick did not need to be told how to do *his*. Under that great cloth, there was a massive, immensely handsome, polished wooden cross which almost filled the stage (and remained throughout the evening), immediately telling us that what we were to see and hear came from God and Man. Not just God, and not just Man; the two had joined forces.

I had heard outside the opera house in the interval, and read in some of the newspapers the following day, that what we had heard was, of course, wonderful music, but otherwise no more than a political story, with a bad man properly coming to grief and the good man and woman released from their dungeon. Politics, they said, just as we talk about politics, and hope to achieve the release of an unjustly imprisoned man, with Lord Lane getting it all wrong as usual. So glorious is the work, and so marvellously has Vick brought it to life, that I have only just begun to be irritated by those who talk of politics, as though we were truly in the Law Courts. Do, please, broaden your horizon, you who believe that *Fidelio* is an exciting work of music, in which there are goodies and baddies and the baddies get their comeuppance or don't, just like Tosca or Rigoletto. *But Fidelio is not like Tosca or Rigoletto, it is much more like God Almighty.*

The trumpet shall sound; where have you heard those words? Don't bother to look it up, it goes like:

> Behold, I shew you a mystery; We shall not all sleep, but we shall all be changed, In a moment, in the twinkling of an eye, at the last trump; for the trumpet shall sound, and the dead shall be raised incorruptible, and we shall be changed.

If you don't believe me, go back to the ENO, get, buy or steal more tickets, and listen to those final bars. You don't have to be an expert in music, you only have to listen to that stupendous ending, filled with God and Man.

No, I do not think that Graham Vick is the thirteenth Apostle, but he can see a cross and know what it means; more to the point, I would guess that Beethoven knew what it meant too, even if he didn't go to church every Sunday, or indeed any Sunday. (*Christ on the Mount of Olives* is far from Beethoven's best work, but it strengthens Beethoven's deistic feelings, however irregular.)

Perhaps he thought that he had done enough for a day, with the *Missa Solemnis*. But heaven forfend that Graham Vick should ever think that he had done for the day. In the ENO programme he lists some operas he has directed, and some that are in the pipeline, and so besotted am I with Vick's work, that I have sworn, shuddering, to go to *Lulu*, at Glyndebourne, this season, *and on my birthday*.

Let us come back to Beethoven and *Fidelio*. The clumsiness of the libretto and the awkwardness of the unfolding story hardly matter, and even if they did matter – well, the quartet in the beginning of the first Act is in its own right an imperishable masterpiece. But it is not only an imperishable masterpiece; we are talking of Beethoven, and Beethoven does nothing without meaning it. The quartet floats to heaven (for some, the tears begin there – mine start at the trumpet-call), and we are in no ordinary work; from this moment on, we are in the hands not of Man or God, but Man *and* God. But don't forget the box office; Beethoven wouldn't.

The Times, 10 May 1996

Index

Schmidt, Helmut, Chancellor 233
Schneerson, Rabbi 232
Schneider, Herr 145–6
Schopenhauer, Artur 176
Schubert, Franz xix, 104–5; Octet 104; *Quartettsatz* 104
Schultz, John 7–8
Schwarzkopf, Elisabeth 12–15
science, dark side of 220–1
Scott Monument, Edinburgh 198
Scream, The (Munch) 149–53
secret service 31, 33, 34
Sedgebeer, Lauretta 134
Sedgebeer, Trevor 134–5, 136
self-imprisonment 189–93
Seoul, South Korea 27–8, 29, 30
service charges 77–9
sex offences 36
Sezession 150
Shaffer, Peter 102
Shakespeare, William xiv, xvii, 52, 68, 89–93, 161
shame 37; forgotten 39
Shelton, John 210
Shining Path guerrillas 27, 29, 30
shoplifters, young xviii
shopping, topless 121–2
Simms, Denzil xiii
Singapore, probity 97
Skriket (Scream) (Munch) 149–53
slavery, abolition 238
slaves 109–11, 112–13
Smellie, Professor xi
Smith, Maggie 91
smoking: dangers of 220; regulation of 126–7
Social Affairs Unit 209
society: changing xii, xvii, 87–8; horrors of xii–xvi, 26–7, 29–30
soldiers: female 218

Solzhenitsyn, Aleksandr 116
South Africa 16–18, 19, 29, 30; expulsion from 132
South America: Nazis in 47
South Korea 27–8, 29, 30
Soviet Union: expulsion from 132; spies 32, 33, 34
Sparta 59
Speakman, Kenneth 170
Speer, Albert 189
Spielmann, Leopold 226
spies 31–5
Spycatcher (Wright) 217
Sri Lanka 27, 29, 30
Stalin, Joseph 30, 31, 34
stamp-collecting 75
Stavely near Chesterfield 24
Steckbarth, Horst 167
Stephens, Mark 41, 42
Stephens Innocent, lawyers 41
Sudan: slavery in 109–11, 112–13; Southern 112
Suharto, Thogib N J 28, 29
suicide: redundancy and 155–8; selected sites 196–7
Sukarnoputri, Megawati 28
Sun 6, 36, 37, 39
sun, water on 220, 223
Sunday Telegraph 247
Sunday Times 43, 85, 176
Sweden 148; murders in 205; probity 97
Swift, Jonathan 221
swimwear design 41–5
Switzerland: Jewish treasure in 115–16; murders in 205; probity 97
Sydney Opera House 133
Symonds, Andrew 130